Tamar Jeffers McDonald is Reader in Film at the University of Kent. She is the author of *Romantic Comedy: Boy Meets Girl Meets Genre* (2007) and of *Hollywood Catwalk* (I.B.Tauris, 2010).

'Demonstrably a labour of love . . . this is an accomplished study of the very highest quality. It is an admirable example of cultural and historical analysis that manages to be, simultaneously, forensic whilst it also sparkles with wit and erudition.'

John Mercer
Senior Lecturer in Screen Cultures,
Birmingham City University (UK)

DORIS DAY
CONFIDENTIAL
Hollywood, Sex and Stardom

Tamar Jeffers McDonald

BLOOMSBURY ACADEMIC
LONDON • NEW YORK • OXFORD • NEW DELHI • SYDNEY

BLOOMSBURY ACADEMIC
Bloomsbury Publishing Plc
50 Bedford Square, London, WC1B 3DP, UK
1385 Broadway, New York, NY 10018, USA
29 Earlsfort Terrace, Dublin 2, Ireland

BLOOMSBURY, BLOOMSBURY ACADEMIC and the Diana logo
are trademarks of Bloomsbury Publishing Plc

First published in 2013 by I.B.Tauris & Co Ltd.
Reprinted by Bloomsbury Academic 2019, 2021

A catalogue record for this book is available from the British Library.

A catalog record for this book is available from the Library of Congress.

ISBN: PB: 978-1-3501-5068-3
ePDF: 978-0-8577-2279-9
eBook: 978-0-8577-3422-8

To find out more about our authors and books visit
www.bloomsbury.com and sign up for our newsletters.

Contents

Conclusion   223

Illustrations

Acknowledgements

The books with the longest gestations obviously have the longest lists of thank yous and acknowledgements. Over the past 22 years that I have been thinking, writing, and arguing about Doris Day, many people have kindly listened to and debated with me, and I would like to thank them all for their insights and provocations.

Particular debts of gratitude are owed to colleagues and students at: Birkbeck Extra-Mural Centre for Education evening class 2002–3, Warwick film seminars 2002–3, Buckinghamshire Chilterns University College (now Bucks New University), Oxford Brookes University, and the University of Kent, in addition to audience members at conference presentations and invited talks in Reading, Nottingham, London, Kent and Leicester, and Minneapolis, Potsdam, Boston and Glasgow.

Librarians have been particularly generous in their assistance in chasing elusive magazine issues and references, and I would like to thank in particular the staff at the Margaret Herrick Library, Los Angeles, especially Lea Whittington and Sandra Archer; Ned Comstock at the library of the University of Southern California for access to the Constance McCormick Collection; James Lewis, Librarian, CFC New Jersey Information Center, New Jersey; Sean Delaney at the BFI, and staff at the Los Angeles Public Library, in the Motion Picture and Television Reading

Room at the Library of Congress, Washington DC, in the Magazine and Newspaper Center of the San Francisco Public Library and at the Boston Public Library.

Thanks must also go to the Arts and Humanities Research Council, who aided my travels and researches with a grant (AH/I000178/1) in spring 2011, and the anonymous reviewers who appraised my application and helped me improve my research questions.

Finally, special thanks to those who believed in this project long before, and longer than, anyone else did: Richard Dyer and Philippa Brewster; my familial support-team Candy, Chloe, Jessica, and, always, Paul; and anyone else who ever helped me source a pertinent film or article, or listened patiently to me when I explained for the *millionth* time why Doris Day doesn't always play a virgin.

Introduction

Even now, 40 years after Doris Day's last film and 20 since her last regular television appearances, the star's name retains currency: she is often invoked as shorthand for a kind of outmoded sexuality, with virginity firmly maintained until marriage. Although this assumption is widespread, close attention to the facts of Day's own life challenges it, and the majority of her film roles also prove otherwise, with Day most frequently portraying a woman of maturely sexual desires. This book will investigate why the rigid view of Day's maintained virginity should have arisen and become so indelibly fixed to the star, one of the most popular in American cinema during the 1950s and 1960s. Despite this popularity, and the longevity of Day's career, work on the star is curiously meagre, and what material there is generally assumes, without actually testing, Day's supposed maiden status. There has been, then, no previous sustained exploration which attempts as this book does to deconstruct the aged virgin myth by tracing its evolution and exposing its fallacies.

Taking a twofold approach, the project both closely examines Day's film roles and performances, and explores material from other popular media for the source of the virgin myth. First, the project focuses on contemporary popular culture contexts. Using a variety of sources, including newspaper stories, articles from film, fan and lifestyle magazines, reviews and gossip, the developments in Day's screen 'persona' are charted, highlighting changing popular perceptions. Second, key characters and performances from across Day's career are analysed in detail, to see if maidenly qualities are always present. Findings indicate that this was not the case, but that although Day did play a variety of women with different sexual statuses (shy ingénue, brassy chorus girl, wife and mother, dignified widow), most often her characters had clearly defined sexual desires and experiences. Film theorist Richard Dyer affirmed in his 1979 book *Stars* that a star persona was constructed across a range of media texts. These included film roles, but also moments outside the films, both public events such as premiere attendances, and more private ones like changes in partner. With Day, however, neither public *nor* private facts correspond with the aged maiden she is popularly supposed to play and be.

I start with a close analysis of a very short sequence in Day's second film, *My Dream Is Yours* (1949), a fame montage of about one minute in duration. Although rapid, this montage vividly encapsulates the mechanics of stardom in a way which not only comments overtly on Day's *own* rise to Hollywood fame, from singer to movie star, but also on the significance of forces outside the studio in creating film celebrity. Up to this moment, the narrative has been devoted to detailing the efforts of Martha Gibson (Doris Day) and agent Doug Blake (Jack Carson) to launch Martha as a singer. Eventually, Gibson gets her big break when she has to stand in for the man she loves, Gary Mitchell (Lee Bowman), on a popular radio show, when he is too drunk to broadcast. Although she is happy to be hired, Martha is distraught when Mitchell views her performance as a personal betrayal.

At this point, the screen fades to black and the fame montage begins. Fourteen shots tell the story of Martha's meteoric rise; instead of cuts in the sequence, each image is replaced using a very slow fade, so that one picture never fully vanishes before the next arrives. First a newspaper with a column signed 'Walter Winchell' rises towards the screen. A new shot superimposes itself, showing Martha being posed for a photograph (Figure 1). This fades to another similar shot, again showing the new radio star being photographed. Another fade reveals the result of this sitting: a picture of Martha, now printed on the front cover of *Look* magazine (Figure 2). The camera pans backwards to reveal customers reading the magazine, and several other titles all with her face on their covers displayed on the news-stand (Figure 3). Fading into this, so that the magazines are still clearly visible as her image appears, a new shot presents Martha on stage for a broadcast (Figures 4 and 5). An applauding audience replaces this, succeeded in turn by another newspaper, with Hedda Hopper's by-line. Martha appears again, this time wearing a different gown; next comes a superimposition of Doug's delighted face and then mounds of bundled fan mail addressed to Martha (Figure 6).

Figure 1.   Martha Gibson (Doris Day) being posed for a photograph
(*My Dream Is Yours*, 1949).

Figure 2.   Martha on the cover of *Look* magazine.

Figure 3.   Magazines on the news-stand.

A further shot of her is replaced by another newspaper, with Louella Parsons' announcement: 'New Singing Star to be Signed by Major Studio' (Figure 7). Finally a new shot appears: Martha emerges from a limousine, wearing a white fur coat and glittering diamonds, to pose for photographs and sign autographs.

Figure 4.   A slow fade positions the news-stand . . .

Figure 5.   . . . under the superimposition of Martha singing.

Although it takes less time to watch the sequence than to
read this description, a detailed examination of the montage is
justified by its overt acknowledgement of how Hollywood
stardom was made and maintained at this point in time, the

Figure 6.   Bundles of fan mail for Martha.

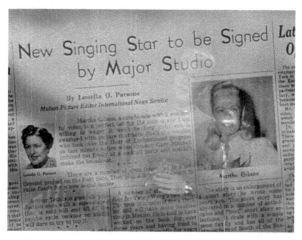

Figure 7.   Louella Parson's by-line lends credibility.

late 1940s. Martha achieves success as a radio star, propelling her into the public eye; once prominent in this field she is then eligible for transfer into a related area of entertainment, the movies. Throughout the sequence the montage testifies to the importance of audience popularity via shots of applauding viewers, and the mound of fan mail, and to the vital role not only played by popularly-known arbiters of taste and purveyors of gossip (Winchell, Hopper, Parsons) lauding the new star's name, but also the importance of fan magazines making sure her image is reproduced everywhere. Furthermore, the saturation at magazine-level leads not only back to Gibson singing in a more glamorous outfit and with more evident confidence, but to the next newspaper review which asserts her fitness for film, and thus national and international stardom.

Besides this highlighting of the importance of extra-filmic agencies in bringing about stardom, the sequence achieves one more thing. As it contains no sharp or clear cuts, but achieves each change of image through protracted fades and super-impositions, the montage demonstrates just how *interconnected* the parts of the fame machine are. Where a cut might suggest a clear distinction between one area of endeavour and another, the fades blend everything – manager's effort, star's active vocal performance and passive photographic posing, audience approval, magazine ubiquity, gossip columnists' attention, fan mail, and more – illustrating the synergy of all these areas, the overlapping, interrelated importance of each enterprise in building and sustaining the star. I have chosen to highlight this very brief scene because it works so well to illustrate the main topic with which this book concerns itself: the formation of a celebrated public persona through *both* the labour of the performer *and* the attention of ancillary media. Richard Dyer's work on stars (1979; 1986) has demonstrated that although viewers think they 'know' about their favourite screen actors, they actually only ever interact with those actors' 'personae', agglomerations of characteristics, attitudes, and traits which seem to be guaranteed authenticity through their presence in the single body of the star. It was equally the task of the movies, and the magazines that both served and fed off them, to create the contrary fantasy that by buying film tickets and viewing a performance, or by purchasing a movie magazine and reading an article, fans were being granted access to some inner truth about their favourites.

Doris Day is a particularly interesting case to examine in light of the constructed aspect of stardom, since much of her appeal was specifically built around how natural and unpretentious she was, at least at the beginning of her career. Her inner truth, then, is not supposed to be buried deeply but worn on the surface, obvious to all. While contemporary stars such as Ava Gardner, Elizabeth Taylor, Rita Hayworth and Lana Turner at times cultivated a 'sex goddess' persona which stressed their exquisite individual beauty and thus their distance from normal female fans, Day's popularity was grounded in the reverse, in an assumption of absolute normality. Actually, this normalcy was far from being found in Day's real life: on the road travelling across America with all-male big bands from 17, twice-married and a mother by 20, she actually experienced a profoundly atypical youth. In a self-referentially circular manner, then, the eventual cultivation of Day's persona as the ultimate girl-next-door was predicated on roles she played in the movies, rather than anything in her own biography.

As this book will reveal, the same is true of her now seemingly inevitable association with virginity. Not only do the facts in her own life discount that Day was ever overly-invested in chastity, was prudish or sex-averse, however; any idea of inherent coyness should be also contrasted with Day's initial fame as a singing star with a particularly husky, seductive and overtly sexualised voice. One reviewer called a couple of her recordings 'as soft and humid as torch songs can be and still be legal' (Roddy, 1950: 109) and Day was well-known for singing not only songs about sexual yearning such as 'While The Music Plays On' (1940), but also for a version of an infamous navy ditty, 'A Guy Is A Guy' (1952), which evokes the well-known dirty lyrics even as it replaces them. Day's now much-vaunted virginity was neither something that originated with her, nor present throughout all her career. In her first few films, for example, she plays a series of generally cynical, wise-cracking and worldly-wise chanteuses. Martha Gibson is less irreverent than other initial Day roles Georgia Garrett (*Romance On The High Seas*, 1948) and Judy Gibson (*It's A Great Feeling*, 1949), but like them, her chastity is also not at issue, as she starts the film already a single mother. Just like the girl-next-door persona, then, that virginal prudish maiden associated with Day actually originates in *films* – and in later films – rather than in her biography. I want to explore how, once established in filmic vehicles, this figure began to dominate the star's persona to the point that extra-filmic material, like fan and lifestyle magazines, had to try to incorporate it into their accounts of the star, with many resultant torsions to narrative logic in their stories.

What I want to do in this book, therefore, is explore Doris Day's star persona, charting developments from its early establishment when she first appeared in Hollywood, building on her success as a radio and recording star, on through its evolutions as her roles changed and her popularity grew over time. In so doing, I will inevitably be taking note of events which enlarged her profile professionally, such as her films, as well as occurrences in her personal life which prompted widespread media coverage, such as the death of her third husband in 1968.

Day's popularity as a film performer commenced with her very first movie appearance, and thereafter waxed and waned in interesting ways that did not always correspond with how she was presented onscreen. The consonance or dissonance, therefore, of her presentation across other media with her portrayal in films is one of the principle objects of examination in this study. In tracing the evolution of her star persona across the period of her main film and television stardom, from 1948 to 1973, I will thus be looking not only at Day's roles and performances, but also, crucially, at how these interacted and chimed with, or alternatively varied from, the Day that was being presented in other media, chiefly film fan and lifestyle magazines.

My main areas of investigation have now been introduced: I want to analyse what is written about the star at various periods, pulling apart the writing to explore the play of fantasies, desires, and anxieties underneath, and to return these writings to their originating contexts as far as possible, to read them as contemporary viewers would have done, alert to topical references, in-jokes and allusions. Alongside this is my other main task, that of reading the film roles and performances, also in their contemporary contexts. Fresh examination of her film performances is necessary in the same way that pulling apart the written pieces on Day is necessary: what has been said about the star before cannot necessarily be taken as true, since all too often those authors who have written about Day have done so without the aim of challenging old assumptions about her.

By going back and forth between the films and the magazines that supported, surrounded and fed off the films for information and opinion on Day, I hope to contextualise both the film roles and the periodical material, noting moments of smoothness, when all the narratives on the star seem to be in accord, as well as occasions of unease when, for example, a film role suggests one thing that the magazines then work hard to deny – or vice versa. The structure of the book is thus threefold; a short initial section sets out the historical contexts of my investigation, including the contemporary fascination with an active female virginity aroused in the American public by Kinsey et al's 1953 'Report' on *Sexual Behavior In The Human Female*; it then presents evidence that

Day has, over time, become a cipher for the coy, manipulative, or pathologically sex-averse aged maiden. Thereafter the in-depth exploration begins, with the second section dedicated to investigating the magazine material, and the third the performances. The periodical section begins with an overview of Day's persona as it was first established on her arrival in Hollywood and then was subject to various alterations, refinements and deteriorations over the length of her main film and television career. Importantly, the 'Virgin' trope proves to be the very final one which evolves, beginning around 1961; this is very noticeable given that a full 50 per cent of the 32 total repeated common ideas – tropes – concerning the star had been in place since 1948, and 12 more arrived by 1952. Next, a section details the collection of the project's raw data: 479 articles from film fan magazines and lifestyle periodicals from 1948 to 1986, which were analysed for the tropes clustering around the star[1]. These 32 tropes were found to be reoccurring across the range of pieces on Day, but while the regularity of these terms' usage seemed to hold remarkably steady, their meanings changed over time, especially as tropes which began as positive became increasingly slewed to the negative over time, eventually shading into pathology. This chapter focuses on the tropes themselves, drawing them individually out of their magazine contexts to analyse their meanings, ponder their longevity, and see how such notions as 'Cleanliness' and 'Energy', initiated early on as compliments to the new starlet, eventually became associated with the idea of a sexual innocence stridently maintained long after it was healthy or wise to do so. The final chapter of the section looks at all the tropes operating in individual articles taken from four key moments in Day's career. This chapter importantly reverses the trajectory of previous ones that removed the tropes from their immediate contexts; by returning them to their originating articles and issues, the variety of tropes operating and their interplay can be studied in situ, as the whole magazine becomes part of the mechanism through which Day's stardom was perpetuated and her persona framed. Examination of the magazines as physical artefacts reveals the significant part played by the design, colour, and placement of the articles on the star in constructing, maintaining or attempting to transform her persona.

The third section of the book then takes these same four key moments from Day's career – her first film in 1948, the first overt assertion of a mature sexuality in 1955, the conscious portrayal of an aged maiden in 1961, and the self-referential play on Day's known personality and history in her television show around 1972 – to discover whether these same tropes played out in her performances. Close reading of *Romance On The High Seas*, *Love Me Or Leave Me*, *Lover Come Back* and several episodes of *The Doris Day Show* reveals that notions and performances of Day's screen innocence were demonstrably absent from her earlier films, as borne out not only by the star's acting choices but also the films' narratives, scripts and costumes. This chapter's analysis then demonstrates that Day's filmic virginity was not a constant presence in her acting; instead it was a quality which manifested itself not only late on in her career but also at a time when it ran counter to other dominant messages about the star's mature and active sexuality. Arriving in the early 1960s, the virgin trope does turn out to have links to aspects of earlier Day roles and performances but, fascinatingly, appears in texts and ways that might not be expected. Although, therefore, this book seeks to undermine the idea of the monolithic aged maiden being all that Day could play, it also works to uncover the origins of this idea and elements that tended to support it.

Finally, why is the book called *Doris Day Confidential*? I developed the title because it seemed to evoke the prurient promises nestling inside all the articles on the star, not just the ones in the particularly trashy scandal rags such as *Confidential, Hush Hush, Whisper* and *Top Secret*, but also in the middlebrow film fan magazines and the upmarket lifestyle and current affairs periodicals. In his fascinating study of the developments of Hollywood stardom, Richard deCordova analyses what is at the heart of the star's appeal and concludes that it is always about sexualised secrets (1990: 141).[2] Following Foucault's lead, he suggests that this is because the sexual is always viewed as the ultimate truth about a person's identity. In order for the fan to find out, therefore, the 'real' truth about a favourite star, s/he needs to discover the truth about that star's sexual secrets. To a certain extent, magazines at every level of respectability did seem to operate a policy of catering to the fans' needs in this area, exploiting the potential for offering the ultimate revelation. A problem with this idea, however, impacts my twin study of the periodicals and Doris Day. With all the possible sexualised secrets in circulation – adultery, nymphomania, homosexuality, even incest – virginity disappoints the reader and undermines the entire edifice of stories built on the fact of revealing 'what really happened'. A nothing, a *not-yet*, virginity nullifies the excitement of seamy revelation by stating bluntly that nothing has *ever* happened. Not only, then, is virginity an odd attribute to assign to a woman in her 40s who has been married three times and has a 20-year-old son; it is one that would challenge the salacious selling point upon which the success of the periodicals was supposedly predicated. By returning to the variety of stories on the star printed during her career, it is possible to build a more accurate picture of the magazines' changing presentation of Doris Day during the 25-year period of her live career, and thus to demonstrate that the maidenly obsession obtained both relatively late and relatively partially.

As the tropes attest and the film performances bear out, there was a central core of meaning clustering around and seemingly evoked by the name 'Doris Day', but within this core was a multiplicity of elements which variously increased or diminished at various points across the span of her onscreen career – and the idea of sexual continence or abstinence was only ever a tiny and partial part of them. This multiplicity brings me back to an image from the fame montage in *My Dream Is Yours*: Doris Day as Martha Gibson, her face repeatedly reproduced on the covers of different magazines on a news-stand. This multiplicity of Doris Days on the *outside* of the magazines echoes the multiplicity of Doris Days *inside* them, in the various stories the periodicals present about her talent, life, interests, and film projects, as well as her loves. It is this awareness of the multiple, rather than the monolith, that needs to be recovered and returned to Day's career. My argument throughout this book will be, therefore, not only that Day didn't 'always play a virgin' in her films, nor ever conduct herself like one off-screen, but that there is no *always* about what she did – or, in aggregate, how the magazines presented her.

SECTION 1
Contexts

Since I have declared that the current monolithic view of Day as a coy old maid persists so strongly partly because it is never taken apart and investigated, but always taken for granted, it behoves me not just to take for granted myself the fact that it is an established – if erroneous – fact. If 'everyone' really does believe Doris Day always plays a virgin, I should be able to demonstrate instances where this has been asserted or insinuated. Beyond this provision of evidence, however, I think a greater historical context is also necessary for Day's career and press reception, in order to explain why the issue of her sexual status should ever have arisen. Put in the context of today's celebrity-saturated mediascape, where the internet records every peccadillo, affair, liaison, DUI and drinking binge of a bewildering array of stars and wannabes, Day's pillorying for *not* doing something – which is what virginity means – seems non-news, tame rather than compelling. What was it about the particular period of her stardom, then, that meant a mature woman, thrice-married and a mother, could be associated with sexual innocence, and this association be found intriguing, even perversely stimulating? In order to answer this question I will look here at a specific moment in American popular culture when the virgin female became the object of intense scrutiny, debate and mingled anxiety and excitement.

Exploring the virginity obsession of the mid-50s to early 60s alongside invocations of Day the virgin, this section attempts to provide twin backgrounds for this study's twin foci.

Released in 1953 with as much careful preparatory fanfare as the most skilfully ballyhooed film, Kinsey's second 'Report', his *Sexual Behavior In The Human Female*, set out to do what his first investigation had done for the male six years before: comment dispassionately on the norms of human sexual behaviour, based on the findings within his sample. Although the Report meticulously presents data solely on the sample of 5,940 unmarried white women, his audience – fellow scientists, church leaders, social critics, journalists, and the mass of general readers – inevitably extrapolated the findings to make assumptions about *all* unmarried American women. When he mildly noted that the popular presumption that unmarried women were virgins had, based on his sample, proved to be erroneous, Kinsey seemed to have little idea of the 'K bomb'[3] he was unleashing:

> Because of [the] public condemnation of pre-marital coitus, one might believe that such contacts would be rare among American females and males. But this is only the overt culture, the things that people openly profess to believe and to do. Our previous report (1948) on the male has indicated how far publicly expressed attitudes may depart from the realities of behaviour – the covert culture, what males really do. We may now examine the pre-marital coital behavior of the female sample which has been available for this study.
>
> (Kinsey et al., 1953: 285).

It is possible that this broad assumption, that an unmarried girl was likely to be a virgin, was actually a post-hoc invention, a nostalgic notion which became more mourned at the moment of its perceived demise than was previously ever believed to be true. What does seem clear is that, from the moment Kinsey published

Sexual Behavior In The Human Female, the majority of his findings and observations were ignored. Only one was discussed and circulated in the media storm that greeted the book's publication, the most obviously newsworthy revelation: that 50 per cent of the unmarried 30 year olds in his sample had ignored the traditional idea that 'nice girls don't', and had done.

This finding elicited not only solemn, in-depth analyses and counter-claims in serious periodicals and further scientific tomes, but also intensely curious examinations and requests for more information in women's and family magazines, cartoons, jokes and smutty stories in many different media (Jones, 1997: 711). This media storm seems both a reaction to, and an attempt to assuage, the anxiety the revelation evoked societally.

Although less frequently noted by the contemporary media, Kinsey's other achievements were no less significant. By the very act of taking women's sexual activities as the topic of the book, Kinsey assumed a parity between women and men, the subject of the first report in 1948. In counting women's activities, Kinsey thus made women's activities count. Moreover, by listing the variety of sexual activities that the women in his sample chose to indulge in besides actual coitus, Kinsey's report informed the reader how to experience various sexual pleasures without giving up virginity through penetrative sex, noting such techniques as:

> Simple kissing [...] deep kissing [...] breast stimulation [...] mouth-breast contacts [...] manual stimulation of the female genitalia [...] manual stimulation of the male genitalia [...] oral contacts with female genitalia [...] oral contacts with male genitalia [...] genital apposition.
>
> (Kinsey et al., 1953: 251–259).

This listing of various activities also importantly served to expose a hazy nebulousness over what 'virginity' meant contemporaneously. If the word was used as shorthand to indicate no experience of penetrative sex, then nothing was breached by such 'petting' activities as those cited above. If, however, 'virginity' was endowed with some sense of moral value, seen as an intrinsic guarantor of innocence or purity, then *any* sexual experience nullified it.

An uneasiness about the notion that virginity is subject to gradations of loss, rather than being an either/or, is observable in the contemporary concept of the 'technical virgin', a woman who had done or permitted everything but the act of coitus itself. If virginity was supposed to matter, to be a guarantee of the woman's lack of sexual history, then technical virginity undid this guarantee. The technical virgin threatened the status quo since she had arrived at her own independent concept of how much she could do and still retain her virgin status, as a *Playboy* writer bemoaned: 'Each girl seems to have her own peculiar and rather precise idea of just how far she can go without losing it' ('Smith', 1954: 9).

Kinsey's Report had thus, in effect, informed America that the popular cultural concept of the 'technical virgin' was factually-based and statistically proven; worryingly, therefore, the division between virgin/post-virgin could not be uniform and clear-cut, if it were individual women, rather than societal consensus, who were deciding the definition of 'virginity'. Furthermore, a belief that women were somehow manipulating this borderline, this metaphorical hymen, between the possible meanings of the word, was prevalent at the time. If technical virginity undid the guarantee of absolute innocence, it also undermined the double standard that assumed a man's right to his bride's chastity.

One further strand of contemporary anxiety is observable woven into this fretting over 'technical virginity': a belief in women's detached exploitation of their sexual attractiveness, in their willingness to grant or withhold sexual favours. It was feared that the detached female gave in a little at a time in order to draw the man in, trapping him by implying she would eventually assent to full sex, but holding this back as a final bargaining point until she had gained marriage. This very prevalent notion makes women frighteningly superior to men in their ability to direct and restrain their own libidinous desires and can be observed as an underlying assumption across this period, and into the early 1970s.

Whether his statistic-laden Report actually helped women in their appreciation of the right to sexual satisfaction, as letters to Kinsey suggest (Jones, 1997: 703–4) it is indisputable that the book, through deeming women's sexual activities worthy of discussion and minute record, propelled the trope of the desirous woman into the public arena, to be debated, denied, or supported, making her, for about a decade, an obsessive object of attention and scrutiny across high and low culture.

Kinsey's extrapolated findings therefore seemed to affix a metaphorical question mark over the head of every young woman, and this interrogative urge became overtly employed, not only in Clairol's 1955 hair colouring tag – 'Does she or doesn't she? Only her hairdresser knows for sure' – but in other contemporary popular media texts, including cinema. Three further particular instances of this questioning stand out to me, each reframing a central interrogation. Clairol's question is designed to be asked about the woman by an intrigued other party, but the next topical use of the inquiry turns from ambivalence to probability, introducing self-interest into the equation. A 1956 article in *Playboy* asked 'Will she or won't she?', going on to suggest that a woman who 'would' immediately was not worth cultivating; the only woman worth the investment of 'time, energy and cash' is the *eventual* yielder, who needs gradual persuasion (Archer, 1956: 13). The man's point of view removes the enigma attached to the Clairol advert, suggesting that the question can be definitively answered. By contrast, Nora

Johnson's use of the interrogative in her 1959 article, 'Sex and the College Girl' from the highbrow *Atlantic Monthly*, posits the same question – 'Should she or shouldn't she?' – but inflected by morality rather than feasibility, and, ultimately, without hope of an answer.

Examining Johnson's article in some detail is useful as this text brings to the surface many of the contemporary anxieties and assumptions that coalesced around the figure of the desirous virgin.

The piece exhibits both traditional assumptions – sex is something boys want and girls grant or withhold – and more counter-traditional notions, such as ascribing the wish for monogamy to the male. The article also interestingly reveals, however, an awareness of the nebulousness of virginity as a category, thus chiming with the contemporary anxiety over the idea of the technical virgin.

In her account of the sex lives of her sample – noticeably younger than Kinsey's and more personal too – Johnson invents a college Everygirl, Susie, and her boyfriend Joe, to act out the sexual negotiations she analyses. Surprisingly, it is Joe rather than Susie who wants a steady relationship leading to marriage, rather than a bachelor life of multiple conquests. The boy is pragmatically said to want a reliable girlfriend in order to spare himself:

> ...the bother of starting the whole sex cycle over again, with discussions and possibly arguments about how far he can go how soon. He wants it all understood, with the lady reasonably willing if possible. (This depends on his and her notions of what constitutes a nice girl).
>
> (Johnson, 1959: 57)

Although Johnson here seems to conform to the idea that boys want and girls grant – 'how far he can go' – her parenthesis undermines this assumption while it also contributes to mid-century debates about women's desires, agency and self-control. Susie is posited throughout as more aware of the mechanics of the relationship than the boy, thus fitting with the contemporary idea of the scheming female detached from her body, able to manipulate it and the man who desires it, in order to attain her goal of marriage. Susie permits intimacies gradually, not because of any romantic need for a relationship, or from deficiency of desire, prudishness or morals on her part, but calculatingly, in order to convince Joe that she is 'a nice girl'. If she permitted penetrative sex he would not respect her; therefore Susie feigns the reluctance that reassures Joe what he wants is worth having.

Susie is no stranger to desire, but her experiences are not to be acknowledged since they would counteract the pose of virginity she adopts. A longish passage from the article is worth quoting since it develops these themes:

> Susie has, on the whole, kept her chastity. She is no demimondaine, and she wants to be reasonably intact on her wedding night. She had an unfortunate experience at Dartmouth, when she and her date were both in their cups, but she barely remembers anything about it and hasn't seen the boy since. She has also done some heavy petting with boys she didn't care about, because she reasoned that it wouldn't matter what they thought of her.
>
> . . .
>
> She has kept Joe fairly well at arm's length, giving in a little at a time, because she wanted him to respect her. He didn't really excite her sexually, but probably he would if they had some privacy. Nothing was less romantic than the front porch of the house . . . or in the back of someone's car with only fifteen minutes before she had to be in. Anyway, it might be just as well. Susie and Joe have decided that they will sleep together when it is feasible, since by now Joe knows she is a nice girl and it's all right . . . She will

sleep with Joe, if they become engaged, because he wants to, and if she becomes pregnant, they can get married sooner.

(Johnson, 1959: 58–59)

These passages testify to the force of the contemporary double standard, and the prevalence of the idea of 'technical virginity'. They also indicate how women could manipulate the boundaries of the good/bad girl dichotomy to which these notions both spoke, the double standard in attempting to impose such binary categories, and technical virginity in subverting them. The account of Susie's sexual history is a fascinating one since it indicates the topical masquerade of chastity girls were adopting while still going about the business of sexual experimentation.

Susie can believe herself to be fairly virginal not because she has had *no* experience, but because her experiments have been with unimportant men. She maintains the stance of the virgin with Joe, who counts because he is marriageable material; the intimacies permitted when drunk with the boy at Dartmouth College do not matter to her, both because she is now unaware of them and he is not still on the scene. In other words, she remains innocent because she cannot remember her experience, and no one else knows about it; thus her reputation is intact both internally and externally. The extent of the intellectual negotiations Susie undertakes to maintain the illusion of inexperience undercuts the concept of purity and chastity. These become not qualities in themselves but goods on the market, not devalued if no one has seen them being handled.

Johnson's assertion that Susie has petted with boys who did not matter contradicts the traditional assumption that girls need romantic attachment to their partners before being persuaded to have some kind of sexual relations; Susie has experimented with 'boys she didn't care about' (58). Presumably, this is because they are not marriage material: if they were, she would care about them. Susie is being cautious with Joe, not risking him ending the relationship because she mismanages her sexuality. This is why Johnson feels 'it might be just as well' (58) that Joe does not excite Susie, since she wants to retain her detachment and her hold on him, which means sublimating her own desires.

Concluding, Johnson's article revisits the idea of technical virginity; without directly referencing Kinsey, the article shows awareness of the kind of hazy boundaries around virginity that he posited, exploiting the ambivalence of the meaning of 'virginity' (sexual inexperience/lack of full penetration) for the maintenance of the title even if not the purity it is taken to represent:

> I suppose the ideal girl is still technically a virgin but has done every possible kind of petting without actually having had intercourse. This gives her savoir-faire, while still maintaining her maiden dignity.
>
> (Johnson, 1959: 60)

As argued, if the idea of virginity was meant to convey merely the withholding of the ultimate act, coitus, then petting did not contravene this, but if it implied some kind of inherent value in innocence, then any sexual experience negated it. Virginity can thus be seen occupying its own vexed terrain, being *perhaps* subject to binary rules – one is either a virgin or a post-virgin, with no middle ground – but *perhaps* able to support a gradation of experiences. In either case, that it was the woman who seemed the one to decide the status of virginity provoked unease. Susie may be subject to internal debating about yielding, but it is still the female debating; furthermore, that the debate is internal means that, as long as she keeps her composure afterwards, the woman's eventual decision need not be visible. This brings us back to the ultimate anxiety, the invisibility of the experience being discussed and the fact that, if virginity is not discernible, then it can be faked.

I have noted elsewhere that this invisibility and the impossibility of definitive ocular proof caused as much anxiety to cinema, a medium predicated upon the visible, as it did to contemporary society (2006 a; 2010 a); fittingly, then, the final instance of this virginity question I want to mention is a filmic one. It does not come, however, from the group of films I posit were topically engendered by the K bomb and its fallout – what I call the 'virginity dilemma' cycle (Jeffers McDonald, 2006 a: 74) – but from a Doris Day film, *Lover Come Back* (1961). As will be discussed further, this film overtly inaugurated the character of the mature maiden played by the star. It seems significant, however, not just to this brief overview of the importance of the contemporary virginity obsession but also to Day's persona that the character, Carol Templeton, should be a *mature* maid, and not a girl like the other exemplar virgins, both of the 'virginity dilemma' cycle and the majority of those discussed in coterminous texts, such as the *Playboy* and *Atlantic Monthly* articles. Critically, Carol is nearer in age to the women in Kinsey's sample but by 1961 is being viewed as an anomaly – not part of the 50 per cent of Kinsey's group who *hadn't* in 1953, but seemingly, eight years later, one of a much smaller number of women still clinging humorously to outmoded mores. When Carol asks herself, therefore, in the film's moment of virginal crisis, 'Should I surrender?' it is a self-interrogation designed to appear comical rather than meaningful. It is in this altered context that, the following year, the media was overtaken by another best-selling book, viewed as being as news-worthy in its moment as Kinsey's report nine years earlier. This was Helen Gurley Brown's *Sex And The Single Girl*, a text which openly asserted 'nice girls do' (206) and that men were glad of it. Brown urged her readers to enjoy the men that came their way before Mr Right, training themselves to be the perfect, experienced partner qualified to entrap a highly marriageable man. Unlike

Johnson's Everygirl who allowed herself a certain amount of sexual freedom with boys who did not matter, for Brown every man matters because he will teach or *give* her something. In this latter point Brown's sexually amenable girl is not that different from the seemingly dichotomous figure of the manipulative maid: both barter intimacies for material goods, the main difference being that the Single Girl does not withhold the ultimate intimacy. Furthermore, the experiences garnered by the Single Girl will not be later denied, innocence feigned, when Mr Right turns up, but converted into yet more material goods: the most radical part of her message is not just that 'nice girls do', but that they assert it and can turn it to their own advantage:

> Should a man think you are a virgin? I can't imagine why, if you aren't. Is he? Is there anything particularly attractive about a thirty-four year old virgin?
>
> (Brown, 1962: 212)

Brown could almost have Day's Carol Templeton in mind as the 'thirty-four year old virgin'; the immense distance travelled from Kinsey's findings nine years before is laid bare in the fact that virginity is an inexperience now coming to seem harmful to, rather than essential for, good marital prospects.

It is important to be sensitive to the changing backgrounds which appear behind the figure of the virgin female across the period under study. The 1950s did not present a monolithic view of virginity, always working to close down female sexual agency; instead, a variety of conflicting views obtained at any one time, and offered sufficient challenges to previously assumed beliefs to shift widespread ideas about innocence and experience over time. Brown's advice to the Single Girl comes in a changed context, when not only was the contraceptive pill removing the fear of unmarried pregnancy, and thus challenging the double standard, but the media was beginning to recognise and represent this important change too. Brown confirms her still-provocative but now more acceptable attitude in a sentence that taps into the zeitgeist she shares with her readers: 'I don't think anybody is even asking anymore "Does she or doesn't she?" They just want to know where can they get that color?' (Brown, 1962: 202–3). This allusive line sums up her own philosophy on contemporary female sexuality, while nodding to the slogan that inspired her own line, 'Is she or isn't she?' (64). Understanding the implicit sexual interrogation in the hair dye advert, Brown suggests that, in the decade after Kinsey and Clairol, what women are pondering about is no longer whether others are having sex, but how they can have some too.

I have been asserting that Doris Day does not always play the virgin role as is so often assumed by other writers – in fact, Carol in *Lover Come Back* is the only explicit mature virgin that Day portrayed. I will be presenting my case for Day being so much more than this prudish old maid in subsequent sections, but where is my evidence that this is indeed the dominant view of Day? In order to contradict what I see as the stale orthodoxies endlessly repeated about the star, I first have to present some of those stale orthodoxies. That is the work of the next part of this section.

As will be seen in forthcoming sections, the initial reaction to the star on her launch in Hollywood was almost unanimous praise. At a certain point, however, the meanings accreting to Day began to have negative connotations, and although she was still lauded in the film fan magazines, it became fashionable among higher-brow publications to mock the star and the values – including an outmoded attitude to sex – for which she seemed to stand. The chapter on Al Capp's demolition of the star in his 1962 *Show* article will illustrate this inauguration of this trend.

If it became modish for intellectuals to despise Doris Day at the start of the 60s, to a certain extent I do not think this tendency has waned. In finding and exhibiting instances of the Day-as-virgin myth, I have discovered examples which are less excessive in their language than Capp's but still fundamentally similar in deriding the star because of attitudes and mores with which she is, unquestioningly, associated. Many are from academic books, dedicated to opening up new areas of interest or putting forward innovative views on a topic; that these should be content to advance their own new areas by adducing tired and untested assumptions about Day seems particularly frustrating. However, Day's name seems also to have entered a more casual public lexicon where she, as a multi-purpose symbol, can also be also evoked in fiction, biographies, and reviews. Again, as with the academic writers, the authors who choose to use her name are generally not doing so in order to say anything specific about Day herself, but about the sexual prudery or hypocrisy she is supposed to embody.

For example, in the 1990s, a television reviewer for *The Times*, Joe Joseph, invoked the star in his account of a programme about teen sexuality: 'By the time [teenagers] are 13 they already know more about sex than Doris Day had ever figured out' (Joseph, 1998: 47). Joseph here uses Day as a rhetorical device, a touchstone to evoke ideas around a vaguely sketched past, creating a fuzzy nostalgia for an unspecified time when, supposedly, children of 13 were allowed to be children, to seek innocent, rather than sexual, pleasures. What he means to evoke by use of the Day name, then, is the kind of old-timey appeal inherent in one of her films set in the early years of the twentieth century, *On Moonlight Bay* (1951), for example, set in 1915. But because he uses the star's actual name rather than working a little harder to gesture towards her films, he falls into the trap of assuming or suggesting that Day was not only inevitably playing roles with these characteristics in her film performances, but was *herself* a woman who was prudish, inexperienced, coy.

Joseph's invocation is meant to contrast age with youth, experience with ignorance, and depends for its sting on the unexpected way in which these pairs combine, surprisingly allying maturity with inexperience, tender years with sophistication. He has no business, then, in attempting to ameliorate this snapshot of Day as an older woman wilfully unacquainted with sexual matters. Interrogating the myth to which he contributes by adding yet another misleading reference to the long list of similar epithets is not his concern. But it is mine; and unpacking what he was trying to do with his rhetoric enables me to expose the hollow foundations of this lazy entry in the Day-as-virgin catalogue. Therefore, one of the ways in which this book hopes to recapture some of the multiplicity of Day's star persona will be by just such dissection of pieces written about her. Revealing the assumptions underlying the writings, as well as suggesting their motivations, should help expose how Day is being perceived and used. It will not be a matter, then, of gauging which texts are 'accurate' about the star, and which continue to rehearse the same old tired fantasies, but rather to assess each piece as something which emerges in a particular historical context and which fits – or fails to fit – the ongoing development of Day's media persona.

Like Joseph, both academic and popular writers tend to use Day as a quick way of evoking key tropes or conventions, idea-clusters that would take longer to conjure up if they went into proper detail. Doris Day is, for them, a shortcut to the prudish 50s, to virginity, to an irritating overabundance of energy. They are not interested in the actual Day herself so much as in gesturing toward something swiftly as an emblem. Unfortunately, these are the more numerous uses of her name, and the idea-clusters they are evoking are exactly what I want to contest in this book.

The most obvious word that Day's name suggests is 'virgin'. She is hailed as either representing attitudes against sex or being herself without sexual impulses; as being sex-averse, prudish or just asexual. Writers who see her in this way invoke her and her characters relentlessly, naming her as 'virgin' (Collins and Davis, 2004: 124; Miller and Arnold, 2004: 72; Maier, 2009: 151), one of the stars playing a 'virginal type' (Monroe in Finney, 1994: 178), performing in 'dumb virginal comedies' (Miller, 2007: 39) and representing 'always the virgin' (Quart and Auster, 2001: 55).

Next, there is an emphasis on the particular period during which Day was a star. She is used in this way as an emblem of 'The 1950s' to contrast later times' more permissive views on sexuality. Thus Day and her films are compared with the 70s as evoked by Woody Allen's film *Annie Hall* (1977). When hero Alvy (Allen) defends masturbation, he calls it 'sex with someone I love'. Joe Garner comments that 'This was not the sort of pillow talk you'd find in a Doris Day comedy' (2004: 164). Day's name here acts to contrast the staid 50s with the hip 70s, as well as the innuendo-laden sex comedy of the late 1950s and early 1960s with the more overtly sexual and realistic romcoms of the later decade. Similarly, dance historian, Sally Banes, writing about avant-garde art practices in Greenwich Village in the early 1960s, comments on the repressed nature of physicality in the previous decade, which Day has so often been taken to represent. She contrasts her full account of the polymorphous dance and art scene in the Village with *That Touch of Mink*, summing up the whole of 1950s and early 1960s cinema when she alleges that Day 'breaks into hives at the mention of pre-marital sex' in the film (1993: 232). Obviously, not only is Day being used as a symbol of a static, conformist and pathological view of sex here, but furthermore just *one* of her films – and one not from the 50s but from 1962, the same period she discussed – is inaccurately invoked to exemplify both the star's and the entire decade's views on sex.

Day further represents the 50s when this period of supposed conformity and consensus is contrasted with the distance 'we' have come from it 'now', whenever and whoever 'now' and 'we' are. Novelist Fannie Flagg not only signals a Noughties heroine is outmoded by overtly commenting 'She was hopelessly out-of-date', but also by providing an example: 'Doris Day was still her favourite movie star' (2010: 74). Day is made to evoke the 50s as a far-off time, a bygone society, which could not have any relevance for today and marks her fan as out of touch with contemporary mores. Similarly, the *Cult Guide to Movies* uses Day as paradigmatic of all that is square, lauding the psychedelic effects in one animated cartoon at the expense of another. To inflate the weirdness of *Hugo The Hippo* (1973/1976), the writer says *this* cartoon makes *Yellow Submarine* (1968) seem about 'as far out as Doris Day' (Simpson, 2010: 16). This unhip quality links to her perceived sexual prudery, and underlines again the distance between the conformist 50s and the swinging, drug-laden 60s and 70s. Camille Paglia has often denounced Day for ruining her girlhood by setting up a standard of golden passive perfection the author never felt she – as brunette, Italian and non-submissive – could meet. In *Sex, Art and American Culture* (1992) Paglia again indulges her dislike of the star, denouncing her not only as an emblem of a gender essentialism that continues to affect contemporary feminism, returning it to a set of 'Doris Day Fifties clichés about noble womanhood' (87) but also seeing Day as the 'applecheeked dictator' of the entire period (111).

While Day is frequently employed in this way as a simple historical marker, symbolising the 1950s as a decade, another of the most common methods that academic authors, in particular, use Day is as a chronological emblem specifically in contrast with another period; they can then set up this – whenever it is – as more liberal, exciting or independent, both within Hollywood cinema and in American society itself. Day is constantly indicted as a debased female star representing a decline in her roles from the active, independent heroines of, most generally, 1930s and 40s screwball comedies, and 1940s films noirs. Sara Evans writes about Day's 'silly, fluffy roles' in contrast to the stronger ones performed by stars like Katharine Hepburn or Joan Crawford (1989: 248); Barbara Monroe similarly finds Day performing 'cute-when-she's-mad' characters out of keeping with those in earlier films (178). Again, Jasmine Paul and Bette J Kauffman contrast the 'perky, wholesome marriage-prospect-next-door' as performed by Day (in Valdivia, 1995: 169) with wartime worker Rosie the Riveter, and Bernice Murphy alters the description of Day only slightly when she includes Day in the 'cheery girls-next-door' who again contrast with the 'sassy, sharp-witted and sexually aggressive career women [...] that had dominated the movie screens during the late 1930s and 1940s' (2009: 53).

Not only does the name of Doris Day, however, act as a form of shorthand for everything these authors want to deride in order to praise what they perceive as the stronger female roles and actresses of other times; the star also does duty as *the* symbol of 1950s conformist housewives even when she is not being contrasted with others. Susan Hayward sees Day as 'the dutiful wife at home supporting her husband (by staying out of the job market)' (2006: 381) despite the star's frequent films where she has not only a job but a career. Rachel Shteir, writing about Rose Louise Hovick, who became the famous stripper Gypsy Rose Lee, chooses to contrast her heroine by constructing Day as her opposite, the true epitome of the 'domestic consumerist' (2010: 155). Gay Smith goes one step further; not only does she set blonde Doris up as the ultimate emblem of 1950s wifeliness, but she conjures her as contrast to another famous 50s woman:

> Different from the popular 1950s wife image of the blond Doris Day, All-American-Girl type, Ethel Rosenberg was small in frame, dark haired, implacable and enigmatic in demeanour. Ethel was Jewish, the daughter of immigrants, Lower Eastside, poor...
> (Smith, 2010: 172)

Pitting Day against Rosenberg in this way seems to set up the star as somehow complicit in the eventual execution of a woman here presented as her Manichean opposite. But the account not only simplifies the politics behind Rosenberg's arrest, trial and execution, it elides all similarities between the two women – such as their shared status as descendants 'of immigrants'. Both could, in fact, despite the enormous difference in their fates, be seen as victims manipulated by the contemporary media.

Two final circuits of meaning revolve around Day on the occasions she is used as shorthand: the first is to do with cleanliness, a purity of mind and body which clearly gestures back to her perceived asexuality; the second is a reading of her boundless good-humoured energy which begins to view this positive gift in a negative light. Although both were perceived at the very beginning of her movie career to be associated with the star, when Day's name is evoked in relation to them now, both become indicative of the seemingly pathological need for Day and her characters to cling to their chastity.

Day is constantly commented on as being 'squeaky-clean' (Hayward, 2006: 80) of presenting a 'squeaky-clean image' to the world (Burke, 2002: 308), of being so 'squeaky-clean' that she is 'antisexual' (Doniger, 2006: 80). Paglia again derides the star for being 'so well-scrubbed' (12), while Leonard Quart and Albert Auster manage to link the two final tropes around the star, describing her as conveying a 'super-hygenic wholesome cheerfulness' (55). While none of these critics would surely suggest being clean is a bad thing, it is the words chosen to qualify this basic cleanliness which hint at a perceived pathology. Day appears to be so pristine and spotless that her unsoiled state can only be the result of constant vigilance and hard work. She must destroy dirt compulsively, attempting to rid her body of odours and stains until she seems medically antibacterial. This may be laudable, but it is not *sensual*. By hinting through their language choices that there is an obsessive urge in Day to keep herself sanitary and uncontaminated at all times, the writers reinforce ideas about her frantic clinging to sexual, as well as somatic, purity.

Finally, Day's genial liveliness is made suspect. Interestingly, one of the most over-used words applied to Day throughout the period of her live career is 'bouncy'. In my sample of more recent invocations of the star, no author uses this term, although Paul and Kaufman, and Camille Paglia use the word 'perky' to describe her. In earlier uses, this phenomenal energy of the star's was celebrated; at that point it carries no ostensible taint of criticism. The idea of bounce and get-up-and-go seems attractive, rather than off-putting. Over time, however, this notion of liveliness becomes another point against her, the implication being that she remains annoying and coy because her galumphing energies are channelled into affable high-jinks rather than sexual activity. Similarly, Peter Redgrove, the British poet and a friend of Ted Hughes, used Day as a symbol in an interview about Hughes and his wife Sylvia Plath which he gave to Hughes' biographer, Elaine Feinstein, in 1999. Looking back on changes he perceived in Plath after she returned from a stay in America, he commented on her seeming 'bright and ebullient but rather false, like Doris Day. She had a Doris Day mask' (2003: 97). This comment seems less an old response recalled now, so much as a more recent reaction to the meaning Day has latterly come to assume in popular culture. Redgrove uses Day here as an emblem of the early 60s, picking up on the vitality found in her by contemporaneous and subsequent commentators, and finding it to be a performance, a masquerade. The fascinating fact about this is it is something which was fore-grounded by Day and her vehicles consciously. Redgrove criticises Plath through his dismissal of Day's fake persona, without realising this quality of masquerade was one intentionally created by the star later on in her career.

In conclusion, while these invocation texts demonstrably vary over their goals, either denigrating the actor or using her to gesture towards abstract notions she seems to symbolize, they unite in conjuring the name 'Doris Day' without investigating the accuracy of the connotations being used to condemn her. The star persona of Doris Day becomes much more interesting and varied when looked at afresh, rather than when viewed via the mass of inherited stale assumptions about her.

Although it is one of the main tasks of this book to see when and how her persona gained its various meanings and these meanings shifted with time, it is the other main aim of the research to reveal the sheer multiplicity of these connotations and the wider historical and societal contexts which prompted them. Rather than simply revisiting unchallenged ideas *about* the period, this book will examine actual artefacts *from* the period, in the form of film fan magazines, lifestyle publications, newspaper and trade journal reports, and advertising material as well as Day's body of work. In this way it will demonstrate that what 'Doris Day' meant was never monolithically established and uniformly accepted across the period under investigation, but was always much more subject to flux and contestation, just like the views of sexuality she was taken to represent. By returning Day's films and performances as much as possible to their original backgrounds, and looking anew at all of these – films, performances, changing historical contexts, press response and accreting meanings – the easy suppositions that are endlessly repeated about both Day and the virginal status she is often seen to represent can be problematised.

SECTION 2
Film Fan Magazines

1 Overview

In the previous section I briefly sketched the historical and social backdrop against which Doris Day's career became, and stayed, highly prominent. Her recordings, film roles, personal appearances and media persona in general all not only formed a part of this backdrop, but also specifically received weight and inferences from it. In considering Day's work and persona, then, it is important to examine the contexts in which these were operating. In this middle section of the book I move from examining the widest context, narrowing the focus to concentrate solely on Day's presentation within popular magazines. These magazines were important to the film studios because they worked to foster reader awareness of stars in the run-up to new releases and, just as importantly, to maintain this awareness in the gaps between film appearances. Magazines were thus a conduit for delivering Day to audience members outside her film vehicles. They sought to entice readers to see the latest films of their favourite stars, but also served as a means of keeping in touch with them, maintaining a relationship, when the movies were over. Unlike the films, which alone could deliver the thrill of seeing the star in action, magazines could only deliver stories and still photographs; but also unlike the films, they *lasted*, were available to be poured over again and again, at least until a new issue or another magazine story supplanted their interest. And there were many, many magazines. During the major period of Day's stardom, there were approximately 64 monthly film magazines, with others operating on a bi-monthly, quarterly or annual basis too (Slide, 2010: 234–245)[4]. In addition, women's service and lifestyle magazines, as well as Sunday supplements to newspapers, specialist arts magazines, current affairs journals, and the scandal rags paid attention to stars, although less regularly.

The frequency of Day's appearances in the film magazines fluctuated across the course of her film and later TV career. At certain periods she achieved almost blanket coverage of the published movie magazines, both issue after issue within the same publication, and across the range of periodicals available. For instance, in 1952, an illustrated article on Day appeared in every one of the 12 successive issues of *Movie Stars Parade* across the entire year, a fact one reader finally complained about, asking in a letter published in the December edition:

> Why is it that Doris Day is splashed all over every issue of your magazine? You've neglected other stars like Liz Taylor and Van Johnson! *Mario Mendoza, Mexico City, Mexico*
>
> (Anon, 1952 g: 85)

Although undeniably thorough in its coverage of the star across the 12-month period, however, *Movie Stars Parade* was only following the general trend that made 1952 the year of Day's highest ever media profile. The star appeared in at least 75 magazine articles across the year. Interestingly, this did not correspond with a particularly successful or innovative film role. Charting a star persona's presence outside of her films provides a pattern of peaks and troughs which can vary enormously from an account based on her movie chronology, which is why it is so important to look at the magazines themselves, in taking account of her media persona. Even in her busiest years, 1950 and 1951, in both of which she released three films and was busy making three more, the movies alone could not keep her in the forefront of public attention. This power rested with the film magazines, which returned to her again and again, signalling her significance by profiling her so repeatedly.

In this section, therefore, I will explore the film magazines' treatment of Day, detailing the fascination they reveal with getting at the truth about her life, love affairs, career choices, personality, indeed her very *essence*. Not having new facts to report every month did not deter the magazines from publishing new articles on the star in issue after issue; authors ruthlessly plundered each others' works, recycling interview materials in new forms, so that a chance comic remark (allegedly) made by Day in one story would turn up relayed with all seriousness in another. Similarly, the 'facts' of Day's childhood and early career were repeated so consistently that by 1952, just five years into her film career, she could confidently tell one reporter:

> Everybody who has ever read a line about me knows how Barney [Rapp, her first band manager] dropped off that German surname of mine and borrowed that professional surname from the song 'Day After Day'.
>
> (Waterbury, 1952: 88)

This would not stop the magazines from repeatedly feeding 'everybody' the same story again and again in the future, however.

This section starts with an account of how Day's persona was conceived in the film magazines across her career, beginning with her arrival on the Hollywood scene, continuing through her major stardom, career dips and transformations, and on into her television years. Although there was often a dissenting voice or two, the overall presentation of Day among the magazines was remarkably consistent at any one moment. While the persona was thus constructed consistently within periods, it also radically changed over time.

The second chapter in this section is devoted to closer consideration of the repeating concepts occurring in the magazines' coverage of the star. Here too there is a remarkable consistency in the key terms, notions and metaphors used to evoke, and evoked by, Doris Day. Of the 34 recurrent tropes I found in press pieces across her career from 1948 to 1986, 24 were in place within the first three years of her film career, six more came on board within the next five years, and only two began later. Beyond this, these repeating tropes also carry across into the afterimage of Day, with many of them recurring in the more current invocations of the star isolated in the Context section. It is important to note, however, that while the concepts remain steady, the *value* attached to them varies considerably. As will be seen, tropes like 'Energy' or 'Clean' start by being weighed positively in their first contexts, but become, over time, associated with more negative aspects, eventually seeming symptoms of pathology.

The final chapter of this section narrows the focus still further to examine four specific articles in greater detail. This is important to show how more than one concept or trope evoked by Doris Day could be worked through in any one article. Of the specific pieces I have selected from my wider field of 479, two are articles which came out around the time of a change in the types of role Day was playing, introducing concomitant new inflections to her perceived meanings, while the other two come from either end of her career. The first therefore was published just as Day was starting out as a film actor, and the last comments overtly on her television persona, while acknowledging the debt this has to her movie roles and characters too. This final piece comes from

Mad magazine, the satirical American periodical. The analysis of the *Mad* piece raises one further point: that although my sample of 479 press items is largely made up of articles from film magazines (roughly 89 per cent), it also includes 48 stories from newspapers, lifestyle and women's service magazines and other monthly periodicals which enjoyed different, and generally higher, regard than the rather lowly film magazines[5]. However, I have not included pieces from the trade papers among this catchment; periodicals such as *Motion Picture Herald*, *The Hollywood Reporter* and *Variety* helped to convey and perpetuate Day's persona within the industry in fascinating ways, but since they were largely read by industry insiders rather than members of the public, I have excluded them from the sample interrogated here.

My method of investigation with these periodical and magazine articles is not only to analyse a specific text and the myths that seem to underlie it, but also to see, wherever possible, what else in each issue contributes to, or detracts from, the overall message being propounded. The film magazines in my sample often include more than one item on a star, and can employ the full range of contents to play a part in her build-up. There seem to be three main ways the magazines do this. Most rarely there is the *star trail*: here a star will appear on the cover of a magazine, then be commented on in the table of contents roundup; there might be an advert for a forthcoming film, a mention in the gossip column and then an editorial piece on her, accompanied by photographs. Each of these provides a separate occasion to vaunt the star, but taken cumulatively they are much more weighty and impressive, with the shorter items setting up a trail for the star which leads the reader to her while magnifying the sense of her importance. The star trail works through the iteration of items about the same person; alternatively, when the pieces on the same figure do not build to a larger piece on a new film role or activity, but just serve to keep her name current, a form of *star saturation* is achieved, especially when this proliferates both across successive issues and over other magazines. As an example of this star saturation for Day, the September 1949 *Screen Guide* works well: the reader would not only find the star on the cover, but also commented on inside on page one ('our pixie-like cover girl'), with a snippet of gossip about her on page six and an article on her 'favorite recipe' on page 74. Although these items here do not build to a bigger piece on the star, but are small and dispersed across the issue, their frequency emphasises Day's importance. Indeed, I suggest that because there are these four different sites for her display, she is actually being highlighted more than if there were only a single sustained article. Finding her here and there throughout the magazine, the reader is given the sensation that Day is *everywhere* right now, is the new big thing. This feeling would have been even more inescapable when Day was appearing simultaneously in other magazines at the time: in, for example, 28 separate articles in 1949, or, as formerly mentioned, in each of the 12 issues of *Movie Stars Parade* in 1952.

While the trail is relatively rare in my sample, Day experiences a sizeable amount of this saturation in the film magazines. One further common way the fan magazines arranged their material was to orchestrate a *shared coverage*; here several stars would each have four of five items on them spread throughout an issue, with others receiving two and three pieces. This seems the most common form of publicity organisation within my sample of film magazines. All three methods of assembling the movie star promotion within any one issue can be perceived as a form of product placement, given that the star was a product like any other. However, where magazines accept paid advertising for material other than film-related items, a form of tangential advertising is in operation. This is most common outside the film magazines, being found instead in the lifestyle periodicals. Here a star featured in an article will also receive another, tangential, mention in the advertising material; with Day, this was usually the promotion of a record album.

The star trail works to set up a reading path which affects the reader's movement through a magazine. Such movement through the contents is commented on in two different theoretical pieces, a book-length study *Decoding Women's Magazines* by Ellen McCracken (1993) and an article by Sally Stein, 'The Graphic Ordering of Desire' (1992). Stein takes an innovative stance: where I am metaphorically taking the articles on Day to pieces, Stein *literally* takes her magazine subjects apart, 'exploding them' (149) in order to see how articles and advertisements were stitched together to make the whole item. Stein examined copies of *The Ladies Home Journal* from between 1919 and 1939 and found that editorial pieces were increasingly cut up and dispersed across the body of the magazine in order to maximise exposure to advertisements; to follow the narrative of a specific story, the reader would have to turn more pages, be exposed to more promotional material, than if the article were laid out on consecutive pages. That this was an obvious policy of the magazines became clear when Stein performed her analysis across sufficient material: readers were being directed to follow certain paths through the magazine in order to take them past the maximum number of adverts. As Stein puts it:

> The interruption of articles may appear to the average reader as a commonplace if inconvenient occurrence, but the resulting movement back and forth also serves as a form of entrapment. Thus the reader will find it considerably more difficult to confine her time and attention to a single article. She is forced to flip through the rest of the magazine in order to pursue her immediate interests.
>
> (Stein, 1992: 149)

McCracken's analysis of many 1980s women's magazines, by contrast, suggests that this delay in consuming the whole article is actually one of the *pleasures* of magazine reading (1993: 8). This intentional delay is both, at different times, inconvenient *and* pleasurable; the various reading strategies promoted by the fan magazines, including the star trail, star saturation and shared coverage, can thus be compared to the competing gratifications presented by the cinema and by the magazines themselves.

The placing of an article or picture within a magazine therefore proves to be as potentially significant as what is being said or portrayed. My method is to examine items on Day in their widest possible contexts, then. Combing available contemporaneous material for mentions of Day, I build up an evolving picture of her star persona, comparing notions suggested by the fan magazines with the star's own career developments, roles and exterior life events. Miriam Hansen has recommended this broad-cast net of references be sought so that, as much as possible, a 'horizon of reception' (Hansen, 1991: 93) can be established for the star being investigated which relies not only on the filmic texts which showcase the actor, but also works on:

> the public discourse surrounding [the star] – reviews, interviews, studio publicity, articles in fan magazines and the general press, popular biographies – sources that at once document, manipulate and constitute [the star's] reception.
>
> (Hansen, 1991: 94)

This 'public discourse' which served to 'document, manipulate and constitute' Doris Day's star persona was largely constructed through the magazine articles devoted to her across her career; it is thus vital to examine these in order to trace the evolution not only of her mass media persona, but the assumptions arising from this persona.

2 Account of the Persona

Doris Day signed a personal contract with director–producer Michael Curtiz on 15 May 1947[7] which affiliated her with Warner Bros. and began work on her first film, *Romance On The High Seas* the very next month. Production lasted from early June to early August 1947[8] and by the following March, when she began filming her second feature, Day had already secured mentions in the film magazines. The first few pieces on her chose to highlight her established stardom as a singer and recording artist, but also noted that she made a good impression in her first acting role. Day was hailed as a new star by *Motion Picture* in August 1948, and other magazines were also quick to award this appellation.

The material on Day across the first few years of her arrival on the film scene was overwhelmingly positive about the star and her talents. The pieces published in the first two years or so were devoted to familiarising the reader with the new star's biographical history, her likes and dislikes, her family set-up, so much ink was spent describing her house in the Toluca Lake district of Los Angeles, where Day lived with her son Terry, mother Alma, and dogs, as well as outlining her redecorating plans and preferred activities for leisure time. Her clothes – at this stage always casual – were usually described and highlighted in photographs, and there was inevitably also a mention of her latest and forthcoming vehicles. In this way the articles act as not-so-covert advertisements for the star and her next movie under the guise of offering fun facts and vital statistics about a new Hollywood arrival. One other factor much mentioned at this point is Day's status as a twice-divorced single mother. Although the accent is on her care for Terry and her eagerness to romp and play with him, there is also a charge around the young, attractive, single woman. Men friends are referred to, both in articles where the studio probably had a hand in setting up a date for the magazine's benefit, as with 'Day and Date' (Anon, 1948 g: 50–53), and in reports over which they presumably had less sway, the snippets which came out in gossip columns suggesting more personal relationships established outside of studio control. For example, 'Inside Stuff' in the January 1948 issue of *Photoplay* queried whether Day was in a relationship with Jack Carson, her first co-star (Anon, 1948 a: 12); in 1949 an item in *Screen Guide* also hinted at an affair with another actor[9].

When Day married her agent, Marty Melcher, on her 29th birthday in 1951, the film magazines' interest in her love life underwent a significant shift. Now ensconced in her third marriage, with Terry, Alma and Marty living with her, Day stopped being perceived in terms of a new starlet, a bouncy young girl-about-town, and began to be seen more as a settled Hollywood matron, a young housewife and mother whose job just happened to be being a movie star. Articles become intent on establishing Day as a woman 'Just Like Us', just like the readers of the film magazines. Like 'us', she is a 'demon shopper' (Anon, 1952 b: 34–37) and loves to go clothes-hunting, has a home to run, a son to bring up, a husband to take care of, dogs to feed and exercise, furniture to polish, even if, unlike us, she also has a maid to take care of the housework, a live-in mother to do all the cooking, and a day job that involves weeks of dance and vocal practice, intensive hours of filming, and a high degree of press attention at all times. While the articles often attempt to elide these latter facts, they cannot help but refer to them when they also follow the magazine rule of promoting the latest film vehicle, and, as they so often do, noting in a magazine article the frequency with which Day is dealt with in other magazine articles. This self-reflexive, 'Meta' turn of the magazines is a strand which runs right through the length of Day's media career.

If the articles of the early years of her marriage portrayed Doris Day and Marty Melcher as being like any other young newly-weds, with an interest in their home, child and each other, the insistence on the couple's refusal to 'go Hollywood', to fit into the movie colony's hedonistic way of life, became increasingly noticeable until about 1953. After this the theme took on a more negative frisson, as the pair became known not only for shunning fancy parties and premieres, but also for eschewing smoking and alcohol, for installing a soft drink soda bar rather than a hard liquor one, and for daily Bible reading. The Melchers became known as devout adherents to Christian Science, despite the fact that many of the articles that mentioned this fact also mention that the pair did not want it well-known, least they seem 'preachy'. From being 'Just Like Us' in not going to Hollywood parties, but preferring barbecues in their own backyard, the Melchers had, together, by about 1954, gone so far beyond this preference for the simple life that they had become *unlike us*: in the severity of their religious practice they had, seemingly, forgotten that star worship has a large component of wish fulfilment and vicarious living. If fans can't go to premieres in fancy gowns and furs to drink cocktails with movie stars, they want movies stars to do so! For a couple who could, to choose to stay home and drink chocolate malteds instead, seemed not upright and inspiring, but prissy and perverse.

Around this low point in the press attitudes to the Melchers together, Doris Day also suffered a personal setback. Having worked on 15 films in a seven-year period, and just finished the physically-demanding title role in *Calamity Jane*, Day found a lump in her breast, according to biographical sources (Hotchner, 1976: 120; Kaufman, 2008: 1620). Christian Science teaches that prayer is the only effective cure for physical problems; devotees shun professional medical help. Eventually Day had to see a doctor and the lump, removed, proved to be a non-cancerous cyst, but the anxiety this had caused her, and the necessity of countering one of the major tenets of her religion, made her depressed and in need of a rest. Melcher and Day cancelled promotions for her next picture, *Lucky Me*, and filming itself was postponed. Magazine writers did not react well to this; already beginning to feel disenchanted with the narrative Day and Melcher were trying to establish about themselves as a couple and Day as a star, the authors en masse took the new publicity ban badly and began to write negative articles about Day. Even when she capitulated and began to give interviews again, there was a tendency to rehash the damaging rumours and conclusions, even in articles where the author was ostensibly trying to combat these.

The Hollywood Women's Press Corps, a body of magazine and newspaper writers which each year awarded the Sour Apple to the male and female stars who had proved Least Cooperative, gave Day the award in 1954. This rift with the press, even though ostensibly patched up, marked the first low point in Day's relationship with the magazine authors. It was a point that affected attitudes on both sides in the long-term, even when both pretended otherwise and attempted to carry on as before. Day had been made aware of the power of the press to damage her persona, and the press had learned how much they resented a star who attempted to insist on her privacy. Neither side forgot the incident.

Luckily for Day, a new film role soon distracted the magazines from their antagonistic stance. *Love Me Or Leave Me* (1955) led to an evolution of Day's persona, taking it from its well-established first stage, in which the star was perceived as a likable, energetic and talented tomboy, its second iteration which involved her modulating into the 'young married' character discussed above, and now directing Day's cluster of meanings in a different direction. Playing Ruth Etting, the 1920s Broadway star and recording artist, seems now a natural enough choice for Day: she had the vocal skills to tackle Etting's well-known songs as well as the dancing ability to recreate approximations of some of her production numbers. What attracted contemporary press attention, however, was the *dramatic* skill required. Etting had been a small-time showgirl in gangster-controlled, Prohibition era Chicago, rising from the chorus to become a star through both her own talents and the efforts of mobster boyfriend, Marty 'The Gimp' Snyder. After marrying and later divorcing Snyder, she had a relationship with her pianist, but Snyder shot and wounded him, for which he was imprisoned. The mature themes thus inherent in the biography seemed to call for a very different kind of performance from those Day had given in the light romantic and musical comedies in which she had previously starred. 'Acting' at this point became a key trope associated with the Day name in the articles on her, as magazines celebrated the performer's new maturity, her convincing portrayal of an ambitious, manipulative and eventually tragic figure. Some of the points habitually associated with the star's persona were given new inflections at this moment: the usual mention of her sartorial style now took notice of her much more revealing onscreen gowns, the display of her cleavage that had not been seen before, as well as a turn to more formal attire in private life, away from the denims and checked shirts highlighted earlier. From a young married woman with a normal middle class lifestyle, 'Just Like Us', Day now emerged anew as something unlike fans, and desirably so: she became *starry*. As will be discussed in the detailed analysis of an article from around this time, in this section's final chapter, *Love Me Or Leave Me* renewed both the star's persona and media currency by reinforcing several of the dominant tropes usually associated with her, such as energy, talent, voice, looks and clothes, but gave them new – and occasionally ambiguous – resonances. The main resonance was sex, and it was much needed to ensure the star's survival at this point. By bringing sex back into the mix, even if tacitly, Day and her management accomplished the first partial revamping of Day's cluster of meanings, recovering some of the enthusiasm for the star that had obtained when she first appeared, as a sexy single mother, on the Hollywood scene.

After her performance as Ruth Etting had earned Day favourable media attention as a more mature star in a newly mature dramatic role, press material on her reverted almost immediately to presenting the previous incarnation of the star, the modest, fun and home-loving girl next door. Articles appeared in which Day herself (allegedly) seemed to backtrack on the Etting persona; despite pieces promoting the film which vaunted how much she loved her new, more sexualised look, now articles appeared which denied this, and reaffirmed Day's habitual commitment to more modest clothing and behaviour. This reversal could perhaps be read as the actor's attempt at 'damage limitation', a conscious decision to reaffirm her well-established 'nice person' image after her portrayal of Etting had perhaps hinted that Day too might be ambitious and calculating. According to Day's 1976 autobiography, she received large amounts of fan mail protesting at her onscreen behaviour in *Love Me Or Leave Me*, with objection being taken to her drinking alcohol, for example (Hotchner, 1976: 144). Day's interviews in the following months' magazines might therefore be seen as attempts to pacify fans and to reassure those she had alienated that she had not really changed.

Interestingly, however, she did not immediately revert to the safer roles in light musical comedies that had previously made up the bulk of her film work. Freed from her contract with Warner Bros. after seven years, Day seems to have taken a conscious decision to work on a run of darker films, dramas which, seen together, not only demonstrate her serious acting skills, but also consistently highlight the gender inequalities enshrined within contemporary American society. *Love Me Or Leave Me, The Man Who Knew Too Much* and *Julie* all present a central female character who is unhappily married, dominated and tyrannised over by her husband, and, in the last and most melodramatic of the three, actively at risk from him. While this run of films now presents a very interesting career move on Day's part in committing herself to presenting a dystopian view of marriage, at the time these roles generated no specific interest from the film magazines; these carried on treating her in the usual way as the fun, energetic housewife whose job just happened to make her internationally famous and incredibly wealthy. There was no attempt to read off a worrying commentary on Day's marriage to Melcher from the roles she played; though there had been hints of marital problems added into her illness and depression around the time of the magazines' first disenchantment with Day around 1954, this did not surface now when she was publicly performing matrimonial discontent. This disjunction between onscreen role and magazine persona is not the only point at which there is a clear divergence between the two.

The roles the star played after this darker trio of the mid-1950s attempted to tap in again to the dominant, tamer, persona established before *Love Me Or Leave Me*. Musical and light comedy roles reappeared as her main fare; but this time the public response was not so favourable and, as gossip columns noted, Day's management looked for different vehicles in which to place her in order to boost her popularity again. This was the moment of the second conscious revamping of her persona; and again sex came to the rescue. Day was persuaded to participate in *Pillow Talk* (1959) a witty and risqué sex comedy, the daring quality of which – for its period – was only exceeded by its extremely glossy production values. For the first time, Day appeared as a chic, urban career woman, not only in Manhattan, and in a highly paid job, but in Technicolor; her extensive Jean Louis-designed wardrobe showcased her trim figure and was accessorised by real jewels and furs. The combination of lavish mise-en-scene, witty script, sexual situations, expert character acting and handsome co-star, in Rock Hudson, as well as adept comic playing, swept Day to her highest financial success and, at the same time, subjected her star persona to another evolution. Now Day was being perceived as one of the best-dressed women on screen, in Hollywood, in America; her maturely sexual body highlighted by the clinging, sophisticated outfits of the film's wardrobe, she seemed perfectly in control both of it, and her own desires.

Pillow Talk was appreciated as a departure for the star because of her 'spicy' role, (Anon, 1960 a: 32), her more sophisticated appearance now marking Day out as a 'gorgeously-gowned, worldly doll' (Tusher, 1960: 27), and her character, Jan Morrow, a 'sexpot' (Lippert, 1960: 56). As with any Hollywood success, as soon as it had been achieved, a number of players began to look to repeat the elements that had made it popular. Day's team, the film's producer Ross Hunter, and the studio all wanted to make another film which would emulate *Pillow Talk*'s bankability. While she worked on two other pictures in 1960, therefore, there was already a sense that these were placeholders until the next Doris Day sex comedy could be found and made. It appeared in 1961, with the same team of producer, studio, co-stars Rock Hudson and Tony Randall and half the original writing team.[10] But instead of confirming the Day 'sexpot' screen character, and perhaps conferring an element of mature adult sexuality permanently onto Day's media persona, the vehicle, *Lover Come Back*, was responsible for a different long-lasting torsion to her image. With this film and the press material around it, the word 'virgin' comes into play for the first time.

Lover Come Back in fact achieved such a revisioning of the Day character that previous roles began to be read in its light. While it was the only film to insist explicitly that Day was playing a mature maiden, after its release writers in both the film magazines and the wider press began to see the immensely sexy *Pillow Talk* in the same way, and to view these Day heroines, *and* those of later films, as being prudish or at least sexually inexperienced. There was a sense of there being 'a Doris Day formula' for a film (Capp, 1961), which would ensure box office success and involve sexual skirmishes from which the heroine would inevitably emerge unscathed, unlike the hero who, in the period's misogynistic formulation, would have suffered irreparable damage by becoming married (Walker, 1968: 231–251).

Bizarrely, however, at the very moment that these chaste conceptions of the typical Day film and heroine were being established in popular media understanding, Day was also simultaneously being held up, by the same film magazines, as a figure of sexual intrigue and scandal. Magazines announced her imminent divorce and speculated salaciously about men who had become Day's lovers. New potential husbands were announced and appraised, with the May 1963 issue of *Movie TV Secrets* going so far as to trumpet 'Wedding Bells for Doris Day'; further asking 'Is there a baby on the way?' the cover showed her snuggling, in a seemingly candid shot, face-to-face with actor Van Johnson. The article inside the magazine, however, performed the usual *volte face* in denying the facts proclaimed outside, attempting to ameliorate the outrageousness of its claims by suggesting Day's *friends* alleged there were three main contenders for Day's hand (Anon, 1963 b: 22–25, 58, 60). And all this while she was still married to Marty Melcher.

One of the main topics of interest in the account of Day's (alleged) illicit love life at this time was her supposed interest in black baseball player Maury Wills. Many magazine items hinted that Day and the married Wills were involved in an affair; the worst was surely *Movie TV Secrets*, which sold itself on the titillating cover story, 'The Trouble Doris Day Has Had Since The Mixed Marriage' (Anon, 1961 c). This story was actually about the marriage of Day's father to a black woman, but the title suggests that Day is its subject. The entire piece manages not to mention the Wills rumours, although in the topical context it was an obvious reference. Rumours about the star and various black male sportsmen and musicians continued to circulate during the period of her stardom.

Around the same point (from about 1960 onwards), one further trope became associated with Day's persona: age. Although early and middle period press pieces had regularly mentioned how old Day was[11], this was more in the spirit of giving the reader vital information on a favourite star; now, with Day on the cusp of 40, for the first time comments began to accrue that stressed her age as a potential problem. The resurgence of references to her son, Terry, now grown up and in his early 20s, perhaps necessitated this attention to Day's maturing. With a son of 20, she could no longer appear to be 30 herself. Magazine articles began to give her age to establish, sometimes tacitly, sometimes overtly, a juxtaposition with a role she was playing onscreen, or actions off-screen. In this way, two 1964 pieces claim Day is 'the oldest teenager' in Hollywood (Madison, 1964: 30–31) or indeed 'the world' (Anon, 1964 a), while a 1961 item on the Doris Day formula film refers to her character's 'mature yet girlish' charms (Capp, 1961). This snide comment intends to suggest that Day's sexual reserve is bordering on the unnecessary. The 'forty year old virgin' persona coalesces the last two tropes centring on the actor, and crystallizes the negative attitude that began to obtain. Day thus appeared to play, and in some articles was perceived to *be*, a prudish sex-averse woman who, in Molly Haskell's evocative phrase, was busily engaged in 'defending her maidenhead into a ripe old age' (1974: 265), jealously guarding her virtue long after anyone could be interested in relieving her of it. Yet articles toeing this – eventually dominant – line, were found on the same magazine stands and even in the same magazines as the other Doris Day, the multi-adulteress who seemed, in Day's own phrase 'Lady Bountiful of the sheets' (Hotchner, 1976: 202). From the beginning of the decade, then, until 1968, the film magazines oscillated between several positions on Day. Articles frequently espoused one of a few positions towards the star: she was impossible, ageing, pious and coy; she was impossible, ageing, and a torrid man-eater; she was the nicest possible person to work with, cheerful, fun and so popular that her very presence in a film guaranteed her and her co-workers success and money.

Day's husband and manager Marty Melcher died suddenly in April 1968 and the magazines went into overdrive. From occupying a place of relative, and relatively new, obscurity in the magazines' attention, Day came back to full prominence as an object of intense interest and speculation in the years following his passing. Notably, the articles in my sample mainly took a sensationalist route, dramatizing the moment of death itself as if the writer had been present ('Doris Day's last words to her dying husband!', Bascombe, 1968) or obscurely hinting at some murky secret connected with Melcher's illness ('What Doris Day Will Never Know About Her Husband's Shocking Death!' Anon, 1968). In the immediate months following Melcher's demise, as Day tried to grieve for him, fulfil the contractual obligations for a new television series, *The Doris Day Show*, to which he had bound her, and return her life to something approaching normality, the film magazines did not help by giving her the space she needed to adjust but instead monitored her every move obsessively. Debate flourished around two main topics: who would Day marry now, and how would she cope without her Svengali? The answer to this second point was soon found by the magazines: Day was moulding her son to take over Marty's role as her manager. The star's resonance as 'mother' began to receive a new valence: now she alternated between different magazines or different monthly issues of the same magazine as either Terry's victim or his persecutor. She was a terrible, unnatural, monster mother, sucking the life from her child and ruining his chances of romantic happiness so that she could keep him for herself (Miron, 1969; Stephens, 1970; Anon, 1970); she was a loving, doting, kindly mother, preyed on by her hapless, cold, unnatural, *hippie* of a son (Solemn, 1970; Cameron, 1971; Night, 1972; Wheeler, 1972).

With Day's love life, speculation continued for much longer; different candidates were suggested, appraised, discarded, and sometimes considered again. By 1970, according to the fan magazines, Day seemed certain to marry Don Genson, one of the producers of her television show, despite the fact that Day, Genson and Genson's *wife* all denied this. During this period, an older trope, 'Tragedy', was resurrected and put into play anew. The idea of tragedy attaching itself to Day had been introduced early on in articles about her, then being used to show how the star had persevered towards her goals despite the obstacles life had thrown her way: the unhappy childhood, the 'broken home' caused by her father's adultery, the car crash which had shattered both her leg and her ambitions to become a dancer. Now the idea of tragedy dogging Day's footsteps was brought out again, as unrelated and sporadic occurrences seemed to resolve themselves into a fated sequence of terrible events. In this version of the Day master-narrative, the star seemed doomed to be haunted by heartbreak. Marty's death was followed quickly by the suicide of Genson's wife; devastating news that Melcher and his lawyer had embezzled Day's funds was swiftly succeeded by anxiety over Terry's erratic behaviour, drug taking, romantic instability, drunk driving and finally a serious motorcycle crash which left him hospitalized. The magazines relished every opportunity for hinting that Day and Genson's relationship was somehow to blame for his wife's death while resolutely managing to avoid outright statements that could result in litigation. And because of her problems with Terry, Day could be cast as a *mater dolorosa*, with article after article portraying her desperate attempts to save her child from his self-destructive impulses.

Meanwhile, Day was still working on the TV show and enjoying a fair measure of success with it. The original format, which had seen her as a widow living with her two small sons and father on a farm outside San Francisco was tweaked several times, first to give the Day character, 'Doris Martin' a secretarial job on a magazine in the city to which she commuted, then to move her and her kids into the city itself, and finally to remove the children entirely and to promote Martin to associate editor. Magazine articles noted the vagaries of each season's changes of format, and that the Day persona continued to evoke memories of her film image, using associations from her film career. For example, Doris Martin's clothes were an important point of focus within the show and in the press items on it, with reviewers noting sarcastically that she managed to build an amazing wardrobe on a weekly salary of $85, and the star herself and costume manager countering by confirming all outfits came from San Francisco department store I. Magnin's, and thus were within reach of many career women (Archerd, 1972: 8; Haber, 1970). Day's cluster of meanings received more constant usage in the television format, where episodes revolved around her energetic attitudes, upbeat personality, and ability to triumph over (comic) adversity on a weekly basis. The parodic *Mad* magazine article from 1971, 'The Doris Daze Show', discussed in this section's final chapter, indicates widespread public awareness of the Day image and its well-established collection of aspects.

Day's high press profile, which had lasted from the start of her film career in 1948 for 20 years and more, as she went into television, finally lapsed when she ended *The Doris Day Show* after the completion of the last of the five seasons for which she was contracted. While she did occasional specials and a series devoted to animal welfare in the mid-1980s, the focus of her working life shifted from performance to charity fundraising, as she began to campaign for animal rights full time. What returned Day to the media spotlight was the 1976 publication of her autobiography, *Doris Day: Her Own Story,* which was co-written by Al Hotchner, a writer whose previous biographical work had been on Ernest Hemmingway. Although Hotchner was supposedly reluctant to accept the assignment at first, fearing that Day's life story would be an uncomplicated account of phenomenal movie success alongside a rehash of her sunny life philosophy, hearing about the tragedies and disappointments that had actually beset her, he agreed to undertake the project, bringing Day's 'true story' to the public. Hotchner organised the book to consist of separate sections narrated by Day, by her family and friends, and by himself. Tagged by one reviewer as a volume in which 'Miss Goody Two Shoes kicks back' (Kirsch, 1976), the biographical project set out to vanquish the 40-year-old-virgin persona by retelling the story of Day's three marriages and other sexual relationships. Day acknowledged liaisons with Jack Carson and Ronald Reagan, but did not provide the name of a lover she had during the run of *The Doris Day Show,* nor confirm the pervasive rumours that she had had an affair with Maury Wills. Instead the biography noted that the star was often linked with black men, Sly Stone being another potential suitor; *Movie Stars* had indeed printed a story suggesting Stone was her lover, in July 1973. Day's biography attempted to establish the star as a sexual woman fully in keeping with then-contemporary discourses about feminism and women's rights to self-fulfilment, acknowledging that her first two disastrous marriages had been based on enormous sexual attraction, while her more stable marriage to Melcher was sexless in its last five years. After the book's revelations, magazine articles which dealt with Day proceeded to use the information, especially on her sex life. Day's marriage to Melcher, hailed as being one of the great Hollywood marriages (Anon, 1968) just after his death, was now dismissed as another unhappy one, while articles by the star herself (allegedly) acknowledged Day was a modern woman with a healthy sex drive (Dahl, 1975; Ardmore, 1976 a; Ardmore 1976 b; West, 1977).

As magazine interest in Doris Day waned, the occasional articles surfacing about her reiterated several key facts about her: her love of animals, former immense popularity, status as American icon, and vastly unhappy life. When her fourth marriage ended in divorce in 1981, this became another in the list of tragedies besetting a star who had, paradoxically, habitually portrayed characters enjoying great happiness. To a large extent the tone set by these articles of the 1980s is maintained in pieces printed on the star even now, 20 years later. Every few months *The Globe* magazine trots out an issue which blasts Day's imminent lunacy or demise on its cover, then carefully backtracks inside to prevent the same kind of litigation that the star brought against it in 1991[12].

Day herself commented in a 1965 piece on the tendency of the film magazines to lead with a salacious and lurid headline, then backtrack in the inside article to avoid law suits, also noting, however, that the damage was already done before the reader could absorb the ameliorating explanation. Tacitly citing *Movie Mirror's* September 1960 piece, 'Is Doris Day Losing Her Husband?', the star relates:

I thought to myself, hundreds of thousands of people will buy this magazine. Many will read the entire story, but millions more will see only the black headline on the magazine stand. All of them will think Doris Day and Martin Melcher are having domestic trouble.

(O'Hea, 1965: 68)

Overall, the material presented in the film magazines on Doris Day offered a remarkably coherent view of the star at each stage of her career. Although occasionally there might be a less favourable mention during her times of supremacy, or a defence mounted at a time when it was more fashionable to criticise the star, in general the media treatment of Day was very consistent. To a certain extent this can be explained by the fact that the magazine writers often borrowed, pillaged and cannibalized each others' work: stealing a story from another magazine might therefore easily result in stealing its view on the star. But magazine authors also managed to borrow the meat of an interview or feature and apply it in a completely different way; Day's supposed comment, first published in the 1960 *Photoplay* piece 'Is Doris Sick of Being A Good Wife?', that she is a difficult person to live with because she is so clean and tidy, ends up being reported as a serious confession of a phobia of dirt and germs later (Anon, 1960 g). It is not just because they reuse and recycle the same raw data, then, that makes the press material on Day so homogenous. Why are the contra opinions on the star so rarely expressed, regardless of whether the field is pro or anti Day?

Perhaps the answer lies in the frequent recurrence of the self-reflexive trope in the articles on her, those film magazine articles that reference Day's treatment in, and attitude to, *film magazine articles*. I did not expect to find this particular theme before undertaking the in-depth analysis, unlike some of the other concepts such as the girl-next-door idea and the association of Day with food and with animals. While these latter themes had been apparent in casual reading about the star, the 'Meta' theme, the obsession of the magazines with Doris Day's relationship with the magazines, had not been predicted in the early researches. Yet, as the number of articles which deal in some way with this theme indicates – with 95 out of 479 articles – it was a very real aspect of her stardom. Roughly 20 per cent of the pieces in my sample discuss Day's appearance in pieces just like the ones in my sample.

This specific trope can therefore perhaps indicate reasons for the generally coherent attitude of the film magazine pieces towards Day. They were significantly interested in her relationship with the publicity machine, with her attitudes to magazine authors, interviewers, newspaper men and women. When she appeared to be antagonistic to this personnel or to its aims in discovering the story on her, the authors closed ranks and adopted a negative party line. The result is a high number of articles which self-reflexively comment on Day's relationship with the very magazines which made and perpetuated the star's media persona, and then blamed her for having this image.

While this chapter has attempted to take the long view of Day's entire career, and chart repeating themes and elements of her persona across this, the next narrows the focus to look at these tropes and specifically examines four that seem to be key to her 'perpetual virgin' image.

3 Tropes

In this chapter I build on the account of Day's media persona provided in the previous one by analysing in greater depth some of the key tropes – those recurring ideas and clusters of concepts that accrue to a star – which circled around Day during the years of her major film and television stardom. In subjecting each of the articles and items of my sample to dissection and close reading, I built up a list of the repeated words and assumptions which Day prompted, noting the consistency with which these tropes occurred. These repeating idea-clusters appeared during the time of her live career, but also very much fit with the resonances still set off by the Day name in more recent texts, as noted in the book's Context section.

There are 32 key terms which I found operating across 34 years' worth of articles (Table 1). As seen, 24 of these were in place within the first three years of the magazines' dawning interest in Day, six more in the next five years, while only two began later, around the cusp of the 1960s. It should be noted that although all 32 tropes were quite prevalent in the material examined, in this subsection I only analyse the ones that seem to me to pertain specifically to her supposed virginal status, as this motif is the central topic of the book. Some of the other tropes were fascinating to see occurring, repeating, vanishing for a time and then returning, slightly altered or significantly developed; space, however, dictates the disciplined focussing on the evolution of the elements in Day's star persona which arose innocently enough but were eventually twisted, slewed to become part of the negative reading of the star, or became interwoven with other ideas to develop in different directions. It was interesting to see how a seemingly positive aspect could be suborned, somehow ending up confirming a criticism of Day.

In the chapter which follows, then, I explore those tropes which eventually become associated with the 'aged maiden' slur. I explore here in detail four key concepts or clusters of ideas that the star's name seemed to conjure up in the articles under examination: 'Energy', 'Natural/Clean', 'Food', and 'Girl-Next-Door/Virgin'.

Energy

This is one of the most recurrent terms at the start of Day's career: nearly every article on the new star takes pains to stress

Table 1. Chart to show themes in DD media persona.

Themes	48	49	50	51	52	53	54	55	56	57	58	59	60	61	62	63	64	65	66	67	68	69	70	71	72	73	74	75	76	77	78	79	82	86	Total
Energy	*	*	*	*	*	*	*	*		*	*	*				*						*													10
Natural/tomboy		*						*		*	*	*															*								9
Natural/clean	*		*	*	*	*		*		*			*	*	*	*			*	*	*														14
Talented/star	*				*									*							*														10
Voice	*	*	*		*											*					*	*													6
Looks	*	*	*										*		*		*	*			*													*	8
Freckles	*	*	*	*	*	*	*	*	*	*		*	*	*	*	*	*							*	*							*			19
Blonde	*	*	*			*			*				*		*			*					*	*	*										7
Food	*	*	*	*	*	*	*	*	*	*	*	*	*	*	*	*				*	*	*	*	*	*	*	*					*			23
Can't cook	*	*	*	*	*	*	*	*	*	*		*	*	*	*	*		*	*		*	*	*	*	*	*		*				*			17
Clothes	*	*	*	*	*	*	*	*		*	*	*	*	*	*	*							*	*								*			21
Name story	*	*	*		*	*							*																						4
Mom		*	*		*	*		*							*							*		*	*	*	*	*			*		*	*	12
Animals/dogs		*		*				*									*				*			*	*	*	*	*		*					13
Tragedy	*	*			*		*							*				*	*					*	*	*	*	*	*	*					12
Money	*	*	*	*	*	*	*					*	*		*	*		*	*	*	*	*	*	*	*	*	*	*			*		*		20
Feminism: for, vs	*	*		*	*	*							*					*						*	*										12
Witty	*				*	*			*	*														*											6
Meta	*			*	*	*	*	*	*	*	*	*	*	*	*	*	*	*	*	*	*	*	*	*	*	*	*	*	*	*	*				26
Bio story	*		*	*	*	*	*	*	*	*	*	*	*	*	*	*	*	*	*	*	*	*	*	*	*		*	*		*	*		*	*	21
Awards			*		*	*	*	*		*	*		*	*	*			*	*	*	*	*													12
Love life		*		*	*	*	*	*	*	*	*		*	*	*	*	*	*		*	*	*		*	*	*	*	*	*	*	*	*	*	*	22
All-American			*	*	*		*	*	*	*		*	*	*	*	*	*	*	*	*	*	*	*	*			*						*		17
Pathology	*		*		*	*		*		*	*	*	*	*	*	*		*	*	*	*	*											*		14
'Just Like Us'					*	*	*	*	*		*	*	*	*		*												*							9
Religion			*		*	*				*		*			*				*	*	*			*								*			12
Girl next door				*	*	*				*		*	*	*	*			*	*		*		*		*	*		*		*	*	*			13
Sensationalized								*		*		*	*	*	*	*		*		*	*	*	*	*	*	*	*	*		*	*	*	*		22
Dramatized							*	*					*	*	*	*					*	*	*	*	*	*	*	*			*	*	*		12
Acting										*				*	*	*	*			*	*	*	*	*	*			*	*			*	*		13
Age								*	*		*		*	*	*	*	*	*	*		*	*	*	*				*	*	*	*				10
Virgin										*	*	*	*	*	*	*	*				*	*		*				*	*	*	*	*	*	86	13

* means an article employing this trope was found from this year in my sample.

her bouncy personality, drive and vigour. This lasted from her entry into the Hollywood scene in 1948, with iterations each year until 1957. It reoccurs thereafter less frequently. By 1969, Day's vitality is being portrayed as surprising in a woman of her age (47), since the article stresses her 'youthful bounce' (Caldwell, 1969: 94).

The authors introducing the new star to their reading publics devoted much energy themselves to finding words, phrases and metaphors which would appropriately sum up or convey this key characteristic of her personality. She is hailed as 'vivacious' (Anon, 1948 b: 72), 'refreshing' (Anon, 1948 d: 91; Anon, 1948 f: 50), 'bubbling, sparkling and pert' (Lynch Vallee, 1948: 45), is said to be 'the most bombastic personality to hit Hollywood in years', with all the 'exuberance of a puppy' and possessing 'bounce', as well as 'a million volt personality' (Shelly, 1948: 37). The comparison to energetic animals is maintained when another writer in 1948 asserts Day is 'more like a frisky puppy than a movie star' (Pomeroy, 1948: 76) and another uses the same adjective six years later, finding her 'as frisky as a mink' (Mathews, 1954: 47). In between, another article announces she has 'a puppy's bounce' (Anon, 1952 d: 62). The magazines also make frequent references to Day's own dogs at home (Anon, 1949 a: 30; Anon, 1949 b: 105;). The use of her poodles in photo shoots with the star further underscores her boundless energy by comparison with theirs, as in a piece which relates the 'zestful star [...] gives Beany and Smudge a tussle' (Henaghan, 1951: 33).

Another metaphoric strand which articles find useful is one which conjures up Day's energy by comparing it to that released in an atomic explosion. This seems particularly resonant in a mid-century Cold War context. One *Motion Picture* article from 1948, examined in detail in a subsequent chapter, announces that Day 'explodes into stardom in her first film' (Pomeroy, 1948: 39) while, continuing the bomb theme, she can also affect 'anyone who's within radiation distance of her' (38). This metaphor is hyperbolic but attests the huge impact Day's arrival had. The atomic bomb metaphor was given visual treatment in another early reference to the star: the cover of the January 1949 issue of *Modern Television and Radio* provides a large image of her face as well as a small picture of the star, full-figure, surrounded by the lines, and accompanied by a yellow dot, that indicate the atom and its nucleus (Figure 8). This nuclear conceit was still in circulation in 1955, as evinced by *Photoplay*'s 'Atom Blonde' article (Roberts: 39–40, 80–84). It is interesting to compare this image to others which treat Day in terms evoking another source of intense heat and light – the sun. With that metaphor, which was frequently used in combination with her surname to provide titles like 'Sunny Day' (Anon, 1951 b: 25–26, 78–79l; cf Wheeler, 1952: 54–55, 104–105; Anon, 1960 d), however the emphasis seems to be on her naturalness and warmth, rather than the almost ferocious nature of her energy, which the nuclear comparison makes seem dangerous[13].

Day is further hailed as having 'zing, zest and zip' (Hale, 1949: 32) and 'champagne ebullience' (Howe, 1950: 73). Two early pieces similarly imply her energetic nature by hinting that she is packed with vitamins. 'She's Got What It Takes' from August 1949's *Screen Guide* calls her a 'freckle-faced vitamin kid' (Anon, 1949 d: 66), although this cannot top *Motion Picture*'s hyperbole: the 1948 article suggested that she was so energy-laden that 'vitamins should take Doris!' (Pomeroy, 1948: 38).

These action-packed metaphors are brought to life when the magazines print photo-articles. A 1948 piece in *Movie Life* shows the energetic Day in action: she is pictured with her ice-skating stand-in (Anon, 1948 j: 62–65). As if skating is insufficiently energetic, bouncy Doris is also shown hamming it up for the cameras, prat-falling as she 'clowns around' (64). A similar

Figure 8. Atomic energy: the cover of *Modern Television and Radio* January
1949 positions Day as the the nucleus of an atom.

photo-essay in June the following year shows Day at Bob Hope's
Palm Springs house being constantly thrown into the pool –
sometimes fully-dressed – but taking the soakings in high good
humour (Anon, 1949 c: 34–37). These articles make Day's energy

visible to viewers so they need not be so overburdened with energy-conveying language.

A similar 1950 photo-essay piece details all the events in, and occurring for this, 'Busy Day', concluding that although the star has been tearing about she still looks relaxed and rested at the end of it. Expending energy is thus seen as Day's natural state of being: she can bounce all day and still look good, as the article's caption implies: 'How to look as though you'd spent the day luxuriating in a bubble bath' (Anon, 1950: 31).

'Bounce' is indeed often used as a key word for this trope throughout its active period from the start of Day's career. A 1948 *Photoplay* piece asking the reader to 'Choose Your Star' recommends Day for stardom because she 'Has bounce, a voice...' (Anon, 1948 h: 103). Day is said to have 'as much bounce as a new tennis ball' (Shelly, 1948: 37) while *Movie Stars Parade* notes the 'bouncy way she walks' (Allen, 1952: 31), *Movie Life* calls her 'bouncy Doris' (Anon, 1954 c: 33), and her brother Paul (allegedly) writing in *Silver Screen* affirms the star 'still has the same bounce' as when a kid (1955: 12). The following year, *Cosmopolitan* relates how Day 'bounced into the room' for her interview (Shipp, 1956: 58). No wonder, then, that Day was voted 'Miss Bounce' 'by a firm of rubber manufacturers' in 1949[14].

The energy trope also interacts with others in the list of recurrent elements in the Day persona, for example with the food trope, so that Day's enormous vitality is explained by the vast amounts she eats and, in turn, her potentially unseemly appetite is excused by fuelling the habitual Day bounce. 'The Lady In Pink', an article in the January 1956 issue of *Modern Screen*, for example, lists the usual contents of a Day breakfast but explains their necessity:

> The early big breakfast is a habit of long standing with Doris [...].
> She always eats a full-scale meal too. When they were first

married, it amazed Marty that his wife, with her mere twenty-three-inch waist, could put away more food than he. But it figures. Doris expends a tremendous amount of energy. Her buoyancy and bounce has to come from somewhere and one of her trade secrets is that she eats a towering breakfast of protein-rich foods....

(Peterson, 1956: 75)

It is actually difficult to see how Day's large meals could be counted as 'one of her trade secrets' since, as the section on the food trope will show, practically every article on the star mentioned her huge appetite.

It is interesting that, once the magazines have come back to her after she alienated them during her 1953–4 sabbatical from the press, the trope of energy is used as a touchstone to reassure readers (and perhaps the magazine authors themselves) that Day has reverted to her former, cooperative self: while 'sick Doris' was deemed 'disturbingly subdued' (Anon, 1954 a: 34) 'wan, sometimes tearful' (37), 'well Doris' is again described as a 'dynamo' (Anon, 1954 b: 31), 'the old, sparkling, bubbling freckle-faced kid' (Anon, 1954 d: 33) and possessed of 'even more vitality and vivacity than she displayed in the past' (Benedict 1954: 31).

The energy trope ceases to be so pervasive once the star falls into disfavour with the magazines. While other tropes will be turned to the negative, 'energy' is only hinted at being read critically once in my sample, significantly in a piece which purports to be by the star herself. Protesting against her traditional portrayal as Miss Bounce in an interview (supposedly) given to *Screenland and TVLand*, August 1954, Day condemns the epithet as it makes her seem so unworldly, naive and saint-like:

'They voted me Miss Bounce of 1950!' she recalled with a sweeping gesture as she put her hand incredulously to her head.

'They hung that one on me! Miss Bounce! Well, I don't bounce all
the time....'

(Benedict, 1954: 63)

This version of the energy trope ties in well with the implication,
so often conveyed in the 'virginity dilemma' movies mentioned
earlier, that the comic virgin is a disaster zone of impulses and
urges which, because she is not channelling them safely into
sexual activity, threaten to burst out in violent spasms.
Significantly, however, as the chapter on Day's performances
will reveal in greater detail, the star does not employ this
performance mode in those of her films which might be seen to
participate in the virgin mania, even though this contemporary
report suggests support for this notion could have been found in
her early persona.

Natural/Clean

The idea of 'naturalness' being connected to and evoked by Day
is found everywhere in the press pieces on her. The material
can be split into two separate angles on naturalness, however.
The first, often associated with the idea that the star, though an
attractive woman, is a 'tomboy', starts as soon as Day's name
becomes familiar to the movie magazines. Here there is a stress
on Day's naturalness in the sense both of her preference for
unfussy behaviour, foods, activities, commenting therefore on
her down-to-earth pragmatism and refusal to 'go Hollywood',
but also in the sense of the star eschewing the usual feminine
movie star glamour in terms of interests, pastimes and outfits.
Look's 1951 profile article dubs her 'The tomboy with the
voice', which establishes an interesting tension between
resonances conjured on the one hand by the unfeminine
nature of this persona and, on the other, the seductive quality
of her breathy tones.

Tomboy Day is portrayed continually romping with her dogs and her son, attired casually, or actively playing sports. Similarly, on her honeymoon trip to the Grand Canyon, she is photographed while exploring a Native American house. It is accessed by wooden ladders and 'the tomboy bride' at once clambers up to explore (Anon, 1951 c: 18). Day's role as Calamity Jane in 1953 called forth comparable if sometimes seemingly paradoxical epithets such as 'glamorous tomboy' (Anon, 1953 b: 12), but all these titles served to suggest she was 'unpretentious', another favourite magazine concept ('Melcher', 1951: 26–27, 50; Anon, 1952 c: 33–36: Mazella, 1957: 68). The natural/tomboy trope declines after about 1957, with *Pillow Talk*'s revamping of the star as a 'sexpot' in 1959 finally ending this strand of resonances.

However, the other frequently-found circulating strand of meaning that involves the idea of 'naturalness' and the star does continue on into the 60s and beyond. Naturalness associated with 'Cleanliness' begins at the same early point but becomes more heavily accreted with negative meanings as time goes on and persists today, as demonstrated earlier. 'Cleanliness' again starts from the same roots in unpretentious behaviour, but is inflected differently. One of the key early terms for describing Day is 'refreshing' (Anon, 1948 d: 91; Anon, 1948, e: 50) which emphasises her natural personality but also her looks. Many of the articles about Day stress that she prefers to avoid makeup off-set, and to flaunt her freckles instead (Barnett, 1950: 16; Mills Goode, 1953: 75). Hence there are items which describe either her face alone or her whole self as 'well-scrubbed' (Howe, 1950: 75), or sporting a 'scrubbed freshness' (Scullin, 1957, a: 105); she is a 'soap and water siren' (Anon, 1952 f: 41). Alongside her scrubbed face, there is already by 1952 the first hint that that this clean look requires constant vigilance and carries over from Day's person to her home; in that year, one article speaks of her 'passion for cleanness and neatness' (Trent, 1952: 91), another notes her always 'clean hair' (Ransom, 1952: 63) and another her clean clothes (Waterbury, 1952: 88). She is perceived to be 'spotless' always, even when playing sports (Anon, 1952 e: 63) and even when younger as a tomboy (Riley, 1952: 90). This sets off an interesting potential clash of resonances, since the word 'tomboy' somehow implies getting into all sorts of messy scrapes that more 'girly' girls would reject. Day is described as 'fastidious' (Goodwin, 1953: 105), not only about herself but her house too: she reports that she used to scrub her home for hours ('Day', 1953: 52), and still insists her house is 'as clean as a surgery' (Hall, 1953: 76). In this latter article too her hatred of dirt is described as a 'phobia' (76). By the time of another similar article, supposedly self-authored, in *Screen Stars* in January 1958, her constant attention to her home is implicitly criticised: Day confesses that she is *too* good at housework, her insistence on the home remaining pristine making others uncomfortable:

> I'm a whiz at cleaning. I love dusting [...] and I'm known to be quite fussy about seeing that everything is completely dust-free' [...] I even think I'm too particular, too efficient.
>
> ('Day', 1958: 32 and 62).

The cleanness trope here begins to darken and to seem an indication of more sinister symptoms; in an unpleasant simile, Day herself is described as being 'scrubbed so that she shines like a billiard ball' (Asher, 1952: 43). Billiard balls may be shiny and clean, but they are also hard and cold to touch.

In further iterations of the trope, the actor is often described as looking like she has 'just taken a shower' (Oppenheimer, 1957: 76) or 'just stepped out of the bath' (Wilkie, 1961: 60); regular reports reveal that this just-cleaned look is apparently achieved by actually taking multiple showers a day. A 1961 article asserts this is three per day (Davidson 1961: 39), although it used to be more – *Pageant* hints at five daily (Friedman, 1960: 28). As the 60s dawn and the 'Doris Day film' comes to signal sexy but ultimately safe skirmishings, the cleanliness trope is applied across the range of Day activities from her person to her movies. The films provide Day with 'happy, clean parts' (Anon, 1960 b: 121) while Day is now hailed as possessing 'antiseptic good looks' (Macdonald, 1962: 58) or 'antiseptic freshness' (Anon, 1963 c: 107). By the end of the 60s her attractiveness is condemned in a particularly cruel metaphor as 'pasteurised', that is, like milk, heat-treated to ensure a longer shelf life (Waterbury, 1968: 45). The comparison of Day to foodstuffs will be considered in a later subsection; comment here on this final jibe can be restricted to pointing out that it is entirely consistent with the strand of conviction, which can be observed growing across the later 50s and into the 60s, that Day's eventually *off-putting* cleanliness is a sign of some inner pathology. Perhaps her obsessive insistence on cleanliness is a mark of a hysterical nature refusing to admit to human faults, frailties, sins, *bodies*; articles on the star attempt to psychoanalyse their subject and to read her outward behaviour as indicative of inner turmoil, whether caused by her relationship with her strict father (Carleton, 1954: 80), sensitivity about her looks (Anon, 1960 c: 62), impulses towards suppressing all tension in her third marriage and in her career (Williams, 1954: 78), or other neuroses. In this way Day's aversion to dirt eventually comes to indicate an aversion to sex, in that her scrupulous attempts to keep herself and her surroundings clean are read as symptomatic of a dislike for messy corporeal urges.

One author back in 1953 had attempted to tap in to the cleanliness trope in a different way. *Modern Screen's* Carl Schroeder went on a trip Day and Melcher took after the star's first big falling-out with the media, when she was still trying to improve relations with the press corps. He was attempting to catch sight of Day in a new red bathing suit she had purchased for the vacation, but although the magazine article teases us that he – and the readers – will see photographs of the garment, Day manages to be fully clad at all times. Still, coming down to breakfast early one morning the writer catches her looking 'scrubbed and slightly sexy' (42). A contrary chain of associations could, then, have been built up around Day which stressed her accessibility, her status as a star 'just like' any normal woman, who looked her best when happy and romantically fulfilled, rather than draped in diamonds and ermine. Day and Melcher tried to perpetuate this idea of Day as a 'soap and water siren', with authorised articles in the media drawing on their shared preference for high necked gowns, simple coiffures and light makeup. Melcher's pronouncement that glamour is not 'a plunging neckline' but 'a cake of soap' (Rowland 1955: 68), bears out the approach Day and her managers were taking with her image. Unfortunately for them, when combined with some of the other resonances set in motion by Day's complex star persona, the accent on soap and water became indicative not of an alternative and more achievable allure but an anti-glamour that also proved easily legible as anti-sex.

Food

One of the most recurrent tropes in the material on Doris Day is that of food. Of the 479 items in my sample, 14 per cent make reference to Day's healthy appetite, love of eating, delight in vast portions or, in the other major strand of significance for this trope, suggest the star *herself* is somehow like a food product.

The first mentions of Day and food begin in 1948, with the first film magazine, newspaper, and other pieces on her noting her appetite alongside her famous 'bounce'; *Motion Picture* in

August of that year managed to use both food and energy tropes together when it proclaimed 'Doris never stays still except to eat' (Pomeroy, 1948: 38), and in fact these two are often associated, at least in the early years, when the accounts of how much Day likes to consume are generally coupled with assurances that she needs the volume of food to cope with her energetic lifestyle; her rather unfeminine hunger and the amounts needed to assuage it can seemingly be excused if the unrestricted portions represent fuel more than self-indulgence. Sidney Skolsky, writing a Doris Day 'likes and dislikes' column, notes her food preferences are distinctly ordinary, calling the starlet 'Strictly a meat-and-potatoes character' (Skolsky, 1948: 22), while a photo-essay on Day in the November 1948 issue of *Photoplay* also contrived to make her seem traditional in both her tastes and her gender roles, since she as the woman caters the 'Picnic In The Park' to which other new stars are invited. (Mulvey, 1948: 60). Calling her 'an old-fashioned miss' (61) the article reassures readers that Day may be a glamorous Hollywood starlet, but still observes the societal strictures that suggest women should prepare, and men consume food[15]. For this reason the 'Picnic' article is a rare piece, since Day is more usually the recipient rather than the donor of meal-time efforts (Anon, 1952 a).

Most early pieces stress that Day's mother Alma is her live-in cook, while later ones note the existence of a housekeeper (Anon, 1953 a: 37; Hall, 1953: 76) who performs this function. 'Katie' is even photographed – in the background – preparing breakfast in Day's kitchen, in one magazine piece (Peterson 1956: 41).

The frequency of references to Day's interest in eating rather than cooking continues once into the 1950s, as seen with the number of articles which employ the 'Can't Cook' trope. The articles often have to work hard to insist that Day is 'Just Like Us' in her eating habits when she also has this contra-domestic element to her character. Occasionally an item will buck the trend by insisting Day does cook, but others try to combine the very well-known fact of Day's aversion to cooking with her equally well-established adoration of sweet things, such as an item where the author purports to peeping through the star's kitchen window and seeing her making fudge – out of a box (Asher, 1952: 42). By 1968 this has changed somewhat so that Day now admits to baking 'a great deal' (Ardmore, 1968: 60), an idea that is tapped into again in 1972 where the star bakes cakes, selling them on the set of *The Doris Day Show* to support animal welfare charities (Anon, 1972 a).

Food-trope articles continue to proliferate: in 1953 it is constantly reported that Day likes to eat large amounts. Sometimes this is a comment to the reader from an observer – 'Keeping this girl fed requires mountains of food' (Schroeder, 1953: 43) – but often such remarks are presented as if confessions from the star: 'My appetite is something that must be seen to be believed' (Hall, 1953: 28); 'I love to eat – period. Fortunately I have no weight problems....' (Holland, 1953: 40).

There is a dip in 1954, with just two mentions, but in 1955 the trope is back in force again (Jacobi, 1955: 49 and Anon, 1955 a: 112; Parsons, July 1955: 16; Anon, 1955 b: 67) as with an aside in a *Filmland* article in which Day is called 'A steak plus dessert girl – and she never gains an ounce!' (O'Leary, 1955: 58). Alongside more of the usual in January 1956 (Peterson, 1956: 41), *Modern Screen* also presents the sole article which avers Day has to watch her weight: all the others have dedicated themselves to asserting the absolute opposite, but here Day herself is alleged to confess she needs to keep an eye on her food intake and occasionally 'do a bit of dieting' (Weissman, 1956: 64).

After this anomaly, the magazines revert to the usual line about how Day's active lifestyle keeps the pounds off; for example, the January 1958 issue of *Screen Stars* has the actor affirming that she plays tennis every day and burns calories 'with my nervous energy' (62). When dieting is mentioned again, its target is the reader, rather than the star. An article in the March issue of *Photoplay* presents a diet plan intended for the reader's benefit. It seems rather unfair here to use Day as the spokesperson for the article – it is addressed to 'you', and purports to recount a conversation between the star and the female author – since the young women she is admonishing for being overweight and unhappy with their looks are therefore urged to change their habits and restrict their treats by someone whom everyone knows never has to do this herself (Greer, 1959). In addition, the photographs accompanying the article seem to be recycled – as so many things in the film magazines were – from a story in a different magazine published two years earlier (Churchill, 1957: 14–19) where the star is featured exploring the stalls in the Los Angeles Farmers' Market, tasting, smelling and generally revelling in a sensuous enjoyment of food which is presumably going to be taboo to the prospective dieters.

This article also indicates some of the contradictions that one well-established trope connected with the star could represent towards other equally well-known elements of her persona. As noted above, the idea that Day was 'Just Like Us' was one which began to achieve prominence around the time of Day's 1951 marriage to Marty Melcher. While Day's 'meat-and-potatoes character' could fit neatly with this latter idea, the constantly reiterated factoids that she never had to diet, deny herself any food, or restrict portion sizes, serves very much to cut her off from the majority of female magazine readers. Even the articles that excuse Day's need for so much food through emphasising her hard-working professional and leisure life inevitably end up noting that she will expend any calories gained by her ceaseless activity, both on and off set. Again this contradicts the idea that the star is 'Just Like Us' because most of 'us' cannot rely on keeping excess pounds off by hours dancing at work, nor do most of us have the court and pool necessary to play volleyball and swim at home. The general sense of Day's unpretentious character is thus undermined by this other turn of the food trope which yet was also originally invoked to emphasise her down-to-earth personality.

The other main strand of the food trope is that Day herself is somehow edible. In this formulation of the food idea there are constant comparisons to various foodstuffs, whether playing on her fair colouring, her wholesomeness, or, perhaps more suggestively, the fact that she looks 'delicious', so that people want to consume her orally.

The 1948 *Motion Picture* article which coupled her energy and food intake, as noted above, also employed this strand of the food trope in suggesting that Day was so healthy looking she 'could pose for Wheaties' (Pomeroy, 1948: 38)[16]. While the writer perhaps meant to suggest Day could be a model for the product, especially given her predilection for bouncing around, and Wheaties' association with athletes as spokespersons, it is also possible to read this line to suggest the star could portray the flakes themselves, given her blonde colouring and fair skin-tone. Day is definitely conjured up as edible in the 1950 *Modern Screen* piece which reports that her husband describes her as being 'as wholesome as a hotdog' (Anderson, 1950:81), while an article from the following year relinquishes even the partial cover of using a simile, to expostulate bluntly 'What a dish! Freckles and all, Doris looks good enough to eat!' (Anon, 1951 a: 85).

A 1954 item concurs, listing the items Day chooses for lunch in the commissary at Warners' (lamb chops, French fries, fruit cocktail and a glass of milk, *and* ice cream). Despite the accent on the food, it is the star who gets the compliment, when the author declares 'She looked delicious' (Mathews, 1954: 47).

As the 50s wear on, this Doris-as-food usage becomes the dominant strand of the trope, largely replacing the appetite emphasis. A 1957 magazine piece comments on the star's 'lettuce-crisp flair' (Swisher, 1959: 14), while a 1960 item goes slightly overboard with its range of food-metaphors: in this piece Day has 'yellow-butter hair', 'freckles like cinnamon on a bun', a 'church-supper face' (Friedman, 1960: 26) and a 'hot-buttered-sunshine-smile' (28). This seems to mark the pinnacle of metaphor frenzy, since afterwards other pieces can only echo the range of images set off here: a 1961 author employs 'butter-yellow' as a descriptor for Day's hair (Davidson, 1961, 43). Film critic Dwight Macdonald, writing in *Esquire* magazine the following year, reverts to the Wheaties-type image when he pronounces: 'She is as wholesome as a bowl of cornflakes, and at least as sexy' (Macdonald, 1962: 58). Now the food trope becomes negative: while occasional articles mention Day's dislike of cooking but love of food over the next few years, the predominant use of food imagery is to compare Day herself to something overly-sweet, although the 'apple pie' which Day is often now said to be as American as, was introduced as a simile quite late on. (Haber, 1970). An article from 1963 calls her both 'the buttermilk girl next door' (Kahn, 1963: 63) and compares Day to a stale ice cream soda 'One that's been left overnight. The fizz has gone' (62); her supposed reclusiveness and ivory-tower mentality are condemned as her own private 'ice cream world' in 1969 (Caldwell, July: 95). The star's well-known preference for, even addiction to, sweet things like lollipops, Tootsie Rolls (Mazella, 1957: 68) and chewing gum begins to be used against her, symbolising the saccharine nature of her persona. In addition, whereas the earlier accounts of her vast and boundless appetite for huge portions might be seen as a covert way of signalling the star had an enormous appetite for life – or for sex – by the later 60s when the trope seems to exhaust its utility, the frequent iteration of her love of sweet foods, especially ice cream, sodas, gum and candy[17] seems to hint that she is compensating for an underactive sex life, or transferring her sexual energies into a more publicly acceptable compulsion.

The food trope can therefore be seen as being paradigmatic in offering itself to many different inflections; it can blend with 'Just Like Us', since the articles that list her likes and dislikes always stress she prefers hotdogs and ice cream to caviar and oysters; it can support the Energy trope by explaining what fuels her ability to bounce all day, or it can cast a shadow over Day's sexuality, shading into the pathological as the star is pictured obsessively cramming sweets into her mouth in an attempt to fill the emptiness the magazines insist is inside her.

Girl Next Door/Virgin

Although not the most frequently-found tropes in the material on Day in my sample, I have chosen to track and analyse those of 'Girl Next Door' together with 'Virgin' because they are so obviously central to the objective of this book: exploring how, when and why Doris Day became known as playing or being an aged maiden. The girl next door element emerged in 1951, three years after Day arrived in Hollywood, while the virgin trope, significantly, had to wait another decade to appear on the scene. This one fact alone would seem to support my basic argument that Day was not initially constructed as a virginal type; however, looking at the material which highlights these two aspects of the Day persona, it seems to me that the situation is more complex. These two tropes are somewhat elided, with aspects of the girl next door image blending into the virgin one once it becomes live. I propose here, then, to look at this pair of tropes together, seeing how they both complement and complicate each other.

What do the writers mean when they say 'girl next door'? Although, as the section on Context indicated, what 'virgin' meant was, contemporaneously, the subject of much debate and disagreement, it still appears at first glance to have an either/or meaning which is more well-defined than this earlier label. The girl next door seems to me to partake of some of the other tropes with which Day was being associated, especially the Natural/Tomboy/Unpretentious strand of meaning, and the 'Just Like Us' one. The girl next door is typed by her gender and location: she is thus rendered domestic, cosy, near geographically but also symbolically. With Doris Day, the term would seem to apply best to her 1950s run of nostalgic musicals and biopics[18], although these films actually post-date the announcement that her time as the girl next door is over. The first usage of the term in my sample, in a 1951 piece in *Movie Stars Parade*, suggests this 'tag fitted as recently as three years ago', but is not applicable to her now (West, 1951: 72). This would place Day as conveying the girl next door image in 1948, but this seems to me doubtful. Day's earliest films, around the time the article insists 'the tag fitted', were as a smart-talking, street-wise chanteuse in *Romance On The High Seas* (1948), a tender but determined songstress in *My Dream Is Yours* (1949), and a perky waitress prepared to do practically anything to break into movies in *It's A Great Feeling* (1949). The last of these films does perhaps contain a germ of the girl next door idea, in that Day's 'Judy Adams' has come to Hollywood from a small town, to which she eventually returns: Goerkes Corner, Wisconsin. Is the character's small-town provenance enough to secure her the girl next door title? A combination of ambition and naivety, drive and kindliness, Judy is prepared to lie, cheat, masquerade, and drive a studio executive insane in order to become a star. These do not seem the traditional attributes one would assume a girl next door possessed. In other words, although associated with the girl next door idea in the press quite early on, Day's playing of such a role *on screen* seems to be problematic. Perhaps, then, what is found with the awarding of this appellation early in her career is more a reflection of Day's *off-screen image* than her film work.

Many early press and magazine pieces on the star worked to create a portrayal of her down-to-earth personality, 'regular folks' habits, her enjoyment at living with her son, mother and dogs in a normal house in a normal Los Angeles suburb. A 1952 article has Day herself affirm that being like her audiences is her ultimate goal: she has come to realise that 'real happiness is normalcy' (Larkin, 1952: 54).

Even the trope that regularly insisted Day 'Can't Cook' played a part in this, paradoxically, since pains were often taken to offset this seeming rejection of normative feminine responsibility with accounts of what Day did around the house instead, including buying or maintaining antiques (Anon, 1952 b: 34–37; Anon, 1952 c: 35), cleaning ('Day', 1953: 60), sewing (Anon, 1951 d: 24) or making cookies (Anon, 1949 a: 31; Asher, 1952: 42). The next iteration of Day as girl next door, in fact, arises in a similar fashion out of a discussion of her domestication. In the insightfully entitled 'Doris Day: her gimmick is – YOU!' (Maynard, 1953: 34–35, 58), the author acknowledges that the star's appeal is her naturalness, the fact that she really is sincere, unforced. It is an essential part of her charm that she is actually *is* this, rather than having been crafted by the studios to *appear* like this.

> [Doris Day is a] ... freckled, gamin-faced woman of 29 whom this magazine tabbed before all others as the Everything Girl and whom everyone feels they know. Films never really had The Girl Next Door until Miss Day moved in....
>
> (Maynard, 1953: 35)

Day is confirmed here as 'the perfect Girl Next Door type' because of her 'natural manner' (58) and her freckles, but it seems particularly interesting that the author puts such emphasis on Day being one of us:

> You do know her. She knows you too. She most certainly is one of you.
>
> (Maynard, 1953: 58)

If Day's 'gimmick' as a star is us, the viewers – and magazine readers – it is because she comes from us, speaks to us, is 'most certainly one of' us. Yet the 'most certainly' seems to hint at the writer's slight desperation in trying to assert this point. How many of 'us', after all, are movie stars, live in Los Angeles, and make movie star money? The author anticipates this objection, however, and continues to affirm Day's unity with her audience: 'She goes to work earlier than you, gets home later and presumably makes more money, but that's the only difference' (58). Finally, Day is ultimately tied down to the everyday by her failure at ordinary domestic chores: the article ends with the acknowledgement that 'she can't get her fudge to harden' (48). Not only, then, is she not superior to the average female reader – despite all the money and success which might make one think otherwise – the reader is in fact superior to her because, after all, *her* fudge does harden.

Despite this insistence that Day personifies the girl next door, after this the aspect dropped out of use in my sample, returning in 1956 again only to have the appropriateness of the appellation again questioned. Day is named as being formerly 'Hollywood's girl next door' (Shipp, 1956: 58), at a point when her role as Ruth Etting seems to mark her as having left this tame role behind. Similarly, an article in the following year explains that Day is now saying goodbye to the girl next door, a persona she adopted on screen but never personally inhabited, and indeed could only impersonate so well because she intensely envied the stable lifestyle embodied by that character (Scullin 1957 b: 111). In another 1957 piece, Doris herself (allegedly) writes that she is bidding the character farewell along with the dual immature roles *and* outlook she embodies, since she is now growing up and facing life as an adult ('For every woman there's a time to grow up. For me the time is now....' Ardmore, 1957).

The girl next door persona seems permanently to exist in the past, then: not only in the past of a performer associated with playing her, but in the past of the country too – a simpler time, the assumptions imply. The girl next door evokes nostalgia: she is associated with earlier times, smaller towns, more local, familial, even rural notions of life. Day herself clearly did not fit with these, as press material often noted – one 1952 piece calling her 'jet-propelled before the camera, as modern as tomorrow' (Anon, 1952 b: 35) – but the run of roles set in the past, from *On Moonlight Bay* onwards, seemed to have attached this small-town character to her. From small-town person to small-town-values is a short step; this is perhaps what links the girl next door to the virgin persona, since, as embodied in the occasional film roles where Day did seem to play her, the heroine asserts her lack of promiscuity in opposition to a sexual sophistication associated with the big city, inevitably Manhattan. It is doubly interesting then that Jan Morrow, the first of Day's sex comedy roles to make a real impression at the box office[19], is both so resolutely urbanite and sophisticated.

It seems, from studying the usages of the term in my sample articles at least, that the concept of the girl next door only becomes applied to Day without reservation around the cusp of the 1960s – that is, paradoxically, only once she also becomes associated with the new, sexier roles inaugurated by *Pillow Talk*. The 'girl next door' persona is re-inflected, once producer Ross Hunter brings his gloss to the star and her films as a 'glamour girl next door' (Anon, 1961 b: 31) and an 'All-American girl next door' in an extensive (but rather negative) article in *Look* the following month (Davidson, 1961: 42). By this point in her career the magazines had overtly begun to comment on Day's image and to seek to find fault with Day as if she – and not they – were guilty of manipulating and perpetuating it:

> The Doris Day image, even to cynical Hollywood, is that of the nice, clean-living, uncomplicated, all-American girl next door....
>
> (Davidson, 1961: 42)

The article goes on to suggest that this 'colorless and incomplete' (43) image has been set up by Marty Melcher to protect the Day brand, although it does not suggest which kinds of criticism it could be serving to deflect. If Melcher really was insisting on the maintenance of this bland image, he was not helping the star; on the contrary, many of the magazine pieces of the time denounce the pair for pretending the girl next door was real and unchangeable. Paradoxically, too, such articles emerged at the same time that others were hailing Day as a 'Lady Bountiful of the sheets' (Hotchner, 1976: 202). Thus, even while the magazines sought to portray Day as firmly wedded to her old-fashioned girl next door image, they were *also* publishing articles with sensational headlines hinting at Day's disillusionment with her current marriage ('Is Doris Sick Of Being A Good Wife?' Anon, 1960 e) or openly declaring its dissolution ('Doris Day Will Divorce in 1961!' (Anon, 1960 g). For all the fascination with which articles detail the evolving nature of the press–star relationship, there does not seem to be a single piece which acknowledges the perversity of these different images being held up simultaneously as presenting the 'real' Doris Day.

And the situation was just about to get worse. The year 1961 also saw the publication, in the 27 July issue of the *Los Angeles*

Mirror, of a short piece by humorist Al Capp. 'All That Doris Day Wanted Was To Get Wed To The Guy', is a simple, 500-word affair in which Capp concludes that a person can earn a lot of money writing 'a Doris Day love story', and this is easily achieved, because 'there is only one'. Capp outlines the inevitable plot of such a film:

> Doris Day's mature yet girlish beauty has always, will always, must always rouse the wolf in her co-star [. . . while his] good looks and good manners inspire thoughts of marriage in Doris Day.
>
> (Capp, 1961)

By this point in Day's movie career, the films that conform to this template were only *Pillow Talk* and *Lover Come Back*, yet Capp ignores the slender nature of the filmography to suggest through hyperbole that every film with the star in it follows this ludicrous yet lucrative pattern.

Significantly, the newspaper piece does not overtly use the word 'virgin' to describe Day. This is reserved for Capp's longer, more vitriolic, and very influential piece published the following year in the highbrow arts magazine, *Show*. The *Los Angeles Mirror* article seems to have been a trial run for the second, longer version. This similarly examines the idea of what 'a Doris Day film' has become, but also (allegedly) interviews personnel involved in Day's films and pillories her as a controlling diva who micromanages every aspect of her career and image. Its most prominent achievement, however, is to introduce the word 'virgin' openly into discourse about Doris Day. The article from *Show*, 'The Day Dream' (Capp, 1962), is analysed in greater depth in the following chapter; suffice it to say here, then, that in his analysis of the Day film template and her star persona both on- and off-screen, Capp slides from calling her stock character a virgin, to insisting that the star herself is one.

While it is true that both the girl next door and the overt virgin persona, which emerged into the media seemingly with the Capp article from late 1962, are images which relate to the characters Day played on screen, and the by-turns bored, adulterous, or loyal but cheated-on wife relate to the star herself, there is never as clear cut a distinction in the magazine articles about which Doris Day is being invoked. Perhaps all stars encounter the phenomenon whereby they and their roles are deemed to merge, differences between character and performer being elided. Certainly it is a convention of film reviewing to slip into speaking of the actor, rather than the character, as performing an action or experiencing an event. This slippage seems even more acute in Day's case, however, since it requires ignoring not only the facts of the star's off-screen life but also oscillating between three different ideas about her: that she is a coy, aging girl next door; that she is a coy, or a hypocritical and manipulative, aged virgin; and that she is a licentious married woman fed up with husband number three, busily involved in auditioning other men for the part of his replacement.

After Capp's article had used 'the V word' in relation to Day, other magazines soon picked up on it and it began to be the leading signifier which differentiated the star from others. Reviewers and writers from other mainstream magazines adopted the appellation without questioning its appropriateness: *Photoplay* used the occasion of its review of circus movie *Jumbo* to employ the virginal metaphor, noting all the showfolks were so kind hearted that 'instead of fighting for her virtue through every reel', 'Doris Day can relax' (Anon, 1963 a: 6). The slippage between character and star is evident here: it is not Kitty Wonder who 'can relax', but Day herself, finding herself in a narrative that, supposedly, does not require her to safeguard her chastity. This asserts not only that this is the common template for Day movies but also, somehow, that Day herself is usually virginal. The review's one-liner both acknowledges that Day is an actor who plays different roles and simultaneously implies that she herself is the one fighting off wolves. Similarly, an article in *The American Weekly* in June followed Capp's lead, adopting the virginal metaphor when it declared no one was 'more dedicated to the vestal keeping of the Doris Day flame than Doris Day herself' (Gehman, 1963: 4). Day is compared here to the maidens of Ancient Rome who followed the cult of Vesta, goddess of the hearth and home, pledging the goddess their virginity and tending the sacred flame on her altar.

Interestingly, it took the non-mainstream, disreputable magazine *Inside Story* to question the application of the virgin epithet to the much-married star. In an article in the May 1963 issue, 'Why Doris Day was out at home'[20], the magazine disparages one myth about the star, the virginity one, by subscribing to the other, the one which positions Day as an over-sexed adulteress fond of black men. The scandalous piece seems to be citing Capp when it outlines the Day movie template:

> In her long reign as Hollywood's top female star, Doris has never once lost her virtue. Not before the cameras, anyway. The part she likes best and plays most often is that of a wide-eyed virgin who is pursued by a panting playboy.
>
> She may fall into the playboy's pitfalls, may even end up in his boudoir, but she never relinquishes her chastity. In all her movies, virtue prevails and Little Red Riding Hood finally tames her wolf and leads him to the altar.
>
> (Levine, 1963: 16)

Although it subscribes to the Capp line here, the *Inside Story* article moves away from the general adoption of the virgin myth noticeable in other more respectable magazines, instead questioning the roots and appropriateness of the label:

> Studio executives keep reminding Doris that her fans think of her as the sweet innocent 'girl next door'. How she ever got this virginal buildup in the first place is one of movieland's major mysteries.
>
> True, Doris does not drink or smoke. And she simply can't stand cuss words. Furthermore, she will not anylone [sic – presumably should read 'let anyone'] drink, smoke or swear in her presence, which sometimes makes it tough on her less holy co-workers.
>
> (Levine, 1963: 17)

This piece from a disreputable scandal rag actually confronts the unlikely nature of the virgin label, and goes on to speculate about what may have caused it. While *Inside Story* was clearly marketing itself as trash journalism along the lines of the more successful *Confidential* (from 1952 onwards), it voiced scepticism and advanced a reasonable theory which no other authors tried to do. *Inside Story* suggests that Day's well-known religious faith, which necessitated her avoidance of alcohol and tobacco, might have contributed to her being seen as pure and saintly. From this 'holy' standpoint it is a short step to being seen accepting or advocating sexual abstinence too.

The *Inside Story* article links the girl next door and virgin personae more intelligently and more overtly than other pieces published in more respectable magazines. While it too peddles many of the same prurient lines about Day, at least it also advances the idea that Day's fans were intent upon seeing and believing in an aspect of the star that insisted upon her innocence – whether as a small town girl next door or a big-city career woman. The article also suggests who was ultimately responsible for the myth of the pure Doris Day: the studios.

'Studio executives keep reminding' the star that she has an image to live up to: this implies that they need to keep reminding her as she is, herself, eager to get away from this image, a notion borne out once the magazines began to publish what the star herself said about public perception of her as an embodiment of chastity ('I really can't stand all that virginal Miss Goody Two-Shoes bit' – Dahl, 1975: 50; West, 1977: 28).

The studios keep reminding her because they can continue to cash in on the popularity of the image – as long as this popularity lasts. Perhaps the article's reasons for following Capp's lead in spelling out the pattern of the typical Day movie now become clear: the piece sets out to show how profitable these films have been, in order to indicate in whose interests producing another one will be. Although the star will obviously make a good financial return for her labour in yet another sex comedy, eventually she will suffer when audiences tire of the genre, and of her. In the end Day herself was blamed for the calcification of her image, and for the hypocritical attitude to sex which the films seemed to endorse, being prurient in suggestion but cowardly in follow-through.

References to the virginal role Day seemed to be playing continue in the later 1960s and into the 70s. Occasionally a savvy critic will note that there is more to the virgin persona than initially seems obvious; Judith Crist in a 1965 piece in the *New York Herald Tribune*, for instance, suggests that not only Day but her romantic *vis-à-vis* are routinely tamed by the films they appear in, and posits that American audiences prefer their central movie characters to have been fully 'domesticated' (27), by which she means both put into homey situations, and neutered, desexed. Usually, however, the references to Day as virgin remain unexamined by their users, the label becoming something employed because others employed it; it becomes a contemporary touchstone, utilised to evoke the topical, regardless of whether it is actually appropriate or not. A

November 1968 article on the death, in April that year, of Day's husband, invokes the myth in testament to Melcher's management of Day's career: 'His careful guidance, his decision to show her as the virtuous but exciting all-American girl he knew, kept her from going the way of most over-40 stars' (Anon, 1968: 73). This piece seems to suggest Day is *herself* the 'virtuous but exciting' person her screen roles promote: the identification of the virgin character with Day is total here. It is also interesting that, just after he died, Melcher was being publicly remembered as someone who exercised 'careful guidance' over Day's career; very soon, however, this handling becomes read not as sensitive but as misguided, and Melcher himself was blamed for harming Day's career, halting her development as a mature female star. This rather prompts the question: was Hollywood ready for mature female stars in the late 1960s? It has not reliably provided interesting roles for them subsequently. Melcher being held accountable for the perpetuation of the virginal image is the central focus of *Movie Life*'s August 1969 piece, 'How Doris Day became a VIRGIN after marriage!' (Anon, 1969.) The sensationalised headline, complete with wacky font on the v-word, betrays how trivially it will treat the topics it covers; although the item declares that the author 'dropped by the TV set of *The Doris Day Show* one afternoon to sound out its star on a number of subjects', it seems very unlikely to be the record of an actual interview, since every single quoted remark from Day appears in print in other earlier articles. The piece seems designed instead to cash in on the topicality of pillorying Day for endlessly playing 'the last of the Hollywood virgins' (48). The *Movie Life* piece insists that Melcher was the instigator of the virgin persona:

> Undoubtedly, it was due to Melcher's influence that Doris changed her screen image. After Melcher took control of her life,

she evolved from the sweet, girl next door image into a career girl who was interested in sex – only if it came with a wedding band. Marty Melcher, her husband, was quite instrumental in turning Doris into a screen virgin after they married. (72)

By this point the impetus to attribute the establishment of the virgin myth to Melcher has become so entrenched that historical facts are discarded or manipulated in order to promote the story. Here Day is perceived as the 'sweet girl next door' before Melcher's interference – yet, as has been indicated, her early roles before he married her in 1951 were much more sexualised than this description suggests. Furthermore, the account above makes it sound as if the virginal persona arrived with Day's marriage to Melcher, another obscuring of the facts, since it did not begin until a decade after their 1951 wedding. Melcher had been Day's agent/manager through many phases of her career, including the overt sexualisation and maturation her image was perceived to undergo around the time of *Love Me Or Leave Me*. Here, however, the majority of actual film roles and her evolving persona are suppressed, so that the nostalgic Day of *On Moonlight Bay* is transformed instantly into the reluctantly virginal heroine of *Lover Come Back*.

The efforts which the *Movie Life* article undergoes, in order to blame Melcher for the emergence of the virginal persona, suggests that the magazines were, by this point, looking for someone to take responsibility for the inevitable imposition of this character onto Day. This indicates to me that there was an awareness of the problematic nature of the virgin as a way of reading the maturely sexual star, yet an unwillingness to see that the very articles attempting to lay blame on this or that party actually did nothing to dissipate the image but actually assisted its longevity. Instead of holding Day or her husband accountable for the insistence on the coy avoidance of sex – imagined, rather than found – in Day's characters, the magazine authors could have looked to their own works for an explanation of where the 'freckle-faced, forty-year old [...] so straight that she blushed buying bed linens' (Edgerton, 1971: 81) was actually inaugurated.

This section has worked to illustrate how the film magazine articles on Doris Day, from the beginning of her film career to its end and afterlife in television, repeatedly employed a series of dominant tropes or idea-clusters. While my sample of 479 pieces indicates that 23 key terms were in circulation about Day across this whole time, several were deemed to be more significant in tapping into this book's main topic of investigation, her supposedly virginal persona. These specific tropes were therefore examined in detail to see how they contributed to the virgin idea. In putting these centre-stage, I have had to isolate them from their immediate magazine contexts, although of course each of the articles in my sample will have touched on many of the current ideas about Day and combined them in different ways. It will be the task of this section's final chapter to return the tropes to their wider environment, by looking at how four separate articles from across the star's career period chose to handle and inflect those they employ from the many on offer.

4 Magazines in Micro
Introduction

The final chapter of this section narrows its focus to examine in detail just four magazine articles across the span of Day's career. While the task of the previous chapter was to draw apart and isolate the various tropes that occurred and reoccurred in articles about the star, this chapter reverses that process to look instead at how single articles brought together many of the ideas circulating about her at particular times. Thus of the four pieces under investigation – from 1948, 1956, 1962 and 1971 – each includes many of the various inflections of the dominant themes and connotations circulating around the star at their particular moments. As previously noted, of the four dates elected for study, the earliest and latest bracket the beginning and end of her live career, while the middle two relate to the various shifts to her meanings caused at two different moments by the (re)introduction of a sexualised element to her persona, around *Love Me Or Leave Me* and *Lover Come Back.*

In addition to examining the tropes on offer and seeing the ways they modulate over time, I will also analyse the chosen pieces on Day in their specific magazine contexts. The impact that other pieces of copy – photographs of Day or others, advertisements or editorials – as well as their placement and use of colour, will be considered for what they tacitly imply about the star, and how they underline or contradict elements being played up more overtly by the articles themselves. The potential reading strategies fostered by each issue's placement of items on the star will be explored, to see whether the star trail, star saturation or shared coverage technique is used.

'The "Most Everything" Girl In Hollywood' by Laura Pomeroy (*Motion Picture*, August 1948: 38–9, and 76)

This piece, from the first year in which Day appeared on the film scene, sets out the major tropes about the star. Many of these endured for her entire career – and still persist – while others soon evolved in different directions. However, the article's interest goes beyond its examination of the resonances circulating around Day: it provides a prime example of the importance, when studying magazine items, of being alert to their placement and contexts.

The potential buyer picking the August 1948 issue of *Motion Picture* off a news-stand would have been presented with a cover showing a photograph, as the black text confirms, of 'Shirley Temple and her baby, Linda Susan' (Figure 9). The colours of photograph and text present a pleasing visual harmony: the

Figure 9.   *Motion Picture* August 1948 cover.

smiling mother and her small daughter are both dressed in white; Temple's red mouth chimes with the coloured circle in which the white 10c price appears. '*Motion Picture* magazine' is also written in red, while the word 'August' appears in black on the right hand side of the cover, above the text naming Temple. The only other text occurs at the very top of the cover page:

see page 25 … YES, PAGE 25 … look on page 25 … NOW! PAGE 25

Here lower case and upper case alternate across the top of the cover urging action. But what is the reader/buyer being sent to view by the enigmatic text? What is found on page 25 is not, perhaps surprisingly, an article about Shirley Temple – the piece on her and the new baby is on pages 36 and 37 – but a further enigma: a full page bearing a message from the editors of *Motion Picture* confirming their unanimous belief in the arrival of a new bona fide sensation:

Include us in!

On page 38 you'll find a story called 'The Most Everything Girl in Hollywood'. It'll probably strike you as being just another story on just another star.

But …

It isn't. Ninety-nine times out of a hundred, when a star is being discussed or a story judged, one of your editors will register an objection.

This is that hundredth time. This is where your four editors line up together and dive overboard.

[…]

See page 38.

Without naming the new discovery, the four editors, with their signatures printed in facsimile at the end, agree that Hollywood is always abuzz with news of some soon-to-be forgotten starlet. The unnamed new star they are hailing here, however, is the real thing: a genuine phenomenon whose claim to success is 'born of talent and personality and that certain extra something that can't be faked, that has to be there' (25).

Interestingly, the article that eventually follows on Doris Day is not placed overleaf from this display of editorial support, but some eight pages later; the editors' message thus acts as another interest-piquing occasion, a trailer, directing the reader on again through the magazine, delaying the gratification of revelation, increasing the pleasurable suspense. In this way the editorial tactic of highlighting the Day article by first signposting the editors' endorsement and then having that endorsement point the way forward again to the actual piece acts in contradiction to the largely undirected flow back and forth through the magazine which is usually supposed to operate (see McCracken and Stein). Instead, the magazine sets up a rare star trail, a reading path which leads the reader through the issue, via smaller pieces, to the large central article.

While this first imagined reader/buyer is thus taken on a fast-track through the magazine, skipping the contents page, adverts, gossip items and articles, straight to the endorsement and then on to the Day piece itself, an alternative reader/buyer who resisted being lured into the mystery would still not have come upon the 'Most Everything' item unprepared. Taking a more orthodox route into the magazine, progressing from the front cover, the reader finds first the contents list revealing that there is a piece on Day (3); a few pages later, in the gossip section, 'Overheard in Hollywood', there is her name again, as the columnist reveals a droll story about Curtiz' methods for eliciting tears from his new leading lady (8). Opposite this snippet is a full page advert for *Romance On The High Seas*, in which a photograph of Day's smiling face is given prominence among her co-stars, and her name is the only one accompanied by its own little tagline: 'She's DAYlightful, DAYlicious! A new Day for the singing, dancing screen!' (9).

In both instances, then, whether by direct selection or slow progression, the article is reached mediated by anticipation. Getting to the article on Day has been stage-managed, produced to heighten the reader's awareness of the new star's impact before a word of the piece on her has been read. But the stage-management does not end there. For finally arriving at the story on Day by Laura Pomeroy, the viewer finds this occupies a double page spread around the middle of the magazine (pages 38 and 39), where the text is accompanied by a collage of several photographs of the new star, including one where her image seems to point to the article title as if Day is announcing her own arrival, with a ta-da! gesture (Figure 10). The article concludes later in the issue, on page 76, where it occupies the majority of the page. And facing the conclusion to the Day item is a 'Whatever became of….?' piece featuring silent screen star Lynda La Plante, placed alongside a two-column advert for 'Toni Creme Shampoo', which carries a large picture of a curly-haired little girl and a smaller one of the product (Figure 11). The little girl looks somewhat like the young Shirley Temple – the star on the cover. This visual reminder of Temple in her most famous period of stardom sets off a complex relay of associations. In close proximity across the two pages are arranged an item on a former star now retired, an image reminiscent of a child star from the previous decade, and the columns about this new sensation. The article on Day is thus not only led up to by various strategies designed to attract attention to it and its subject, but also surrounded by pieces which tacitly point up her significance, as she is implicitly positioned as the successor to both La Plante's and Temple's fame.

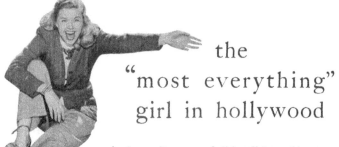

the "most everything" girl in hollywood

by Laura Pomeroy   ● If she couldn't earn a living as an actress, singer, comedienne, dancer and horse-woman (her latest accomplishment), Doris Day could easily keep the wolf from the door by posing for Wheaties.

Doris is the long-legged, peppy blonde you'll see capering around in Michael Curtiz' production, Romance on the High Seas, and we do mean capering. Doris never stays still except to eat. She has bounce and zip, and in this day and age of neuroses it's wonderful to report that here is a girl who says, "I'm happy," and what's more, makes anyone who's within radiation distance of her feel that way too. Someone once asked Doris what vitamins she takes to keep her so full of the *qui vive*, to which a friend immediately answered, "Vitamins should take Doris!"

Doris looks like a cross between a 4-H girl and a Cub Scout with a bit of Sally Co-Ed thrown in. She's healthy and clean-looking and the freckles on her nose should remain uncovered even if it takes an act of Congress to do so. She wears sweaters in a certain casual way, lets her hair fly and has the sort of all-embracing smile that takes in every one of her features. No wonder Michael Curtiz, one of the most astute producer-directors in Hollywood, has placed his chips on her as a winner.

Curtiz, during his twenty-six years as a top Hollywood [*Please turn to page 76*]

Long a star of radio's Hit Parade, she loves to clown in the studio with Sinatra

38   Photo by Robert Perkins

Figure 10.   Day appears to point to the article about her.

As noted elsewhere in the chapters on the various tropes and on Day's media persona in general, the 'Most Everything' piece is significant for confirming many of the themes that became associated with Day. The article starts with a list of Day's multiple gifts – 'actress, singer, comedienne, dancer and

Laura La Plante?

● One of Hollywood's prettiest blondes (both past and present tense), Laura La Plante is best remembered for the many light comedies she played on the silent screen—Beautiful Cheat, Poker Faces, Her Big Night, Cat and the Canary and Thanks For the Buggy Ride. She also starred in Show Boat, one of her last pictures, in the late twenties.

Laura today is Mrs. Irving Asher and mother of an 11-year-old daughter and an 8-year-old son. She lives across the street from Louella Parsons in Beverly Hills and gets a kick out of watching the young starlets of today parade hopefully up to her neighbor's door.

Recently she was told by her Beverly Hills butcher, "Know who you look like? Just like a girl who used to be in the movies—Laura La Plante. Of course, you look like she used to look, not the way she looks now." Somewhere, Laura thinks there must be a compliment in that. ●

As attractive today as she was pretty twenty years ago, Laura is now the mother of two, a boy and a girl

Toni Creme Shampoo

GIVES YOU

Soft-Water Shampooing

EVEN IN HARDEST WATER

It's another hair beauty miracle by Toni! "Soft-water shampooing" with new Toni Creme Shampoo. An amazing new kind of shampooing that brings out all—yes, all the shimmering highlights, all the glorious natural sheen of your hair.

Toni Creme Shampoo bursts into creamy, Lanolin-enriched lather—so gentle it's wonderful for children's baby-fine hair. Just as wonderful for your hair. Leaves your permanent so soft, so easy to manage. Today, get Toni Creme Shampoo in the handy tube or jar.

**ASK FOR
TONI CREME SHAMPOO
IT'S NEW**

77

Figure 11.   Reinforcing Day's new stardom: The Toni Creme Shampoo model looks like Shirley Temple.

horsewoman' – which hints at the aptness of the article title and confirms why Day should be such a phenomenon. This is not the first use of the 'Talented/Star' trope, but it is one of the most sustained early pieces to deal with it. Next the item emphasises Day's 'Energy', her pep and enthusiasm, alludes to her 'Blondeness' ('Wheaties') and notes her 'Freckles', as well as the fact that she is 'healthy and clean-looking' (38). Both parts of the 'Natural' trope, that loading with 'Tomboy' and that with 'Clean', are thus elicited, the former when the article stresses that Day's choice of clothing and hairstyle is generally 'casual', her closet stuffed with informal clothing, and she herself 'as unpretentious as a pair of jeans' (76). In a move which would then be copied by most of the pieces on the star for the next few years, the article lays out her brief biography and includes the story of how her name was changed from Kappelhoff to Day.

Since the piece is likely to be introducing the new star to many reader/viewers who have not seen her before – though it acknowledges that most will have *heard* her, recognising her success already as a recording star – it devotes a lot of attention and some hyperbole to describing her looks, despite the fact that the piece is accompanied by four photographs of various sizes, showing Day in a variety of poses. Besides the one in which she indicates the article's title, there is one with her 'clowning' with Frank Sinatra (38), another showing her full length as she leans on a balcony railing, and a fourth, close-up, in which she smiles into the distance just left of the camera. The tag for this particular image asserts 'With a figure as pert and trim as a saucy sailboat, and a face fairly bursting with animation, Doris Day explodes into stardom in Romance on the High Seas' (38). As noted previously, the piece evokes the new star's persona in terms of an atomic bomb detonation. This metaphor is hyperbolic but attests the huge impact Pomeroy is trying to convey the new star has made.

In all, the account seems most intent to stress the multiplicity of Day's talents, her energy, and her lack of pretension: 'she will have nothing to do with Hollywood hoop-la' (76). This latter is established further by anecdotes which highlight the new star's refusal to put on airs for the camera, hinting at the foundation of the 'Just Like Us' characteristic which became particularly dominant once Day married Melcher. This characteristic is paradoxical in as much as obviously Day is not just like us – she is much more talented, lucky and famous. The article oscillates between playing up Day's *unstarry* star persona – told by her business manager that she can afford a new car, she retorts she might buy a *horse* – and attempting to explain the magnitude of the impact this major new star will have on audiences. This last is the aim of the little story Pomeroy tells, which gives the article the quoted portion of its title. Michael Curtiz, pegged as Day's discoverer, is said to give her the epithet:

> [Curtiz] was on the quest for a girl to play the lead in Romance on the High Seas and the qualifications were sharp. She had to be beautiful, of course. She had to sing. She had to act. But above all, she had to sparkle. After interviewing dozens of girls, none of whom had all those qualities together, Doris was brought in to see him.

> Curtiz looked at her and let out a yelp. 'This is it,' he cried, 'This is the most everything dame I have ever seen'. (76)

While Curtiz here christens Day with the 'most everything' soubriquet – also using the less cultured word 'dame' for girl – the *Motion Picture* title alters this, making the noun more polite and widening the sphere of Day's influence from Curtiz' experience to the whole of Hollywood. Although this quote, allegedly from the director, is what gives the article its impetus, the magazine itself was happy later, when letters from readers arrived to praise Day, to take the credit for spotting Doris Day's star quality, publishing three positive responses to the star (and its own find) in the November issue:

> I really enjoyed your article on Doris Day... as a result I went to see her in *Romance On The High Seas* – boy, she was terrific!

> ...the editors wrote a note telling of a star being born, that star being Doris Day. They said she was 'the most everything girl in Hollywood'. I agree 100 per cent.

> ...I'd like to congratulate you for being the first magazine to recognise Doris Day as 'the most everything girl in Hollywood'. I fully agree with you.

> (Anon, 1948 i: 14)

While letters to the editors can never be proven, especially at this distance, to have been generated by genuine readers and viewers rather than more interested parties (Day's agent or publicist, Warner Bros. employees, even magazine staff members themselves), what the publication of these letters does indicate is that *Motion Picture* was determined to promote Day's stardom across a number of issues, announcing her arrival as a major new player in Hollywood and then supporting this finding by printing supporting testimony from audience members. What the article and its placement in the issue demonstrates, then, is both the foundation of some of the most dominant tropes circulating around the star, and the manner in which a star promotion could be highlighted as significant through its placement and that of the advertising and editorial material around it. Both reading strategies prompted by the article's location – turning direct to the endorsement or paging through the magazine as usual – set the reader off on a star trail which leads to Day and her emphasised significance before a word of the article itself is absorbed, and in this way seek to validate her worth as a new arrival.

'Sex Isn't Everything' by Doris Day[21] (*Motion Picture*, May 1956: 26, 27 (picture) and 67)

This article, unlike the others in this tranche, purports to be written by Day herself. There is probably no way now to prove who authored 'Sex Isn't Everything', but despite this, the article is interesting to analyse for its use of tropes and especially its position on the cusp between two versions of the star's persona. Again, as with the 1948 piece on the star, the article's physical placement in the magazine also provides information which affects its meanings, although the reader of this article comes to it with much less fanfare than the earlier analysed piece. By now Day's stardom was well-established, so magazines did not have to tout her as a new sensation. Indeed, the cover of the May 1956 issues of *Motion Picture* does not mention her; there is no sign of Day until the careful reader scans the contents list on page two: her name appears against the eighth listed story. Going direct to this article, however, would mean missing out on a small item which subtly establishes the terrain for the later piece.

Day is the subject of a little item in the gossip section, 'Under Hedda's Hat', which sprawls across several columns on several pages. Day features on the fourth page, in a snippet about her potential house-moving plans and the title of a forthcoming film. Hopper reports that Day 'has a new name for the musical version of *Anna Christie* which she's doing with Howard Keel for MGM – it's now called *A Saint She Ain't*' (1956: 12). This is the first hint at the type of Doris Day the main article will present: the *sexy* Doris. *Anna Christie* (1930) was famously advertised with the tag 'Garbo Talks!' and had shown the Swedish star in the role of a prostitute. While a musical remake of the story might be expected to tone down the degrading elements of its heroine's life, *Anna Christie* was still sufficiently well-known that most readers would realise it meant the continuation of Day's more adult roles, perceived to have begun with that of Ruth Etting the year before.

'Sex Isn't Everything' appears on pages 26 and 27 of the magazine, text on the left page and a full colour picture of Day on the right (Figure 12). Above the two columns of text, the headline features the word SEX in block capitals, printed in hot dark pink inside a black box, with 'isn't everything' in a cursive font designed to look hand-written. The hot, overt pink colour used for the word SEX underlines the word, and carries on underneath the rest of the headline, across the entire page, having more impact when it rides across the white paper underneath 'isn't everything'. The hot colour also contrasts markedly with the softer, pastel pink jumper that Day is wearing in the photograph. Visually, thus, the two-page spread of the article presents oppositions, even before the story's message is read and

Figure 12. *Motion Picture* May 1956 article.

absorbed: the lurid highlighting of 'sex', through its colour, capitalisation and format, is placed in opposition to the appealing, frank gaze of the star who stares out at the reader as if leaning on a window ledge. Yet Day too is framed against an entirely black background, establishing her as a sign like the word 'SEX' – surrounded by black – and thus potentially equated with it, although this is complicated by the different colour emphasis in the photograph and the opposition of the recto/verso placement. While, then, the words of the headline insist that 'Sex isn't everything', the delivery of this message is complicated by the equation between the word 'sex' and the image of Day. This confusion accords with the mixed messages inherent in the text itself.

Like many magazine articles, this piece does not finish in the two pages on display here, nor is it continued directly over the page, but concludes instead at the other end of the magazine, on page 67. If turning the leaves over steadily, rather than flicking quickly to read the conclusion, the reader may come across another mention of Day before arriving at the end of the 'Sex isn't' narrative, for on page 50 in Sheilah Graham's gossip/opinion column, 'Sounding Off', the author takes Day to task for turning her back on musicals in favour of 'going straight', continuing dismissively that the star 'had a taste of the dramatics in *Love Me Or Leave Me* and liked it' (Graham, 1956: 50). While this comment may seem an entirely negative criticism, it still acts first as an advertisement for the significance of Day as a star, as writers devote column inches to her activities. Graham reaffirms the reasons for Day's original popularity, 'Dodo's marvellous way with a melody as much as her shining, ebullient personality'; however, by concluding that Day may be happier in dramas but her fans, among whom she counts herself, *won't* be, Graham actually underlines the reasons for the star's return to less sexualised roles after her turn as Etting, which the article by 'Day' rehearses. The careful placing of items on Day prepares the reader for the article through the use of frequent mentions – saturation – which contributes not only to the importance of the star at this juncture, but also frames the reception of the story told about her.

The final two columns of the 'Sex isn't' piece appear on page 67. While the article's conclusion appears without much visual impact, it is interestingly placed: opposite a full page given over to the conclusion of a story on Elizabeth Taylor ('The Girl With The Golden Face', tagged 'How could such perfection be so destructive?' 34–35). Postage-stamp sized pictures appear at the top left of each page, to remind readers whose story they are finishing, and it is noticeable that Taylor's presentation is more sexualised, her face three-quarters to the camera, shadowed and with a provocative pout, while Day smiles straight out at the viewer, her gaze direct but unthreatening. Summing up Taylor as brooding and dangerously sexy, Day as self-contained, good-humoured and healthy, the two pictures again do much to reinforce the Day article's *new* old story of the star, returning her to a time before the Etting role.

The piece itself supposedly presents Day's views on sex appeal at a moment when the popular media had just changed its story about Day, acknowledging her, in the light of her mature performance in *Love Me Or Leave Me*, as an adult star in an appropriately adult role. However, in seeming to back away from the more mature persona established by other articles, 'Sex Isn't Everything' returns to an earlier incarnation of the star.

The article quickly establishes itself as having a dual time-frame; 'Day' looks back from the 'now' of 1956 to her childhood in the mid-30s, when her ideas about glamour were comically immature. The article sets up a contrast: between the little girl then and the mature wife and mother now, and further, between the girl's innocent yearning for the trappings of adulthood, and the adult's wiser awareness that true attractiveness comes from within. While most of the article sides with the contemporary part of the dichotomy, as 'Day' goes on to relate how wrong-headed her nine-year-old self was about female sex appeal, there is yet a slight sense of yearning to return to that period which complicates the rest of the article's thrust towards the improvements of 'now'. 'Day' relates how she once went to see a 'fashionably attired woman' play the church organ, becoming enchanted by the woman's 'most beautiful eyelashes' (26). Although, then, most of the piece goes on to stress the adult Doris's dislike of 'provocative' clothing, gaudy jewellery and make-up, the account of her first encounters with long eyelashes and, in a later paragraph, a permanent wave, still evokes a sense of the little girl dazzled by other women and her own future potential for glamour.

'Day' goes on to stress that, as a little girl playing 'movie star', she used to 'bur[y] my freckles in a sea of make-up', although whenever she went anywhere public, her parents 'saw to it that I was scrubbed clean' (26). The general tone of the article is to assert how wrong little Doris was about feminine beauty, but it is very noticeable that, in the full page colour photograph opposite these confessions, not a trace of freckles remains, despite Day's well-known championing of them. The article's attempt to situate make-up on the negative side of the dichotomies running through the piece is thus compromised. Indeed, the whole argument of the article is somewhat incoherent, its oppositions often as confusing as the article's own visual layout.

'Day' here asserts that though she used to yearn for four things, convinced they would give her allure – a perm, high heels, false teeth and a brassiere – she now realises that 'one woman's sex appeal is another woman's poison'. Further, not only is the overt sexiness granted by such false trappings not *her*, the article suggests that *no* woman is improved by such meretricious possessions:

> ...I learned that the term 'sex appeal', in itself, was frequently a contradiction in terms. Actually, I've come to believe not only that sex isn't everything but that, in fact, it isn't anything if it's divorced from the rest of a girl's personality. (26)

In this pair of confusing sentences, 'Day' seems to mean that sex appeal is often unappealing, and that if the external trappings of attractiveness are put on a woman without them somehow arising from her character, they will fail to dazzle. The language used however can easily be read as prudish, anticipating the later idea of Day as sex-averse, if the actual words rather than the context are noted: the article seems to slip from discussing 'sex appeal' to talking about actual intercourse – 'sex isn't everything... isn't anything' – yet the end of the sentence makes clear it is still sexual allure rather than the act that is meant.

'Day' eventually alludes to the most obvious reason for the article's publication: the perception that she has changed since playing Etting:

> After the picture came out, there were all sorts of reports that I had gone sexpot. The word was that I wanted to play nothing but slinky, sensuous females. The general reason behind this alleged transformation was that I loved the low neckline gowns I wore in the picture.
>
> Now, nothing could be more absurd, really. (67)

Here 'Day' seems to disavow her enjoyment of the gowns she had attested in an 'Impertinent Interview' published in the September 1955 issue of *Photoplay*: the article posed the question, 'How do you feel about being sexy for the first time in pictures?' to which her ultimate response was 'I love every second of it' (Connolly, 1955: 4). Other magazines noted the new sensuality in her role, with *Cosmopolitan* calling her 'a full-grown woman of passion' (Shipp, 1956: 58) and *Photoplay* designating her 'Whistle Bait' (Ott, 1956: 48–49, 110–111).

In the quotation above, 'Day' mocks those who call her 'sexpot' because she apparently now favours décolleté, suggesting that the gowns were only appropriate for the Etting story because of the mature storyline. But by sloughing off her supposed preference for low cut gowns she also seems to be belittling *Love Me Or Leave Me*, despite the warm reception her performance had won for its dramatic skill. The article is thus revisionist, seeking to return to the older established wife-and-mother Day of the earlier 50s.

The article attempts to compound this domesticated view of the star through its final strategy in dismissing the 'sexpot' charge: here 'Day' asserts that her dislike of feminine artifice is equalled, even exceeded, by those of her husband and son:

> [Marty] doesn't like a lot of make-up and he howls when my hair is set...He's the same way about my clothes. He hates anything the least bit pretentious or sensational. (67)

The piece concludes with the information that Day's son Terry, then aged 13, also hates 'cheesecake' and is glad that *his* mother does not make a spectacle of herself by wearing scanty clothing on magazine covers. The article firmly equates looks with conduct, buying into then-prevalent notions which dictated women were not entitled to sexual experience – the double standard. 'Day' resolutely condemns women who seem to advertise their availability: '...when a girl looks cheap – no matter how she flaunts her curves – no sane man will be attracted to her'. Women should thus not dress provocatively, and men should not dignify with their attentions those who do. This presumes that all women are intent on marriage, the market from which they disqualify themselves if they hold their own virtue too cheaply. No 'sane' man – that is, no man with marriage on his mind – will consider a fallen woman. This seems a harsh message, especially in light of the plot of *Love Me Or Leave Me*...

In concluding the article, 'Day' presents a final point which takes the piece in a new direction, suddenly offering an extra motive behind the article's writing and stance. Musing that 'The sexiest looking girl in the world can be so unappealing, so uninspiring,' 'Day' notes that the same is true of handsome men. She promotes the idea of a natural, unforced attractiveness which does not require the sight of breast flesh – from either gender: 'Jimmy Stewart never bares his chest or flexes his muscles, but he exudes charm.' This mention of Stewart leads 'Day' to note she has just finished making a film with him, and to offer a final conclusion about clothes: they should be appropriate to character and context. While the article winds towards its conclusion, then, positing that screen costume needs to be plausible and that in *The Man Who Knew Too Much* she needed to dress believably as a doctor's wife, the revelation that the piece is a promotional puff for her new film prompts a fresh examination of the article. The influence of the Hitchcock film can then be seen from the article's tagline onwards:

> When I was a little girl, I had a burning desire to be alluring, seductive, provocative. Now I know that...Sex Isn't Everything By Doris Day. (26; ellipses in original)

The first words of the tag now recall the opening line of the famous song, 'Que Sera Sera' from *The Man Who*... ('When I was just a little girl...'). Instead of asking her mother, what shall I be, here the younger 'Day' seems to be offered counsel by her own, older self. Casting her as the mother figure in the article begins the work of re-establishing the star in this familiar, familial role after the anomalous one of the cynical Etting; this explains the importance of including Terry's ideas about appropriate feminine garb, as the article works to prepare movie audiences for a new mother character from Day.

Several of the dominant tropes identified across the popular media pieces on the star occur in this article, although some are complicated by the fact that it purports to be written by Day herself. For this reason, and because she does not overtly mention her religious beliefs as influencing her ideas about modest clothing, it is difficult to decide conclusively that 'Religion' is being invoked here; her aversion to sensationalised dress *could* be read as being caused by religion, or as suggesting the 'Pathology' trope, or as being good sense, depending on the reader. Other tropes are easier to spot, however: 'Day' employs the 'Natural/Tomboy' idea at points where she notes her preference for bare feet, and the 'Natural/Clean' cluster when she supports Marty's ideas about minimal make-up. The entire article and its accompanying picture concentrate on the star's 'Looks' and 'Clothes'. 'Day' also mentions how she used to want to hide her 'Freckles'. Published in 1956, the piece is one of the earliest examples of the 'Sensationalised Heading' in the literature sampled, while the allusion to the coverage of the star's overt sexualisation brings in the 'Meta' idea, an article on Day commenting on other articles on Day. It is possible to see the whole article, with its look back at a child's naive mistakes about adult sexuality, as a sustained attempt by the writer to prompt acceptance of the 'Just Like Us' trope, with 'Day' confirming that she had a regular childhood in small-town America, as well as making initial mistakes about glamour like many teens. This is probably undone, however, as many of the 'Just Like Us' attempts were, by the severity of the position 'Day' supports. Though no one would like to look 'cheap', the clothing ideas seem prudish; similarly, Marty's dislike of costume jewellery feels particularly out of step with what the majority of readers could afford to own. 'Day' does herself no favours then by confessing she recently had to return a $10 bracelet because Marty hated it, telling her he would rather she 'spent a hundred and had something really good'. The Melchers pass at such moments from being 'Just Like Us' to just impossible. Finally, the reference to Terry's endorsement of her properly dignified clothing evokes the 'Mom' trope, which sits particularly well with the film actually being promoted by the article.

'The Day Dream', by Al Capp (*Show*, December 1962: 72–3, 136–7)

Show – 'The magazine of the Arts' – is a different type of magazine from the two film fan products examined previously, dealing with not only a more varied art scene but also a higher one. Everything about the physical presence of the magazine underlines this emphasis on higher than average quality: its page numbers (138 compared to an average *Motion Picture*'s 72), its size (26 cm wide × 33 cm, rather than *Motion Picture*'s 21 cm × 28 cm) heavy, glossy paper which shows off the full colour photographs, and cost (75 cents compared to 15)[22].

It might be expected, therefore, that the film magazines' habit of laying a reading path through the magazine highlighting a personality before her/his main feature, might not obtain in *Show*, intent as it was on promoting itself less as an indispensible part of the movie experience, and more as a well-rounded arts examination for well-rounded middle class readers. Despite this, there are two different points which reveal *Show* exploiting the inclusion of its star article.

The first is product placement. As this is the December issue, the magazine is full of gift suggestions. On page two there is an advert for Columbia Records, Day's record label, which presents six albums as the ideal way to give 'the gift of music'. Not only is Day's album from the movie *Jumbo* given central positioning for this, but her album also appears above another from Les Brown's Band of Renown – with whom Day used to sing. While she does not appear on this LP, the resonance of her former fame as a big band singer is still set circulating by this reminder. While Day is thus granted a mention before Capp's deflating piece, this probably has more to do with the opportunity an article on her offers the sales team, rather than acting as an assurance from the magazine that it still endorses her talent despite Capp's satire. Columbia Records will have been told an article on their major star would be appearing in the December issue, but not its contents; just as well, as Capp's article goes on to reference this very film while criticising Day.

But the magazine also seeks to critique the star on its own terms, currying favour with author Capp by a sly dig in the Contents list. The magazine provides for 'The Day Dream' the subtitle 'Or Doris, the hottest property in Hollywood' (6). The subtitle is reminiscent of those affixed to melodramas (such as Vitagraph's 1907 production, *On the Stage, or Melodrama from the Bowery*). This manages to suggest that Day's story is as hokey as an early melodrama, peopled with stock characters and trite events, which Capp's sharp humour will expose for its fakery. The article is thus set up as satirical before its own text is reached; it seems unlikely that Capp would have written this Contents subtitle (the 'Or, Doris' portion is not repeated on the article page), so *Show* itself becomes complicit with the satirical treatment of the star which the article perpetrates.

This is carried on in the layout of the text of the piece itself. 'The Day Dream' appears on a double page spread, with two columns on each page (Figure 13). The first column on the left

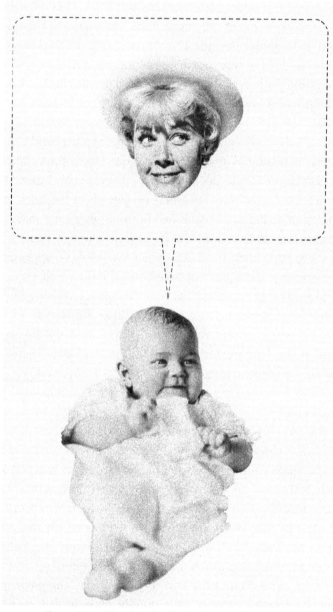

Figure 13. *Show*'s baby Doris dreams of success.

hand page is taken up with a baby photo of Doris with a thought bubble coming from her head in which her older, more familiar self appears: the 'Day dream' seems to be the fantasy the young Doris has of her future self. This perhaps suggests that the persona of 'Doris Day', which the article goes on to attempt to puncture, is so impossibly sweet and good it is as if an innocent – or ignorant – infant imagined her.

Unlike the film fan magazines, which, as seen, generally try to provide further snippets about their stars in the pages between commencement and conclusion of an article, *Show* does not include any other information about Day between the first double-page spread on which the article starts, and the second on which it finishes. The text arrangement on this last two pages, the final double-page of the magazine (pages 136 and 137) is interesting, however: the text appears in an inverted 'U' shape besides and across the top of a large advert for 'The Steve Allen Show'. Rather than provide any commentary on the topic of the article, however, this seems to laud Al Capp through juxtaposing his work with that of the more contemporaneously-famous satirical writer and entertainer.

> Compounded of the wishful thinking of middle-aged matrons, movie moguls' wild dreams of avarice, and the frustrated nightmares of every unmarried, red-blooded American matinee idol, that professionally gelid miss, Doris Day, has become the hottest property in Hollywood. (72)

Thus begins the article that, as far as the available material suggests, inaugurates the association of virginity with Day. As noted before, Capp had written a short piece rehearsing some of the themes of this anti-Day piece in a *Los Angeles Mirror* 1960 column. In this longer version, he takes his assertions further, however, passing from what a Doris Day film means, to what the star herself means. Interviews with some of the personnel involved in Day's films enable him to suggest she is a monstrous diva, controlling and unreasonable. In this way the anonymous comments from 'a producer' or 'a publicity girl' (73) are justified because no one dare overtly criticise her: she is powerful enough to prevent people working again. Though Joseph Pasternak (who produced *Love Me Or Leave Me* and *Jumbo*) seems brave enough to be quoted by name, the article suggests that co-star Rock Hudson is too timorous to do so. By thus obscuring the names of his sources – under the guise of protecting the innocent – Capp can convey that Day is a monster without having to reveal the identities of those who affirm this – or whether they actually exist.

Capp's opening line suggests that Day is herself a dream, a shared hallucination. Middle-aged women, women like her, are cheered by her triumphing in film narratives and support her by attending her movies in droves. Movie moguls see the audience numbers and agree to green-light anything with Day in because the loyalty of her fans assures box-office victory. While audiences and moguls share this fantasy of successful female-driven films, albeit from different motives, every 'real' man in America views these movies as nightmares, since the star and her films support a moral regime which will prevent women going to bed with them. Capp here calls Day 'professionally gelid', a term that acknowledges that it is her job which calls for her to be icy towards men; the rest of the article, however, engineers a slippage so that, by the end, Day herself – despite her marriages and son providing contrary evidence – has become a virgin off-screen as well as on.

A return to the formula-film argument of the earlier Day piece follows this opening salvo. Here Capp describes the male with whom the Day character skirmishes in the sex comedies as a 'handsome New York bachelor, a $250,000 a year executive whose clothes are constantly being ripped off by love-maddened

19-year-old debutantes' and the female character she plays as 'a vinegar-tongued, fortyish, small-town virgin' (73). While Capp seems to draw the antagonists in this battle of the sexes as total opposites, his character sketches do not provide equal information on both. While *He* is wealthy, attractive, sought-after and metropolitan, *She* is bitter, old, small-town and chaste. What he omits is as interesting as what he includes: there is no mention of her financial status, companions or looks, or of his age. Capp cannot mention these aspects as they would ruin the inequalities he is trying to suggest: he is implying that the old-maid character is lucky to get any sexual attention from the handsome bachelor and should be grateful, rather than fighting it. He also cannot mention the man's age as he is either, when played by Rock Hudson, roughly the same age as her or, in the case of Cary Grant, 20 years her senior. Capp's oppositions do not bear too much analysis, which is precisely why analysis is necessary – to expose his motives in creating them. He has crafted the dichotomies to set up Day as an inexperienced, prudish, and ageing virgin by suppressing some elements of the Day formula film and over-emphasising, or entirely misrepresenting, others.

Trying to work out why the Day formula is so popular, Capp decides to go to Hollywood to interview the star herself. He is not dissuaded from the trip even when he hears that Melcher will not agree to the meeting unless he is granted full control over what is written. Refusing to allow this, Capp goes to Hollywood anyway, to interview people who work with Day instead. While he makes this sound like the action of an independent journalist, Capp has actually acknowledged he is not getting his material direct from Day but only from anonymous sources, enabling him to write anything he wants.

Having attempted to prove that Day's formula films are phoney, because they are based on the premise that a handsome bachelor would choose one old maid rather than several lubricious young women, Capp goes on to try to show that Day's 'Just Like Us' persona and reputation for a being down-to-earth, unstarry star, are also phoney. By constantly repeating the words of people paid to work with the performer, the article manages to suggest a more negative truth: the repeated phrase 'warm, wonderful human being' implies that Day is the reverse: not just *professionally* gelid, then.

Capp visits the set where Day is making her circus picture *Jumbo* (Charles Walters, 1962). This enables him to report Day's prudishness in action. When a 'property man' on set drops a chair on his foot and swears mildly, Day breaks from the scene to stare at him reproachfully. Day's dislike of bad language, often reported in other magazine articles, is evoked here, with Capp using the already-established notion that Day's priggishness takes her beyond the merely annoying holier-than-thou to the truly insufferable actually holy.

After the vignettes which purport to give glimpses of the real Day – cold, manipulative, selfish – the account of the inevitable confrontation between Capp and the star herself is rather anticlimactic. While on the *Jumbo* set, Day comes over to Capp. Her words, 'I couldn't let you leave, Mr Capp, without saying hello' (136) seem eminently friendly but the author manages to suggest otherwise: 'She has a neat figure, a cheerful grin and the warmth of a manager of the oldest-established charm school in town.' By ascribing Day's kind greeting to an amiability that is purely professional rather than sincere, Capp again evokes the warm/cold dichotomy which runs through the article. Day *seems* warm, but is actually cold, manipulative, like someone employed to teach others how to be superficially charming. Her onscreen persona of cheerful good humour and upbeat energy seems thus not only false but meretricious, with the star's smiles and amiability items to be purchased.

The article concludes with two more interviews; producers who have worked with Day agree she is the answer to their prayers as she has a loyal female fan-base. One of the producers notes that older women are loyal to Day because she seems to be one of them. He goes on to pitch his theory of how to get these women into the movie theatres:

> 'You get these dames coming and you've got the most loyal audience in the world. But you won't get 'em with kids like Ann-Margret and Sandra Dee. Watching them have romances actually makes the older ones feel sad and lost. But I'll go for a quarter of a million to lure any overripe ex-glamour girl out of retirement. No matter how she's decomposed and discouraged other producers, I find there's always one good feature left.

> 'With one it may be her eyes, with another it's her legs. With Doris Day, it's her fanny. It's the greatest in show business, and nobody made a thing out of it until I took a long hard look.
>
> (Capp, 1962: 137)

The description of 'an overripe ex-glamour girl' hardly applies to Day, who, as has been seen, took great pains not to present herself as glamorous and, at 40 years of age[23] and at the peak of her success, was surely neither 'overripe' nor retired. There is also an interesting ambiguity of phrasing in the line about Day's 'fanny' (bottom) – that 'nobody made a thing out of it' before the producer decided to do so. This could be taken to mean either that no one had emphasised Day's derrière before; or it could mean that nobody had made any money from so emphasising it previously.

Significantly, it is this quotation about the 'fanny' that gives away the identity of 'the producer' in question. Ross Hunter, the Universal producer who has been credited with revamping Day's persona from *Pillow Talk* onwards, declares he discovered Day's posterior in very similar words in Day's biography, suggesting that this was a claim he was known to make[24]. Citing Hunter's words does not mean that Capp heard them from the man himself, however...

While Capp's article was very influential, with a lasting impact on the perennial assumption that Day always played a virgin, this was contested while Day was still working in films. 'The Most Misunderstood Girl In Hollywood', published in *Modern Screen*, is purportedly written by Ross Hunter himself, and while 'Hunter' goes on in the piece to argue against many of the negative comments being perpetuated by the media about his two-time star, he seems to be reserve particular ire for a certain 'New York writer':

> During the past five years, Doris Day has been attacked by almost every magazine published and misrepresented in a hundred ways. A New York writer once told me with a smirk, 'I've interviewed nine people and I've been able to get good digs against Doris from each one. You're my tenth and last source. I hope you aren't going to disappoint me.' What I told that gentleman (?) can't be reported in a family magazine. BUT HE MANUFACTURED A QUOTATION FROM ME AND PUBLISHED IT WITH QUOTES – PROBABLY FRAUDULENT – FROM OTHERS TO WHOM, ALLEGEDLY, HE HAD TALKED. This was certainly a fine example of cesspool journalism.
> ('Hunter', 1964: 35; typography as printed, including capitals and question mark)

The reason that 'Hunter' is angry at being misquoted seems clear and offers an interesting sidelight on the Capp article, suggesting that much of it was made up. If other interviewees had refused to dish the dirt on Day, as 'Hunter' had, whether from genuine respect for the star or fear that her clout could get them into trouble, it would support the idea that Capp does not name most of his sources, not to protect them, but because they don't exist. It seems ironic that the single most influential piece responsible for giving Day her '40 year old virgin' epithet was possibly based on false reporting.

'The Day Dream' contains many of the major tropes found in my sample of Day articles, as well as launching, as mentioned, the 'Virgin' concept, but it often invokes a trope negatively or contests it. In this way, the piece plays up the idea that she is prudish (though he does not declare for either 'Pathology' or 'Religion' being the root of this); Day appears to be 'Just Like Us' and 'Natural' as a down to earth person, but Capp works to suggest this is part of her false persona, and the star is actually as unlike us as any other Hollywood star.

The familiar concepts of 'Looks', 'Clothes' and 'Money' are all conjured up through the piece, as is her 'Age', which last links to her particular existence as a 'Star' – one beloved of mature women. In this way Capp manages to denigrate not just the actress but her fans too.

'The Doris Daze Show', by Angelo Torres and Stan Hart (*Mad*, January 1971: 43–7)

Unlike the two previous film publications, this article from *Mad*, the satirical monthly magazine, does not lay a trail for its reader in the pages before the article on Day; nor does it, like *Show*, present an endorsement of the star through paid product placement. The piece spoofing her is mentioned in the table of contents, and there is a also a cartoon of her in the lower right hand corner under 'Vital Features' (1). But there are no other mentions of the star before the commencement of the piece lampooning her television series. This is explainable, perhaps, because at this time *Mad* did not carry advertisements: with no advertising space to sell, there was no need to solicit companies to take advantage of the presence of the star by placing an advert promoting one of her products. As seen, the film fan magazines regularly included paid promotional material among the other snippets and items making up the accompanying matter in a star trail or saturation campaign, such as the full-page advertisement for *Romance On The High Seas* in August 1948's *Motion Picture* issue. I differentiate this from regular product placement, however, because with this the publication makes no attempt to link the advert thematically to other material on the star, as seen in *Show*. With no advertisers to accommodate, and without the need to promote a popular figure, the opposite aim being its raison d'être, *Mad* has no need to combine advertising and editorial material in an issue.

Mad had a history of TV parodies which had begun the year after the magazine's 1952 inception, with 'The Lone Stranger' in the January 1953 issue. Inclusion in the ranks of the parodied can be considered a kind of perverse compliment, as it indicates the show has become part of the topical zeitgeist. Here the article begins with an introduction about the genesis of the show, under the heading 'Freckles and Her Friends Department'. This taps into *Mad*'s custom of dubbing each of an issue's separate stories a different 'department', but also, with the use of the specific title, harks back to another print cartoon, 'Freckles and His Friends', created by Merrill Blosser in 1915. This strip told the story of Freckles, a teenager living in the small town of Shadyside. Linking Day to this strip works not only obviously, because of Day's own well-known freckled state (prominently featured in each of the story's 27 panels), but also because of her former film roles as a small-town young woman.

The introductory passage begins by asking 'Why are most weekly series TV shows pretty awful?', answering this by blaming the usual 'incompetent Producer', 'inept Director' and 'no-talent Star'. Although Day's position as both star and producer of the show was widely enough known for readers to get the satirical point here, the article ignores restraint and goes for excess:

Now [...] what happens when the Star of a weekly series TV show is also the Producer and has all the power on the show? What happens when the Star makes all the decisions and signs all the checks? It'll probably come out looking remarkably like....The Doris Daze Show. (43)

Although *The Doris Day Show* was into its third season at the point when the *Mad* piece was published, the parody copies the basic formula of the *second* season, in which Day's character Doris Martin lived in the countryside outside San Francisco, but travelled to the city to her secretarial job, leaving her small sons with her father, Buck, on the family farm. The show at this point regularly made comic mileage from the clashes between Doris's city and country lives, as well as the antics of her boys at home and colleagues at work. The third season of the show moved Doris and her sons, without Buck, to an apartment above an Italian restaurant in the city, bringing the restaurateurs and an apartment neighbour into the cast. Why did *Mad* elect to revisit the previous season, which had finished in April 1970, rather than the current one being screened as the magazine article went to print? Perhaps the writer and illustrator had not seen any of the later episodes and were unaware of the format changes; another possibility is that the accent on the country/city dichotomy permitted the authors more satirical mileage.

While it is generally the written gags that contribute the parodic element to the strip, it must be noted that the drawings of Day are also extremely skilful, managing both to capture her likeness and to add to the humour of the skit with details repaying close attention. For example, the first frame of the story contains all the main 'country' characters in their home environment. The written jokes work here, as throughout the story, to portray Doris as a woman with a towering superiority complex, but the drawings contribute to this theme and also enlarge it. While obviously the *Mad* reader takes in both text and illustration together, these elements will be analysed separately here to illustrate the impact of each more easily.

The text begins with 'Cluck' opining that 'it must be hard being both a mother AND a father to these boys!' Doris's answer shows the lack of humility her character will display throughout the strip: 'Oh, I don't know! I do everything so effortlessly and perfectly!' When Cluck persists that it is not hard on her, but on the *boys*, she questions, 'You mean they miss having a Father?'; his rejoinder is 'No, I think they miss having a MOTHER!' Chiming in on this note, the smaller son asks his mother whether there might not be 'some man somewhere who might be good enough for you?' Doris's answer concludes the frame and underlines her hubris: 'Silly! I've told you a million times – the Pope is not ALLOWED to get married!' (43)

Besides satirising the star/character's arrogance, the script here taps into two of the well-established tropes Day's persona mobilised: seeing the Pope as her only possibly fitting mate underlines ideas about the star's image of chastity, as well as piety. Day's well-known status as a mother is also alluded to, not only of her TV show children, but also of Terry Melcher, co-producer of the show and magazine gossip target alongside his mother. This trope is given a negative inflection, however, perhaps deriving its energy from topical press reports about Terry's 'problems' with his mother's neediness (Powell, 1969; Caldwell, 1969) and his involvement with the Manson murders ('X', 1970), to suggest that Day is an inadequate parent, not, as her character believes, as good as two parents but so self-obsessed she is hardly performing the role of one parent.

While the script is busy lampooning the star/character, the drawings which illustrate this panel continue this theme while also adding other significant background details. The family gathers in the living room of a country cottage, lightly but effectively sketched; Cluck is busy whittling a piece of wood into the shape of a buxom naked woman, which he is showing to one of Doris's sons, and Day lifts weights while talking to her younger boy. She wears shorts and a sweatshirt with a drawing of a dodo on it.

These pictorial details can provoke a smile in themselves – like Cluck's whittled woman – or can again bring to mind the familiar persona of the star. Day's dodo sweatshirt evokes her common showbiz nickname, as does her car's bespoke licence plate and dodo flag, seen in a later panel. The emphasis on having her nickname on her possessions enforces the story's overall emphasis on the character's narcissism and self-obsession. It also seems significant that here and in a later frame set at the office Day is seen exercising, perhaps acknowledging that her trim form could not be obtained without a constant regime. By drawing Day engaged with exercise both at home and at the office, the cartoon mocks the pose of effortless perfection presented by the show's main character but also gestures openly at the hard work required by a star to maintain her ostensible physical superiority – more openly indeed than many other texts which purport to examine such matters. While the film fan magazines frequently included Day in articles about diets and exercises, her slender body there was promoted as a model for readers' emulation: Day herself, these pieces constantly affirm, does not need to watch her weight nor engage in serious exercise in order to achieve her svelte form; she eats what she likes because her 'Energy' burns off the calories. When she does take exercise it is parsed as *play* rather than effortful *labour.* She is not seen 'working out' in the film magazines as she is here.

Across the 27 frames of the cartoon, then, *Mad*'s story seeks both to lampoon and comment on Day's persona and the implausibility of its perfection using the text *and* visuals. Although the text has perhaps the most immediate impact, the visuals seem the dominant element of each frame, not only due to the amount of space occupied by the drawings, but also because of the subtlety of their details, often requiring reader attention across a number of frames.

The story begins as 'Doris Marlin' leaves her sons with their grandfather and undertakes her daily commute to the office. En route to San Francisco in her convertible, she arouses the ire of other drivers by enjoying her own 'shaft of sunlight' which cleaves the rain and smog engulfing the rest of them. This personal good weather, Doris explains to a toll officer, is the result of an 'arrangement' she has: 'God doesn't make trouble for me...and I don't make trouble for him' (44). Arriving at work, Doris is told by her boss there is 'terrible crisis' at hand, to which she replies 'Naturally'. While 'Mr Knucklehead' proposes committing suicide, Doris is confident that she can solve everything:

Mr Knucklehead:	...The Bank President is coming over here! What are we going to do?
Doris:	Don't worry! You know that he's bound to fall in love with me.
Mr Knucklehead:	Because you have charm and beauty?
Doris:	No...because I have Script Approval! (45)

The Bank President conforms to expectations, and Doris agrees to go out to dinner with him. She dresses for dinner in a phone booth, causing a female colleague (visually echoing the show's Myrna) to exclaim she now understands 'How you change your clothes every week without going home first!' The dinner with the Bank President takes place in the vault. After small talk, the President begs Doris to kiss him, promising to save the magazine she works for by giving it a loan, but she holds firm against his entreaties until he agrees a low interest rate for the repayments.

Figure 14. *Mad* (January 1971) posits Day working secretly to usher in Feminist rule.

The next day at work Mr Knucklehead thanks her for 'saving the magazine from disaster for the 27th time this season!', and she responds:

Doris:	Doesn't it strike you as a little odd?
Mr Knucklehead:	That you've done it so often ...?
Doris:	No – that I'm STILL just an $85-a-week secretary!

The strip concludes with two final frames showing Doris back in the phone booth again changing her outfit, and Myrna outside talking to her (Figure 14).

[Myrna]:	I've been meaning to ask you, Doris...why are the men in your show always such drivelling,

	emasculated simpletons?
Doris:	That's my whole purpose!
[Myrna]:	I don't understand!
Doris:	I happen to be 'Supreme Propaganda Minister' for the 'WOMEN'S LIBERATION MOVEMENT'!! Today, Television....tomorrow, the World!! (47)

The cartoon's narrative dwells only superficially within the diegesis of the television show, more often operating in a space outside it in order to comment on the repetitious tropes and other absurdities of the episodes. The cartoon echoes other reviewers' criticisms of the show's lack of realism when it notes that Doris, the '$85-a-week secretary', has an implausibly glamorous house, wardrobe, and car, in its foregrounding of the plot machinery in which a crisis is routinely averted because the antagonist likes Doris, and in the general inefficacy of all the other characters compared to the central one, which the strip initially seems to ascribe to Doris's narcissism.

Overall, the cartoon attempts to mock three different targets: *The Doris Day Show*, Day's star persona and her contemporary media position. Despite the overlaps, there are differences. Jokes about the star's glamorous show wardrobe and convertible obviously come in the first category. The God and Pope references tap into the star's well-known persona, here evoking her religious devotion. The more topical references include the younger son's possession of a large marijuana cigarette, unnoticed by his mother: this evokes Terry Melcher's 'hippie' lifestyle, a contemporary topic of interest in the media. It is also noticeable that although both text and visuals are regularly employed in the lampooning of the television show, textual references bear more of the weight of evoking Day's star persona, while the more topical references are generally carried in the drawings.

For example, the text overtly refers to Day's religious devotion (43 and 44), to her frequent former film roles as

'Over-Ripe Spinster' (44) and 'Professional Virgin' (46), her freckles, her power in the show as producer (45), her status as a widow (46) and as not 'that kind of a girl' (47). It remains, however, for the drawings to bring out the full implication of this latter point. Doris dines with the Bank President in the vault. The text has him commenting that he doesn't remember asking the guard to stay late, but Doris responds that she did. This is ambiguous until the viewer sees the 'DM' insignia on the guard's uniform and hat. He is not there to guard the money, but Doris's virtue. Other drawn details round out this allusion to Day's established star persona: although the scene is set for a candlelit dinner for two, and the President has a glass of wine, Doris has a frothy soda instead, which she sips through a straw. This alludes to Day's well-known abstention from alcohol, but the artist develops this image still further: the soda has a cherry on the top, clearly visible in frame 20. When the President repeatedly pleads with Doris to kiss him, in frame 21, and she acquiesces only when he agrees on a low interest for the magazine's loan, the text has her tell him to 'pucker up'. The tension between text and visuals that I am trying to evoke here is best conveyed in the image that accompanies this dialogue; it admirably displays the text's ability to go for a gag while the drawing rounds out the characterisation and then goes beyond this to make both more topical and more subtle points (Figure 15). At the left side of the frame the President reaches out towards Doris, while the guard steps in to guard the valuables – *her*. He has a can marked 'MACE' in his hand and is kneeing the President in the groin. This seems to evoke the figure of the brutal policeman who appeared in contemporary news reports (such as those responding to the protests against the Kent State massacre in May 1970, for example).

Meanwhile, Doris sits curled up, her curvy hips, long legs and cleavage all on display, at the side of the round dining table. She

Figure 15.   Day's cherry-laden ice cream sundae.

proffers the Bank President something on the end of her spoon –
a *cherry*. The fact that another cherry is positioned still in the
soda's froth does not lessen the traditional allusion to virginity
but rather strengthens the point the artist is making here about
the mercenary and calculated nature of Doris's sexuality. While
an old hand at this, she still pretends to offer valorised
inexperience. And although performing coy prudishness to
accompany her repeated chant, 'not that kind of a girl', this
valuing of a falsely-claimed virtue is shown to be not for its own
sake but for what it can buy.

Overall, then, the article showcases many of the traditional
tropes Day's star persona had mobilised, including 'Freckles',
'Clothes', 'Mother', 'Religion'. Several of them are now given a
negative weight by assuming that they indicate arrogance or
hypocrisy by their pretended presence, such as the 'Just Like Us'
trope, which the television show works to employ but fails to
convince with, as the clear mockery of the magazine attests.
Day's vexed relationship with 'Feminism' is given another

mention here too, as the magazine takes it to be the acme of its satire that she should be an agent of the Movement. And it is this specific trope that seems to hold the key to the article's use of a surely outmoded figure, the mercenary maiden.

In drawing Day offering up her 'cherry' for the Bank President only once the price is right, *Mad*'s artist conjures up the traditional trope of the coy woman who holds her man at arm's length, not from a lack of desire or any moral fiat against sex, but because she is waiting for the highest offer, dangling the bait of her own chastity for gain. This is what critics had been saying variously about film females, Doris Day and women in general for a couple of decades, but it is initially surprising to find in a publication from 1971. What seems to generate this return to the now familiar Day-as-virgin trope – seemingly first broached, as has been seen, in the *Show* piece of 1962, nine years earlier – is the cartoon's emphasis on Day as hero of the Women's Liberation Movement. In the cartoon's final frame, Doris emerges from the phone booth announcing that is part of her master plan is to have all the men on the show behave as 'drivelling emasculated simpletons'; she is dressed in a dominatrix outfit, a cat-suit with exposed cleavage, gloves, thigh boots and whip.

The cartoon now finally seems to posit that it is not because of her narcissism that Doris is the centre of the show, nor because she has 'Script Approval' and a producer's credit that she makes all the other characters into minor ones: it is specifically the men who are meant to look inept and idiotic because Doris is secretly taking over the airwaves for Feminism. But Day's status as feminist warrior is portrayed satirically because of her garb – why would a woman interested in not being judged for her gender make so much of displaying its attributes? This leather-look suit is as overtly sexualised as the bare-shouldered, cleavage-showing, tightly-cinched dress worn for the dinner with the Bank President. That outfit was calculated to bring him to heel, and did so; but what is the dominatrix attire meant to achieve, or rather, *whom* is it meant to affect? 'Feminist Doris' seems to be as much of a pose, put on *with* and *as* an outfit, as the earlier virgin-seductress.

Although the cartoon strip makes a valid real-life point about efficient women in the workplace being paid less than their worth (the implausibility of someone as useful as Doris still being 'an \$85-a-week secretary'), the coupling of the mercenary maiden persona with the leather-clad women's libber, in the single person of the show's star, suggests finally that *Mad*'s artist and writer assume *both* roles are only put on by women in order to impress men. The seeming *reductio ad absurdam* of having someone as ostensibly passive, traditionalist and non-feminist as Day secretly running the Women's Movement attempts to belittle feminism, insinuating its demands for female sexual freedom are as much of a calculated pose as the old insistence on female chastity and control. This ends up reinforcing the double standard at the very historical moment that it was facing its most overt challenge, but also indicates the significance of Day as a public figure who, having endured from the 1950s into the early 70s, could be employed to evoke the earlier era and mobilise a range of assumptions about female sexuality, agency and desire.

Conclusion

It has been the task of this chapter to put four individual articles under the microscope and see how, at different moments in her career, the various tropes clustering around Day's star persona were differently inflected. In examining two articles from film fan magazines and two from other periodicals, ones with pretensions to catering to more elevated or more 'cool' cultural tastes, it can also be seen how Day shifted across time as a topic of interest, from being a key film star and personality, to being perceived as a symptom of contemporary media ills, formulaic films in the 1960s and routinely and unrealistically plotted television episodes in the 1970s.

The first piece about Day analysed here, 'The Most Everything Girl in Hollywood' establishes many of the tropes that would go on to dominate the circulating meanings about the star, all, at this point in her career, inflected positively to connote her energy and talent. The article also establishes Day as both starry and unstarry, as exceptional and 'Just Like Us', which, as has been seen, went on to be a defining trope associated with Day. This piece further illuminates the film magazine habit of framing the material around a star, here by the relatively rare star trail, where many snippets or items lead the reader inexorably to the main article, ensuring she reached it fully primed. On the occasion of Day's launch as a new star, *Motion Picture* actually prepares two different trails, one for the reader who heeds the instruction 'turn to page 25...' and jumps into the middle of the magazine, and the other for one who more patiently pages through from front to back.

Day purportedly speaks directly to the reader of 'Sex Isn't Everything', but despite this, the authorial voice does not provide a clear or wholly positive view of her persona. Familiar tropes are invoked but in a muddled way, which now permits negative readings to arise. Confused in both visual layout and verbal argument, the piece shows Day's persona in flux as she, or her advisers, endeavour to recast her in mommy-mode to prepare audiences for her latest role, but reading the piece as an extended advertisement for *The Man Who Knew Too Much* gives the article a coherence it otherwise lacks. Again, the magazine offers a – more minor – star trail to prepare the reader for the slant the article will be taking, chiming in with the domestic presentation of Day endorsed by the piece and reinforcing the importance of her voice to her stardom, neatly cueing the accent, in the Hitchcock film, on the song 'Que Sera Sera'.

The significance of the Al Capp piece in *Show*, 'The Day Dream' perhaps ultimately lies more in the impact it had on the subsequent treatment and memory of Day than its own content. As seen, *Show*, for all its aspirations towards dealing with high art, still indulged in product placement because of its reliance on advertising. The magazine itself contributes to the critical pose the article adopts when it subtitles the Day piece, 'Or, Doris the Hottest Property...', as this is reminiscent of old-fashioned melodrama titles; it also employs the hot/cold dichotomies that run through the article, criticising Day for her pose of warmth which Capp asserts is actually a coolly calculated performance.

Furthermore, the fact that most of his 'sources' are anonymous enables Capp to write what he wants; posing as a fearless crusader for the truth, Capp actually absolves himself of the necessity of adducing any evidence, a point aptly made by the 'Hunter' article in *Modern Screen* two years later. The 'Meta' trope associated with Day is perhaps given its greatest currency here, since the Capp story cites other articles, is so fundamental to other articles about the star subsequently, and receives a debunking in a further periodical piece.

Finally, the *Mad* comic strip sets out to mock the ridiculousness of the routine plot tropes in Day's television show, while also commenting on her extant persona. In doing this latter, it fascinatingly exposes her position in early 1970s popular culture, as a well-known film star now involved in a weekly television show which itself commonly milked the familiar aspects of its star's already-established image. Of all the pieces looked at, the satirical *Mad* is the only one which has no reading strategy or framing device preparing the approaching appearance of the star; it seems hardly coincidental that it is the only one, also, without advertising revenue to find. *Mad's* piece attempts to mock both its star and the current Women's Movement when it associates the former's well-known assumed marketable chastity with the latter's emphasis on female self-fulfilment; what it actually succeeds in doing is both to expose its misrepresentation of feminism as just another pose to get male attention, and to testify to Day's significance as a contemporary media figure. That she had by 1971 endured as a figure of importance and newsworthiness across four decades is not acknowledged by the final piece, but indicates now one of the reasons that makes Day such a fascinating object of study: that she can have a definable specific meaning, and that this changes radically across time, affirms her significance within twentieth-century American popular culture.

5 Film Fan Magazines – Conclusion

This second section of the investigation into the reasons prompting Day's association with the aged maiden has set out to explore the very significant part played by the film fan magazines in constructing and maintaining this persona. Its aim has also been to develop some useful methods for studying how periodicals present and consolidate such an image, paying attention not only to what is written about the star, but how what is written is phrased, what repeating ideas and concepts circulated around her name, and how the articles' layout, including text placement, photograph and colour usage, can affect the narrative they are telling through contrast or emphasis.

The large amount of sources I have had to draw on, which represents only about half the existing material on Doris Day, testifies to the star's impact in the movie magazines from the very start of her career. Although precise figures are difficult to estimate, Day seems to feature in the film magazines more than many female stars now considered 'classic' and 'iconic', such as Marilyn Monroe and Audrey Hepburn, and more too than a clutch of contemporary female performers with whom she might be associated by dint of perceived shared qualities, like energy and good humour, such as Debbie Reynolds, June Allyson and Esther Williams. Day, in fact, seems to appear in the film fan magazines from 1948 into the 1970s more often than any female film star apart from Elizabeth Taylor, whose extraordinary beauty and torrid love life kept her a favourite in periodicals of all types during this period.[25]

Throughout the section, I have tried to show the obsessive interest film magazines paid Day over her personality, biography, marriages and love affairs, career choices, and status as a wife, mother and woman. As mentioned previously, Richard deCordova maintained the ultimate secret of a star, which fascinates audiences and industry alike, is her/his sexual proclivities, and it is the hope that they will one day learn the 'real truth' about these that keeps fans reading, viewing, buying. The film magazines I have studied, however, seem to evince just as compelling a drive to know about Day's real personality, her real self, as about her sexual activities, obsessively building her up as a normal, healthy, regular individual and then subjecting her to such intense scrutiny that the maintenance of this regularity becomes impossible. Above all, what seems revealed is the magazines' own blind spot about the impact they have on their object of study, a blind spot which is paradoxically sustained since these same magazines endlessly point out the harmful effects other periodicals' attention has on the star.

My first task was to give an account of how Day's persona was conceived in the film magazines across her career, charting recurrent turns of phrase and points of interest, which went to make up my list of tropes, those repeated idea-clusters, like 'Mom', 'Blonde' and 'Pathology', which seemed persistently to circulate around Day. I next analysed some of these in more detail, concentrating especially on those which most seemed to provide the potential for reading Day as mature maiden. It was notable across both overview and trope examinations that, while the main view on Day did change over time, with her popularity being subject to dips and surges, there was a remarkable consistency of view being put forward at any one period. When the press falls out with her after her media blackout in 1954, for example, the *entire* press corps falls out with her, and when they experience a resurgence of affection for her, the magazine articles all seem to evince this.

In the final part of this in-depth analysis of the film fan magazines, the focus narrowed to examine four specific articles across the stretch of Day's career, not only seeing how the tropes can combine in various ways at different times, but also viewing how the placement of each article, its immediate context in situ, contributes further to the reading of the star being fostered. This is where I develop the ideas of shared coverage, star trail and star saturation, the first most commonly operating across film fan magazines when they devote much room to a sample of stars, the other two when just one is selected for a major promotion. The star trail builds to a peak when it presents a sustained piece on the star after a path to it has been created from smaller items, while star saturation blankets an issue with seemingly unlinked items which together create an impressive sense of the star's ubiquity and importance. With this saturation technique, the effect lies more in the cumulative impact of seeing Day's name again and again, rather than having small snippets build to a larger piece.

While the *Show* sales team could promise Columbia Records that there was an article on Day in the December 1962 issue, and those responsible for selling ad space in the August 1948 number of *Motion Picture* could similarly assure Warner Bros. that the advert for *Romance On The High Seas* would be accompanied by a nice promotional piece on their new starlet, there seems to be a difference between *Show*'s overt product placement, and *Motion*

Picture's choice to insert star-linked gossipy items or favourite recipes, material which does not obviously promote a specific piece of merchandise other than the star herself. The difference is that a magazine sells advertising space for revenue, but the star trail, star saturation and shared coverage techniques were not employed to promote a specific product in exchange for money, but in order to help build up Brand Day. The ultimate products being sold in this way can then be seen as the star, the magazine and ultimately Hollywood itself, with the periodicals prepared to invest their labour, copy and pages in promoting a new star because she attests *their* importance as conduits of glamour and information between film and the consumer.

SECTION 3
Performance Analysis

1 Introduction

While the previous section may have seemed to imply, in my accent on the dominant part played by the film fan magazines in creating, maintaining, and suborning Day's persona, that I believe the star to have had no agency or input to her image, it is the work of this portion of the investigation to illustrate the contrary, and to establish how Day did in fact actively engage with her performed characters in order to signify, among other things, their attitudes to and experiences of sex. It is not, therefore, that I believe the film fan magazines invented the Doris-Day-as-aged-maiden-persona from a vacuum, a neutral zone in which the actor herself had nothing to say, but rather that the periodicals took up and maintained this persona frequently despite what she was trying to achieve.

In order to demonstrate the fact that the movie publications often ignored what Day was actually doing and instead perversely persisted in reading her in the maiden mould, what needs to be analysed is not only *why* they saw her as a virgin but *when* they did so: it is, in fact, not her early roles that were perceived in this manner. Not until after 1959's *Pillow Talk* was responsible for changing the overt Day image, updating it and making it chic and overtly sexual, did the coy maid persona begin to be mooted. This paradox lies at the very core of this book's project: I want to uncover why at the moment she becomes involved in films which explicitly narrativise the heroine's desire for sexual intimacy, the media decides to brand Day an old maid either too coy or too manipulative to give in to her urges.

My method across the following chapters is to examine four different Doris Day performances, each from one of the significant periods in her career already noted and explored in the magazine section. Thus I will look at the beginning of the period of her movie stardom which corresponded with her initial screen role, in *Romance On The High Seas* (1948), the first significant perceived change to her persona, occurring with *Love Me Or Leave Me* (1955), the sole overt performance of maidenly modesty in Day's roster, *Lover Come Back* (1961), which was to have such an impact on readings of her films, performances and persona, and, finally, episodes from her television series, *The Doris Day Show* (1968–73). Across all the examinations of these various media texts, I will be intent to see whether Day is overtly performing virginity in a way that can be readily recognised by the viewer, or is indeed portraying the opposite: sexual experience.

What would such performances, of experience, of virginity, entail? Before the mid-1950s weakening of the Production Code – occasioned in part by a text actually dealing with virginity, *The Moon Is Blue* (1953)[26] – it was not permissible to include words like 'virgin', 'virginity', 'mistress' or 'pregnancy' in a script; as much of Hollywood's output in the next ten years or so proves, even when such terms were not forbidden by the Code, they were not used as overt terms although they might be incorporated as plot elements. The burden of hinting at sexual status could then be seen to fall upon the actor; her performance would form a large part of what connoted the virgin or post-virgin state.

While, in addition, narrative exigencies, dialogue, costume (Jeffers McDonald, 2005, 2006a, 2010a), and music can help to suggest sexual experience or innocence, these elements, like performance, tend to have most impact in action. Virginity – a nothing, a *not yet*, rather than any positive quality – is best illuminated in these films at moments of crisis or change, since one of the most obvious ways to show it, is to show it under threat. I have noted elsewhere (2006a) that virginity was enacted, in a slew of 1950s comedies and melodramas fascinated with the topic, according to a strict performance dichotomy which allied comedy with an excess of movement, a broad slapstick style, and virginity maintained, while dramatic versions of the virgin story rigidly featured a performance style predicated on stillness and seriousness as well as a crisis moment where the urgent promptings of physical desire would win over moral or social strictures, and result in virginity's loss. At such filmic emergency points, music, dialogue and mise-en-scene could all be recruited to indicate the threat to a young woman's maintained chastity; costume could be relied upon to show the results of the transition from innocence to experience. Performance, however, is above all the method that best allows the actor to portray the imminence of sexual-decision making. I have previously (2010a) contrasted the two comparable moments of sung soliloquy in *Pillow Talk* and in *Lover Come Back* in order to show that, as I see it, the former's central woman, Jan, is a post-virgin, entirely confident in her own allure and intent upon ensuring her desires for physical intimacy are achieved, while it is the excitement combined with hesitation of the latter's Carol which mark her out clearly as a virgin.

Further, across the texts investigated in this section, Day clearly seems to be wearing sexual knowledge with confidence; this is subverted twice, however, overtly in *Lover Come Back* and, intriguingly, also in *Love Me Or Leave Me*. In *The Doris Day Show*, it might be imagined that the star's role as mother to two small boys would be enough to discount the virgin tag, but, as has been seen with the star herself, just being a mother and wife was not enough to ward off the affixing of this label. The performance choices that Day makes as Doris Martin, then, must also be examined, to see how she performs the role. Day's enactments of bodily and sensual confidence as Georgia Garrett and Doris Martin will therefore be examined as assiduously as her portrayal of Carol Templeton's conflicting desires, and Ruth Etting's careful management of her own sexuality in order to manipulate her man.

2 *Romance On The High Seas* (1948)

The first sight of Day in the film is of her standing looking in the window of the Baker Travel Agency. Her back turned to the camera, she then draws attention to her trim figure by raising her right leg a little to stroke her stocking seam, as if to ensure it is straight. Once inside the travel agency, this highlighted attractiveness is compromised by the discussion the clerks have about Georgia; they report to Mrs Elvira Kent, to whom they are much more respectful, that Miss Garrett is a frequent visitor to the agency who 'loads up on literature' on vacations, plans many, but never takes one because 'she's just a singer in a honky-tonk, doesn't have a dime'. Although the clerks clearly see her as a liability, one of them does serve Georgia, and Day gets her first lines of dialogue. These are very much in keeping with the image of her character already hinted at: she uses slang, chews gum while speaking and leans comfortably on the counter, unlike Elvira, who is a model of contained deportment and polite speech. Throughout the scene and several following, Elvira and Georgia are established as contrasts to each other around simple oppositions such as dark/light, classy/brassy, moneyed/poor, educated/ignorant, married/single, although one dichotomy that is never proposed is experienced/innocent. Although married Elvira could perhaps be expected to 'know about' men, and thus contrast with single Georgia, the film makes it very clear through dialogue, costume, and performance that Georgia is *not* inexperienced when it comes to dealing with the opposite sex.

In addition to greeting the travel agency clerk with a breezy 'Greetings, chum!', Georgia is not averse to a little flirtation to get him to divulge what destination she should be thinking about (not) going to next – she leans insinuatingly towards him and dismisses his idea of a canal cruise with a flippant, 'Canals're for schmoes', before wheedling, 'come on, what *really* looks *good?*'. The drawl Day gives to the word 'on' ('ahhhhn'), plus the way her voice and eyebrows rise jauntily on 'really' and 'good' illustrates Georgia's willingness to flirt to coax information. The scene concludes with another glimpse of this: overhearing that Elvira is going to have her passport picture taken, Georgia decides to do the same, smoothly producing a mirror from her bag, primping, and announcing her intention in one fluid sequence. When the clerk remonstrates, 'you've had seven taken already!' she bats her eyelashes and responds, 'But never as a *blonde…*' before sashaying off to the photographer. Again, the purring drawl on 'blonde' indicates her enjoyment at engaging with men and making them do what she wants by such simple manipulations.

Georgia's perky, flirtatious and worldly-wise persona is cemented in the next scene in which she appears, set in the Club Casa nightspot. Elvira has by now hatched her plot to *appear* to go on a South American cruise, leaving her husband alone, so that he can relax, misbehave with other women and be caught by her doing so. All she needs is someone – Georgia – to take her place on the ship. Elvira and her uncle Lazlo visit Georgia at the club to propose this masquerade; the film precedes this expository sequence with the first of Day's musical numbers in the film. Accompanied by a four piece band, Georgia performs the song 'I'm In Love'. While the dialogue afterwards, when Georgia meets Elvira and Lazlo and learns about the proposed impersonation, fits entirely with her tough streetwise broad persona, complete with slang ('schmoes!'; 'natch') and cynical comments about marital fidelity, the musical number is more problematic in its presentation of the singer, and repays some closer consideration.

The main problem I see with the number and Day's presentation in, and performance of, it is that which bedevils the entire film: it does not present a coherent character in Georgia. She is portrayed in an inconsistent way here, via her voice, actions, and, interestingly, costume. For this number Georgia eschews the trim suit and somewhat flashy accessories worn in the first scene; now she wears a more dramatic outfit, a long skirt with a tight top revealing a hint of cleavage. She has 'evening' type jewellery too, and so the first message the outfit seems to be trying to transmit is 'glamorous sophisticate'. A closer look reveals however that this transmission is disrupted by details: the long skirt is a very dark chocolate brown, but the top is baby-blue and made from distractingly shiny satin. While there is a cut-out triangle that reveals some chest-area flesh, the other elements of the outfit, and in fact the number of these elements, somewhat swamp the idea of evening allure – the top actually has a high neckline which runs across Georgia's throat, making the triangle of flesh below it stick out oddly, especially as some blue beads hang there, just above a sewn-in roundel of fake turquoises and diamonds, another of which is similarly found at the end of one sleeve (Figure 16). In addition to this accessory nestling between her breasts, Georgia also has a large blue fabric hydrangea in her hair, and a large blue diaphanous kerchief which she flourishes for emphasis at certain moments in the song. The overall result, then, is not so much urban evening glamour that an adult woman might put on, so much as the overkill of a little girl playing dress-up and putting on *all* the

Figure 16. Costume confusion in *Romance On The High Seas*.

things in the box. Elvira's evening outfit again establishes her as a contrast to Georgia, as it is simple but luxurious, an evening suit and coat of rich dark brown with gold embroidery over one shoulder.

The over-accumulation of details and accessories in Georgia's outfit can be read as a clash of signifiers. On the one hand, the bust accents of the top, its tightness and cut-away revealing skin, the faux diamonds, all suggest grown-up attractiveness; on the other, the baby-blue colour, proliferation of details, plastic beads, and floral headpiece connote innocence, girlishness.

This clash is then borne out in the manner in which Georgia delivers the song also, combining a simple vocalisation on certain lines which reveal Day's pure tones ('. . . on a school house wall'), then a raunchier, more clubby handling of others which conjures more directly her own big band experience singing 'jump tunes', as she bops and bomps her hips to the music, pouts and winks at the audience. Although the succeeding part of the scene, where Georgia hears about the masquerade, has been noted as seeing her revert to her slangy, cynical persona, this song and its treatment provides the first hints at the inconsistencies in the character that will trouble the film.

Again, it is worth stressing that the *Romance On The High Seas* is not trying to set Georgia up as an innocent who only performs an outer toughness; the story does not propose the heroine is misguidedly cynical about men until she discovers true love. The character is just contradictory as performed.

As a further example, when Georgia joins Elvira and Lazlo in the club, the wealthy man tells the singer, 'We've ordered champagne cocktails, if it is alright?', to which Georgia replies with a laconic, 'So I'm stuck with it'. The end of the scene sees the trio toasting the impersonation deal and about to drink. In the Cuban nightclub, and in Rio, whenever Georgia is with Peter Virgil, there are two glasses on the table, one for each of them. Alcohol does not seem to be eschewed by Georgia, then; yet, when depressed because Peter has quarrelled with her, Georgia wanders into the bar, she tells the bartender 'I don't drink'. Overhearing the band rehearsing, she goes to sing with them, this, rather than alcohol, being her way of working herself out of a bad mood. This implication that the singer doesn't need stimulants because music elevates her humour posits a much softer version of Georgia than the rather calculating young woman seen at other times. Singing is not just the way she earns her $40 per week, then, but the way she expresses her emotions and, through expression, transcends them. Unhappy Georgia inveighs against romantic love and its symbols in 'Put 'Em In A Box, Tie 'Em With A Ribbon', singing the lyrics while pouting, crossing her arms across her chest defensively and looking grumpy. As she sings, she recovers her usual buoyant spirits until she is nodding her head in time to the beat, smiling at the musicians as they harmonize with her. The streetwise version of Georgia proposed by earlier scenes would surely have no trouble justifying drinking to alleviate the misery of a broken heart; it is a different, less coarse version who finds relief from sadness in singing.

This lack of continuity in the character could perhaps be seen as just an oversight, if her line of dialogue about not drinking contradicted only one occasion where she was seen with alcohol in front of her, but the repeated romantic settings for dates with Peter continually show the pair with matching glasses. The error seems more fundamentally linked to a tension in the conception of the character, therefore, and this tension, seen in the first number of the film, is again borne out by further musical moments. When 'Mrs Kent' is in the ship's bar with Peter Virgil on their first evening, she listens attentively to the band quietly playing, before opining that she has always wanted to sing. Virgil is somewhat surprised to see this society matron sashay up to the bandstand, swaying to the music, then join in. Once she starts 'It's You Or No One', he is even more surprised, since she sings not only well but with confidence and showmanship – pointing and firing a 'finger-gun' directly at him to underline the amorous words of the song, harmonising spontaneously or singing contrapuntally with the other musicians, as if she were a professional. Of course, Georgia *is* a professional, but she is on a paid vacation, so what makes her step up to the piano and start singing along with the band? Is this another moment where she needs to express her emotions in song, even if still impersonating Elvira? Are her feelings for Peter so urgent that she needs to let them out in the way that works best for her? If this is true, it sets this performance at odds with her first one; the song 'I'm In Love' was delivered with gusto when she was not in love. At the end of the song too, when the other patrons of the ship's bar applaud her performance, Georgia suddenly seems to 'come to', realising where she is and hastily descending the dais. This 'coming to' implies that she lost herself and the remembrance of her impersonation in singing, further suggesting that this might be because her emotions echo the lyrics of the song. When she descends the bandstand and goes back to Peter, the pair go into a dance and Georgia resumes her society lady voice and manner, although her instruction on where he should hold her seems more Georgia than Elvira in its flirtatiousness, regardless of the voice it is performed in: 'Anything above the third rib I consider *formal*'.

Naturally the film needs to allow space for the new actor, Doris Day, to do what she famously does, to sing, but once the plot has got her onto the cruise in the person of a wealthy society matron, such musical moments have to be narratively explained in some way. The film does not work very hard to find a motivation for this specific scene, however, and thus furthers the contradiction in the characterisation of Georgia, positing her both as a professional who can slip instantly into singing with a new combo without rehearsal, and a passionate amateur who relies on singing to assuage the intensity of her feelings.

The musical numbers continue to raise questions about her character as the film progresses. The cruise ship docks for a while at Havana; Peter and 'Elvira' go ashore to buy souvenirs and end up in a club (with two drinks in front of them) as local musicians sing. Georgia hears the tune and begins to sing the film's main song, 'It's Magic', mostly gazing directly at Peter or off in the middle distance. The performance by Jack Carson as Virgil is also interesting in this scene; he looks at Georgia singing at him, looks down, looks embarrassed, looks enthralled. In the middle section of the song when the lyrics drop out for a time, he even comments to Georgia about the song: 'Something about the way you sing it, I dunno, it *does* something to me.' But what is 'the way' she sings at this point? Her delivery of the song, much slower and more romantic than the others heard so far, seems simple and unaffected, but whether this is because she actually feels the emotions being mentioned, or because as a professional she instinctively realises this passionate song demands an impassioned yet unfussy performance, is not clear. The viewer is not let into Georgia's intentions here. There is no clarity over whether she is in love with Peter and attempting to convey her feelings to him through this medium, socially safer, after all, than telling him that she loves him though she is ostensibly a married woman. Perhaps she not does mean to tell him but her response to both song and man is so overpowering that she cannot help the truth coming out. Or perhaps her professionalism is such that she can sing the lyrics and make them sound as if she means them, just because she is an experienced performer. At times, such as when Peter makes his avowal and she merely goes on singing and humming, it seems more like the latter; at others, as when she ends the song looking as if she has tears in her eyes, it feels like the former. There is no definitive resolution of this problem or the character ambivalence it occasions.

But there is a hint that at some point the film-makers became aware of this problem themselves and took some steps to remedy it. For just around the hour-mark there is an odd little flashback sequence, narrated by Georgia to Oscar when he too joins the ship. Although only a few minutes have passed since some of the incidents, they are now shown again, this time accompanied by Georgia's voice as she explains about Elvira's deal, how she met Peter and how he's now refusing to speak to her.

Perhaps this strange flashback is then motivated by a wish to make clear Geogia's feelings when singing to Peter, since, as she narrates over the scene of the two of them in the club, 'By the time we reached Cuba I was in love with him. Head over heels, if you know what I mean. Oh, Havana was heaven....' The same shots of Georgia staring into Peter's eyes when singing are now framed by her voice explicitly expressing feelings that were left ambiguous moments earlier.

It is also both evident and problematic that as the film wears on Day seems increasingly to perform the musical numbers without any overt characterisation, either as Georgia or Elvira, so that on the second occasion she sings 'It's Magic', she delivers it straight and by the final time it provides the emotional climax of the film. Even though she can finally sing it to Peter in her own persona, as all identities are now disclosed, she does not affect her former brassy Georgia voice and behaviour but performs in the same heartfelt manner as the other two times.

As the staged songs progress through the narrative, then, Day's performance of them becomes much less marked by the bouncy sass which has been used to indicate Georgia and the rapid blinking and posh tones Georgia employs as Elvira. Although she uses these markers to differentiate the characters, there is no emphasis in the former of innocence and the latter of experience: Day as both seems to be fully post-virginal. I have outlined previously that virginity is hard to see unless narrativized as under threat. Is there, then, a scene in *Romance On The High Seas* where Georgia seems torn between abstract ideas of morality and the more urgent physical promptings of desire? No; on the contrary, she seems decidedly open to the idea of a physical relationship with Peter, even though she is supposed to be married. She is even more prepared for this than he is, as is illustrated in one scene, where the doubts are given to Peter rather than to Georgia.

Having seen a man in her stateroom at night, and thus assuming the worst of 'Mrs Kent', Peter quarrels with her the next morning, which is when Georgia seeks the alleviation of her bad mood in song. Later that evening, Georgia is seen looking sadly at the couples dancing to an orchestra. On deck, she heads for the side of the ship alone, and begins to sing again the song she had playfully serenaded Peter with before, on the night of their first meeting, 'It's You Or No One'.

She now wears a dramatic evening gown of pink silk and silvery sequins, with her make-up immaculate and hair piled high on her head in a sophisticated up-do, but though she is outfitted in high glamour, Georgia presents a softer side in both her outfit and the way in which she tackles the song this time. In the bar, on the previous occasion she sang the tune, she had been all bounce and liveliness, her strapless icy blue dress with its elbow-length satin gloves and capelet a performative costume which suited her performance with the band. Now the softer nature of her gown, which with its colour but also its design – long-sleeved, high-neck – gestures at modesty, matches the soulful way in which she sings. The tune is slowed down, she has a full stringed orchestral accompaniment instead of the peppy trio, and her voice treats each line caressingly. It should also be noted that Georgia believes herself alone – she does not know that Peter is watching her, so her performance of the song now has the weight of a spontaneous confession: again, when her feelings prove too much for her, Georgia's instinctive response is to seek relief in an outpouring of song.

Her sincerity is also augmented by the simplicity with which she renders the tune and lyrics on this occasion. Instead of bounding through the line 'you'll find that you are still the one', with a slight accent on the 'you', as before, she now draws the line out, with a tiny pause after 'still' which thus emphasises 'the one'. At the end of the line, too, she drops her eyes, droops her head a little, and makes a small gesture with her mouth, a pursing or tightening which seems expressive of barely suppressed emotion: she is singing so that she doesn't sob.

Georgia's passionate version of the song on this occasion is delivered, then, with a voice full of tears which match the glitter of drops yet unshed in her eyes, the silvery sequins on her dress and the diamond clips in her ears. Confirming this sadness, at the end of the song she wipes away a tear and sniffles a little as she busies herself getting a cigarette out of her evening bag and trying to light it.

When a match appears next to her she double-takes in surprise at seeing Peter but lights her cigarette and then turns slightly in readiness to hear what he has to say. It is noticeable that for all the vulnerability she has just revealed in this privileged moment to us, Georgia attempts to hold herself together in front of Peter: she does not want him to know how hurt she is, does not ask if he witnessed her emotional declaration. She holds herself still and watchful as they stand side-by-side looking out to sea. Peter talks about the beauty of the night and she agrees; her answers are short and acquiescent, but still she holds herself in check, wary to see what he does next. When Peter announces, tossing his cigarette away, that the night's loveliness makes 'a man feel he wants a woman is his arms', she copies his gesture, disposing of hers so that she can be ready for what comes next. Her eyes slide to the right as she quickly checks him, then says 'and vice versa'; she moves her shoulders slightly as if both steadying and readying herself, as she anticipates his next move. Unfortunately, it is a reminder that they should not be together:

Peter: If only you weren't married....
'Elvira': Oh, how I wish I could tell you I wasn't...

Georgia's line is truer than Peter suspects; she wishes she could confess the entire subterfuge to him along with her actual single status, and they could enjoy the fulfilment of their shipboard romance. When Peter's next line seems to be another overture, Georgia is ready to accept it and take it as far as she can; he acknowledges that if she weren't married it would be so easy, he would just take her in his arms.... 'Like how?' she inquires, going into his embrace. Play-acting in this way nearly gets them to the desired kiss but then Peter remembers the problem again:

Peter: You have a husband.
'Elvira':   *You* have principles.

Georgia utters this line in the flat voice of one who feels bilked of her desires; her tightening mouth produces a pout and she sets her jaw a little in disappointment. Although the next to-and-fro of the dialogue gets her back in his arms and even nearer to being kissed as she encourages him ('if you can't help yourself, you can't *help* yourself!'), Peter again manages to resist at the last moment and departs, leaving Georgia to gasp with surprise and annoyance, then settle back at the ship's side with a furious pout at the wasted romantic setting.

Interestingly, all her ardent emotions are expressed in this scene in the song she sings alone, rather than conveyed to the man she desires when he is with her. When Peter and Georgia are together she is first very guarded and wary, then fully prepared to act on her physical promptings, but not to tell him that she loves him in person. The softer side of Georgia seems only displayed in the musical numbers, creating an ambiguous characterisation. When the behaviour of the frustrated pair is analysed, Peter is seen to act out doubts and hesitations over whether to pursue the attraction; by contrast, Georgia is completely ready to move forward and accomplish the desired outcome. While the scene had the potential, then, in presenting two characters circling around the topic of their mutual attraction, to show the woman giving way to anxieties about the ethics of acting on their feelings, as it might have done if she were supposed to be a virgin, it instead gives these doubts to the man, and has them narrativized not because of the *initiatory*, but the presumed *extra-marital*, nature of the sexual experience being negotiated.

Georgia is of course not married but neither the pretence that she is, nor any other factor, looks as if it would inhibit her: she is very desirous of consummating her relationship with Peter if he will only let her.

Close reading of the film and Day's performance in it thus seems to confirm that her character is not intended to be a shy virginal type. But how did contemporary reviewers receive Georgia, and Day? The earliest review for the film in the trade press was one of the most favourable; *Film Daily* liked both Day's performance and the film as a whole, dubbing her 'devastating' and 'socko', and predicting the film 'should go $ places', largely due to her: 'Day is going to be spelled dough at the box office'. The 'devastating' label is not a one-off, as the review adds that Day 'makes every appearance register and gives the impression that she is out to devastate the proceedings. And she does too.' (Anon, 1948c: 6) What the review finds so overwhelming about Day's performance is, seemingly, her hold over both musical and narrative segments of the film. There is no hint here that *Film Daily* feels Day is portraying a shy maiden, but rather 'a gal with a glib tongue [...] delivering lines and lyrics with equal zip and punch'. The reception of Georgia is in accord with the way Day has presented her in the early parts of the film, as a wise-cracking bouncy dame, her cynicism tempered with good humour. The softer Day that, as noted, is scripted at times, is not the one who registers here.

Generally, *Film Daily*'s opinion was echoed by all the main reviews – from the *West* Coast. The East Coast critics' disparagement of *Romance On The High Seas* was so noticeable, in fact, that *The Hollywood Reporter* ran a full-page review of the reviews on 30 June, "High Seas' Suffers From Brushoff By NY Critics' (Hoffman, 1948: 14). In this piece ten different reviews are quoted which denigrate the film, although most had a few complimentary words to say about Day herself. Bosley

Crowther's damning entry in *The New York Times* is the most derogatory of Day's performance, opining that 'this bouncy young lady [...] has no more than a vigorous disposition which hits the screen with a thud' (Crowther, 1948: 10). It is interesting that, even in criticising the actor, Crowther picks up on the quality of bounce which, as has been seen, was most associated with Day on her movie debut.

Significantly, then, none of the reviews suggests that Day is unconvincing as a perky chanteuse or posits the part of an innocent maiden as more appropriate. There are no comments which can be interpreted as reading Georgia or Day herself as cast in a virginal mould at this time. Whether a reviewer likes or dislikes Day in the film, the qualities she is said to possess and convey are those of energy and high spirits, not any maidenly decorum or reticence. Sexual status is simply not an issue here.

Two further pieces from the trades merit notice here, both from *Motion Picture Herald* (*MPH*). This was one of the most influential trade publications; it not only carried industry news and film reviews but, since its intended audience was made up of movie theatre owners and exhibitors, also featured an accent on film promotion, regularly including letters from readers about how they had chosen to 'bally-hoo' a particular movie to attract audiences. With this accent on promotion, it is understandable that *MPH* was always interested in stars, and that its September feature in which the 'NATION'S SHOWMEN SELECT THE STARS OF TOMORROW' (Wheeler, 1948: 11) was seen as an important indicator of future success. Whether they worked for one of the Hollywood studio chains of theatres or were independent owner/exhibitors, the 'showmen' were expected to be mindful only of box office potential in selecting the top box office stars of each year and the top newcomers.[27]

Advertisements in *MPH* would thus be expected to reach a readership of movie theatre exhibitors; impressing such an audience might result in a nomination for the 'Stars of Tomorrow' title. It is unsurprising therefore to find Curtiz foregrounding his new signing with a trade advert; Michael Curtiz Productions took out a full-page advert in the 4 September edition of *MPH* (opposite page 28). The ad is interesting, however, in playing up Day's multi-media popularity, noting her success in records and on radio as well as in films, while also quoting the headline of the *Motion Picture* article examined in the previous section, 'Doris Day – The Most Everything Girl In Hollywood'. Here is an instance of the sometimes dizzying levels of self-reflexivity found in the publications of this time: Curtiz is quoting *Motion Picture* quoting Curtiz...

The overall heading of the advert appears opposite Day's face smiling directly at the reader positioned over the bulb of a thermometer: 'The <u>HOTTEST DAY</u> OF THE YEAR!' Many of the reviews had commented on the summer's hot weather and its negative effects on cinema attendance[28]; this advert manages to link Day's new celebrity with the heat-wave, and though it is her topicality which is being hailed as scorching, there is still the indisputable link between Day and heat, with symbolic overtones of the sultry and ardent, which cancel out any idea of virgin or asexual status at this point.

The Curtiz advert lauding Day was followed exactly one week later, on 11 September, by the announcement of *MPH*'s 'Stars of Tomorrow', which included Doris Day in its 10th spot. Lest this achievement seem negligible, the *MPH* editorial itself points out the unusual nature of her case, since managing to appear in the Stars index so early in a film career is very rare:

> Doris Day's election to the Top Ten position on the strength of only one picture, 'Romance on the High Seas', crosses up poll tradition, which usually ordains that a ranking Star-of-Tomorrow be seen and remembered in several widely played pictures. But

producer-director Michael Curtiz, to whom she's under contract, designed that Technicolor musical with the declared purpose of show-casing his new contractee to utmost advantage, which it seems to have done.

(Weaver, 1948: 14)

Perhaps Day's success in other fields, which the 4 September ad had highlighted, had helped put her on the fast-track to movie star fame; certainly, her selection by the movie exhibitors indicates their confidence that she would act as a box office-draw in future years. In this they were correct: Day not only went on to feature in the top-ten line-up ten times, but has also attained the status of the top female box office draw for the most years[29].

Overall, the reception of Doris Day on her initial film outing was a very positive one, as has been seen. Notwithstanding the critical slighting her vehicle received from the New York critics, it was in fact only Bosley Crowther who seemed to be able to resist the new starlet on her debut. Day's reviews are almost uniformly enthusiastic and, more importantly for this examination, never suggest that she is miscast playing the brash singer. Curtiz and Warner Bros. calculated wisely in casting Day in *Romance On The High Seas* as this not only enabled them to present Day in a role believably close to her own established career, but also resulted in tie-in products in the form of recordings of the film's hit songs: as the *MPH* advert noted, her rendition of 'It's Magic' was 'First on Hit Parade'. Her 1955 role in *Love Me Or Leave Me* as Ruth Etting, another nightclub singer, could similarly be seen both creating the potential for tie-in revenue and drawing on the star's own well-known background to aid realism. This easy justification for Day in the role was complicated, however, by two overt factors: because the film was a biopic, Day had to contend with public memory of the real Etting, plus the real Etting had had a dramatic and somewhat torrid love life, which seemed to call not only for a new kind of Day performance, but a new kind of Day herself, as will be explored in the next chapter.

3 *Love Me Or Leave Me* (1955)

Day made 16 films between *Romance On The High Seas* and *Love Me Or Leave Me*, the next film analysed in detail here, over a period of just six years. It is not surprising, then, that her persona had evolved by the time of the 17th film; nor am I claiming that it only changed at this point. Smaller, incremental changes occurred between her first film and the Etting biopic, which will be examined very briefly now.

As mentioned before, Day's first three films all allowed her to portray a perky, bouncy and determined young lady, in films which might have their sad or tender moments but generally would be comedic. Her fourth was a slight departure from this pattern, being more dramatic. *Young Man With A Horn* (1950) presented a version of the life story of jazz trumpeter Bix Beiderbecke, with Kirk Douglas taking the lead role. Here Warners carefully tested the range of the new star by putting her into a drama, but also cushioning her against failure by, again, having her portray what she once had been: a band singer. The parallels with Day's own past are even closer than in *Romance On The High Seas* as her Jo Jordan sings with the same large outfits in big dance venues, rather than the little club in which Georgia performed. Day received complimentary notices for her more straight role but the studio elected to put her back into familiar musical comedy territory for her next two vehicles, *Tea For Two* and *The West Point Story* (both 1950). The former shows how far Day had come, in just two years, from Georgia: her Nanette is much softer, more upper-middle-class, more passive, although her vocal mastery still adds tension to the narrative, as in the scene where professional singer Jimmy (Gordon MacRae) first sings her the title song. Nanette, an heiress, is supposed to be hearing it for the first time, but Day's expertise with the tune, with harmonising and anticipating its significant beats, exceeds his. In the latter film, Day plays another of the close copies of herself, a successful singer who has been on the road with big bands from the age of 16.

Another chance to extend her range into dramatic performance came next, with the low-budget shocker *Storm Warning* (1951), but this dramatic turn was immediately followed by other films which put her back in the musical comedy mould. Warners seem with this pattern to be experimenting slightly with the roles offered to their new star, testing her out in smaller parts in more melodramatic pieces before returning her to star-billing in the big glossy musicals. *Lullaby Of Broadway* (1951) was another in this vein, with Day given plenty of opportunity for dancing and singing old standards. Although the plot is very pedestrian, it added to her popularity, with her performance in it cited as winning Day *Photoplay's* 1951 Gold Medal for most popular female star (Sammis, 1952: 34).

It was her next film which began an association of Day with small-town, old-time values. *On Moonlight Bay*, set in 1915, has Day playing Marjorie Winfield, a teenage tomboy who, as the film progresses, discovers boys and begins to try to dress and behave in the manner sanctioned by society: polite, demure, manipulative. The film was a big success and the studio evidently believed this was at least partly due to the romanticised historical setting. Warners sent Day back in time in five of the eight remaining films she made for them before her contract with the studio expired in 1955, including a sequel featuring Marjorie, *By The Light Of The Silvery Moon* (1953), which revisits the comforts of the olde tyme tunes, period costumes and quaint old-fashioned customs. As the wife of an important real-life man, in 1952's *I'll See You In My Dreams* and *The Winning Team*, Day was introduced to biopics; thus *Love Me Or Leave Me*, when it came, was not a total departure for her generically, although it differed in casting Day as the famous one. Both 1952 films were again set in the past, furthering the association of the star with musical standards of former years and with the persona of a devoted wife, which fit well with her recent real-life wedding to Melcher.

Day's final four films with Warner Bros., from 1953 to 1955, indicate the highs and lows of her times with the studio: all musicals, they vary in tone and effectiveness, but continue to affirm Day as an actress-singer. Music is, at this point, an indispensable part of her roles: only in *Storm Warning* had she had a part without a song. 1953 brought the largely disposable *April In Paris* (Day as a showgirl again), as well as the *Moonlight Bay* follow-up, and then *Calamity Jane*, a watershed role which perhaps showed the full extent of Day's range within the musical comedy format. I have written elsewhere in detail on this film and the significance of its costume within the narrative plot to normalise its central female hero (2007; 2010b); it has also been noted that Day's expenditure of energy on this film reached such a peak that she suffered some form of collapse afterwards, delaying production of the rather woeful *Lucky Me* and leading to her estrangement with the press. Day's last film for Warner Bros., *Young At Heart*, brought Day together with Frank Sinatra in a remake of the 1938 film *Four Daughters*. A romantic drama about the loves of, here, three sisters, the film gave Day and Sinatra the chance to sing a variety of songs, and presented a more muted and adult musical tale of married love *almost* reaching a tragic ending. Day responds well to the more serious material, although Sinatra's Barney Sloan is so resolutely objectionable that her marriage to him seems more motivated by noble self-sacrifice than romantic love. Still, the darker tones of the story perhaps helped prepare her for her next film, her first as an independent artist, made as a one-off with MGM. As noted before, Day appeared to celebrate her release from her Warners contract by entering into a series of three dramatic pictures which seem calculated to undermine the authenticity of her sunny, cheery disposition, showcased so often in the Warner years, and suggest this was just a performance, despite off-screen work, in interviews and other material disseminated by the fan magazines, trying to propose the opposite. Although more downbeat than her usual musical vehicles, *Young At Heart* did not really prepare audiences for the new more adult Doris Day which now emerged with the Etting biopic.

Given that the role of Etting was seen as a significant departure for Day and, as has been discussed, as causing her to go dramatic and sexy, it is perhaps strange to look at this text for signs of virginity in Day's character. However, there is a very significant emphasis on female sexuality in this film which bears careful scrutiny. Although it is never posited that Ruth is a virgin when she meets Snyder – nor that she is *not* – her behaviour towards him up until the film's midpoint entirely fulfils mid-50s anxieties that young women manipulated their men, dangling the bait of their sexual favours, prolonging capitulation for as long as possible in order to make material gains.

Ruth is first seen being fired from her job at the dime-a-dance hall for kicking a customer who got too grabby. When one of the other women employees sneeringly tells her that she won't succeed in showbiz 'til you stop hollering "hands off"!', Ruth retorts that she'll stop hollering when *she* wants to, 'not because the customer's always right'. Although this might be seen to be an important mid-century message about women's right to act on their own sexual promptings, the way in which Ruth proceeds throughout the rest of the film to ignore her own needs for love and sex, and to attempt to parlay the promise of these into success, undermines this stance.

Ruth views with suspicion the offer of Marty Snyder (James Cagney), a gangster whose laundry business provides protection to many Chicago clubs, to introduce her to people who might give her a job. Although initially hostile and certain his offer is just a line to make her obliged to him – as is true – Ruth gradually begins to take his favours, believing that she can delay 'payment' for them through careful handling of the man. Irascible, pugnacious and arrogant with others, Marty's sole soft spot quickly becomes Ruth. When he gets her a job as a dancer at a small nightclub she is ungrateful, as she wants to be a singer, and it is Marty the tough gangster who has to scramble to put things right, not the 'little lady' he believes he is patronising.

Several of the early scenes in the club prove key in revealing Ruth's attitudes towards men. For example, after one dance routine is completed, the dancers return to their shared dressing room; Ruth, who never seems friendly with the other women, is washing out her stockings to make them last, when the club's piano player, Johnny Alderman (Cameron Mitchell) approaches her. They exchange relaxed banter, which culminates in his offer to coach her if she is serious about being a singer, with the stinger being that they will have to rehearse at his apartment. Looking him right in the eyes with a knowing smile, Ruth huskily wonders whether that would not be 'an awful lot of trouble for you?'. She seems to understand Johnny's offer, and has, significantly, not said no to his suggestion, when he is urged to leave by the club owner, who then tells him to keep away from the woman as she is Snyder's, 'bought and paid for'. As he discovers in a later scene, however, Ruth does not consider herself bought, and is happy to carry on postponing the day when the debt she owes is called in.

After 18 minutes of developing storyline, the audience is finally treated to hearing Ruth sing. Until now there has been no diegetic evidence to support her self-belief: now a simple musical number, accompanied only by Johnny on piano, proves to him and the viewers that she does have a very real talent. Uniquely for the filming of the musical numbers in the movie, the camera does not cut away from Ruth for the entire song; this adds to the intensity of the performance, letting the viewer be wrapt in the spell of Ruth's voice. The camera frames Ruth at the side of the piano as she sings 'It All Depends On You', a love song which she delivers simply, unfussily, but with power. Johnny is impressed, and Ruth asks him to confirm to Snyder that she does have talent: she is aware that Marty has been humouring her about the singing, hoping she will get bored and consent just to be his mistress. The film has shown the men – Johnny, Snyder, and his sidekick Georgie – all involved in the conspiracy to humour her until she's ready to quit. Ruth knows but doesn't care what they think so long as she gets her chance to prove them wrong. Now realising that Ruth can sing and has the potential to be a hit, Johnny urges her to try without Marty's help, because he is aware of the payment the gangster expects in return. Ruth refuses to acknowledge this; and, when Marty suddenly turns up at the end of the singing session, tells him the truth about forgetting their date, and apologises for being pushy with him. Marty melts as always, and makes to take her home. There is a very interesting micro-moment in Day's performance here; Ruth says a simple 'thank you' to Johnny for the lesson as she leaves, but Day imbues it with much more: there is a spark of triumph in her face and voice as she looks at the pianist, as if bidding him acknowledge that she does know how to manage Marty.

When she finally does get a featured singing spot, Ruth and Johnny have another conversation on the same subject, a continuation of the one before but more serious as Ruth now owes even more to the gangster. Just before her first performance, Johnny urges her to trust her own talent to make her a success, or to let him help her, but she is both scornful of his motives in offering assistance and insistent that she has not committed herself irrevocably to Snyder – 'I've made no promises'. But Ruth is about to find out that Marty has taken her acceptance of his help as a pledge of sexual obligation. After she has finished the two songs, he comes to her dressing room to insist she go with him to a weekend house-party: there is no doubt whose room she would be sharing. At first Ruth blusters and tries to get out of the conversation by pleading tiredness, but Marty bluntly rejects her excuses: 'Not this time, Ruthie. That's all over'. He is not prepared to postpone payback any longer.

Ruth here proves again that she knows how to play Marty. With her back turned to him as he delivers his demands, her face is set angrily, her jaw set and jutting a little, her eyes cold. She is thinking fast – she turns to him to try to reason but he talks over her, and she sits down, perching on the top of her dressing table chair. After he's told her again, she gives two small nods and says quietly, 'I understand. You got me a break and now....' She stands up, suddenly revealing the height difference between them – in her heels she is taller than Snyder – and says 'Alright, I'll go with you', as she walks away from him again, with a sort of aggressive saunter; then she stands, crossing her arms in front of her body. Behind her, Snyder begins to be delighted until she gives him the coup de grace: 'And then you'll never see me again.'

Ruth is betting on Snyder caring more about her now, being in love with her, so that her acquiescence to sex is not what he actually desires. She gambles but she knows her mark well, and is right; while all the power seems to be on her side, however, he yet has some also, because she still cares about the deals he can do for her. Ruth sits again at her dressing table, toying with one earring as she tries to think of a way to get what she wants without giving Marty what he does. She gets him to admit that he cares about her so that she can use her honesty about not loving him – 'not yet anyway' – as further bait that one day she *might*, and might give him everything he wants from her. The scene ends as usual, with Marty agreeing again to the postponement of her repayment.

In between these two scenes, the rows with Johnny and with Marty, Ruth has sung two songs on stage. As so often in this complex musical, the choice of numbers is significant, and also as so often, Ruth expresses emotions through her performance of tune and lyrics that are entirely pertinent to the action. What is so interesting, however, is that the emotions she expresses throughout the film are usually not her own, but *Marty's*. While the dramatic action shows the manipulative relationship between Ruth and Marty is toxic from both sides, and that neither is guiltless, the songs frequently provide another perspective, allowing the viewer to feel Snyder's pain at being unloved and used. The two featured at this juncture conform to this pattern, letting the viewer appreciate Marty's point of view even while he watches Ruth singing the words. First, she sings 'You Made Me Love You', which neatly encapsulates his feelings of reluctant devotion. The other song, a jauntier number, 'Stay On The Right Side', seems by contrast to serve a narrative, rather than symbolic, function, in proving that Ruth has the confidence and skill to tackle jazzy up-tempo tunes as well as the slower torch songs she has so far sung. In performing this one too she abandons her usual static pose for singing, and starts to move, shimmying her hips, stepping back and forwards, and always using her hands to mark the rhythm. This song warns the listener to beware temptation, and to keep away from the devil, since contact with him will mean 'you'll never get to hallelujah land' (Figure 17).

However, reviewing the lyrics in depth, it does seem as if there can be a symbolic resonance to this song too, with it forming a musical counterpart to Johnny's warning earlier: Ruth is cast as the hero in this Faustian story, with Marty in the role of Mephistopheles; she should resist his offers of help because of

Figure 17.   Day as Etting performs in *Love Me Or Leave Me*.

what she will have to have to sacrifice to him in return. On the other hand, *she* can be equally viewed as the devil, if the sympathies of this song, like the others, are assumed to be with Marty; this view gains in credence since all of Marty's other businesses and relationships are neglected once he meets Ruth. Marty gives up any chance of a place in 'hallelujah land' in order to bully and coerce first other people, then Ruth herself, but she is not innocent in the relationship – the film constantly makes it clear that she has the talent to succeed without using Marty's contacts, and in that way would not owe him anything. But Ruth is seen to be so sure of her manipulation of Marty that she does not believe she will ever have to repay him.

The film develops this into a pattern, showing that after every incremental achievement there is another scene between her and Marty where he demands, and she refuses, payment. At her highest career point, however, he finally rebels. Having brokered her a starring role in 'The Ziegfeld Follies', Marty is anxious that she remember she owes her success to him, but he is ejected from the backstage area during the first performance and Ruth does not object. When she arrives back at the hotel, he is the angriest she has ever seen him, reproaching her for not siding with him but with her New York friends. He reminds her of all that she owes him and, by now sobbing in real distress, she acknowledges, 'Marty, I know what I owe you, but there's no way to pay it ... '. Snyder responds, 'Ain't there?' before grabbing her, forcing her back on the bed and kissing her. Ruth escapes to the next room but Marty follows her slowly with a ferocious look on his face – and in the next scene, they are married.

Hollywood's truncation of the suggested rape makes it none the less significant, and much of the dramatic impact of the sequence is due to Day's performance. Her sobs seem totally realistic, at times coming out high-pitched and squeaky, as she gulps and gasps, sniffs snottily, and seemingly without any vanity over how she looks or sounds, enacts a convincing crying bout. When she manages to fight Marty off and escape for a time to the next room, her racking sobs are particularly high, as if she were verging on hysteria.

After the fade out on Marty's angry, determined face as he stalks towards the room where she has fled, Ruth emerges in the next scene seemingly unscathed, calmly packing her clothes in the hotel room, ready to leave New York. Marty comes in with a breakfast trolley with the morning paper, its headline helpfully filling the viewer in – 'Ruth Etting Weds Martin Snyder'. The film thus economically confirms Ruth's possession by Snyder both physically and maritally. However, although he has forced himself on her, Ruth has one weapon left, and proceeds to use it, behaving calmly and without affect around him. He wanted her, he has her, her behaviour seems to say, but he can forget about her being happy or showing enthusiasm or any emotion over anything, ever again. Thus begins the second half of the film and of Ruth's relationship with Marty, with her passive-aggressive and him increasingly maniacal as he tries to extort some kind of response from his bride.

While, then, there is no firm line from the narrative about Ruth's sexual status before she meets Marty, her general reluctance to give him what he wants from her could be read in this light – especially perhaps by contemporary audience members, who by 1955 were getting used to dramatised narratives around the topical figure of the virgin. Ruth thus appears like other 'ladies of desperate disposition who have their traps out for any fair game', as the *New York Times* review of *The Tender Trap*, released the same year, characterised the film's heroine Julie (Debbie Reynolds) and other young women who used their maiden status as bait. [*New York Times*, 11 November 1955: 29). The film is not free from anachronisms in either the costume or haircuts, outfitting Day as Ruth not in the appropriately slender, boyish costumes of the 20s, but showing off her curvy body in clothes which speak more to the pneumatic outline of the 50s, and with Day sporting not a bob but a short 'butch' haircut. Yet the film's most significant prolepsis is this assignment of the 1950s manipulative maiden role to its 1920s central character.

To a certain extent, this is a problem brought on by the perhaps necessary bowdlerisation of Etting's story, since when the film was made all three of the principals were still alive. Unlike other alterations to the story and songs, however, which, like the change in 'Ten Cents A Dance' of the word 'pansies' to 'dandies', serve to assuage Production Code anxieties about sexual conduct, the decision to present Ruth in the scheming maiden mould turns her story from a tragic love triangle into a cautionary tale about what happens to girls who tease.

It seems ironic that the very film which was taken contemporaneously as bringing a new Day to the screen and proving that the actor could master both a sexualised role and a very dramatic one should thus have such a clear allegiance to other mid-century 'virginity dilemma' texts. Nevertheless, on examination the film's narrative does seem to present Ruth as the type of young woman who attempts to control her man by paying out her favours, with the promise of more to come, on a 'carefully graduated scale', as one scathing suitor denounced in another mid-century text.[30] The usual manipulative maid, cautiously dangling the bait of her sexual favours in order to get what she wants, does differ from Etting in one important particular, however: what *she* wants is marriage. Ruth Etting, by contrast, is playing Marty 'like a fish'[31] not in order to marry him but in order to advance herself beyond his reach. And perhaps the extremity of this manipulation accounts for the extremity of her punishment. Although the basic narrative may suggest that she 'gets what she deserves' when Marty forcibly takes the bait she has been dangling for so long, Day's performance skilfully shows that the penalty far outweighs her crime.

In her performance going forward from the moment of the attack, where she is shown to be first affectless, then cynical, always hiding her unhappiness behind a mask of blankness, Ruth enacts the difference in the way she walks and talks, in her 'real life' as well as on stage, between her pre- and post-punishment selves. The immediate juxtaposition of the very strong dramatic performance Day gives in the scene where Marty assaults her, with its presentation of a sobbing, hysterical, emotional Ruth, and the next with its muted, empty, emotionless Ruth, provides the strongest warning about the risks of gambling with virginity as the stake. Furthermore, as the narrative goes on, it is seen that not just Ruth's off-stage life has been altered; even her musical performances do not give her pleasure anymore.

Symbolically, the next song she performs is 'Ten Cents A Dance', which seems on the surface to hark back to her own beginnings in the dance palace, but also speaks to her new awareness of having been bought and sold as a commodity. The once-vivacious Ruth, who showed off in her performances, as in the kinetic 'Stay On The Right Side', has been replaced with a hollowed-out woman, who performs this next song with the minimum of gesture and movement, apart from two contrasting motions: her hands repeatedly clasp, fingers interlaced, as if in supplication, while she also performs a cynical hip-thrust that sets the beads on her dress shimmying with tired suggestiveness. The gestures suit the song, but one feels they are not a performance, and this is borne out by Ruth's offstage behaviour immediately afterwards. She takes her bow and walks back to her dressing room, opening the door with one hand and reaching for the large drink Georgie has ready for her with the other. It is obviously a practiced routine, and one which strongly contrasts this scornful hopeless woman with the excited performer who ran offstage in giddy glee after other appearances.

After yet another row with Marty, which shows that Ruth has got used to his 'dramatics', his violent outbursts, and does not let them disrupt her general numbness, the narrative permits a little moment to occur which shows Ruth can still feel excitement and, most importantly, wants redemption. Marty has told her she is going to Hollywood to make movies, and she has greeted this news with the same shrug that has met all his other endeavours on her behalf since their wedding. Once she is alone, however, the telephone rings, and she takes a call from Johnny Alderman out in Los Angeles, telling her they will be working on her pictures together. Day's performance in this scene is skilfully calibrated; she takes Ruth from sullen nonchalance to breathless surprise in seconds, as Ruth can only gasp 'Johnny!' at his news, and smile the widest, most ecstatic smile. Marty then returns, and there is a nice throwaway character hint here, in that he has come back again to apologise for his latest outburst, showing that though he has been the aggressor, though he has married her and seemingly therefore possesses Ruth now, he has not lost the habit of appeasing her. Ruth hangs up on Johnny, pretending he is just someone from the newspapers, and at once announces her wish not to go to Hollywood. Marty is astounded and irate, but Ruth can clearly be seen trying not to jeopardise her marriage – even though it is so distasteful to her – by going to work again with the man she really loves. In this, the film makers seem to show Ruth's maturing character, to suggest that the suffering her marriage has caused her has at least made her a better person, one who scruples at adultery.

Inevitably Ruth and Johnny do end up meeting, and when jealous Marty cannot oversee this reunion, he sends Georgie to watch and report back. He need not fear Ruth's loyalty, however: she is shown to be businesslike and distant with Johnny too, even when he greets her ardently. Playing the tease with Marty is seen to have terrible consequences; even though she cares for Alderman, and he avows his own unchanged feelings by suggesting she sing one specific love song, she cannot respond. Alderman passes her the song and she bleakly reads the title.

Johnny: I think you know this, it's an old one of mine....
Ruth: I'll never stop *loving* you, yes, I know it...

Day has Ruth look Johnny straight in the face as she delivers this line; she is acknowledging their old feelings without qualms, but in such a direct, non-flirtatious manner that no one could derive hope from it. They stare at each other for a second or two after this announcement, before he then begins to play the accompaniment, and she sings in an passionate way which suits the words but, coming after her denial of any future for their relationship, seems colder than if she had sung it badly or without feeling.

Although, then, the film does condemn Ruth for dangling the bait of her sexual favours in front of Snyder, Day's performance in the second half clearly shows that she has suffered a terrible punishment for her manipulative behaviour, with her energy and vitality entirely sapped. In this, the film correlates interestingly with the somatic performance of sexual innocence found in other 'virginity dilemma' films; as noted, comic entries in this roughly decade-long cycle had their protagonists act out their maiden status through their excess of energy, while the more melodramatic entries, where virginity would actually be lost, associated sex with a physical stasis and reserve. Ruth, like another unfortunate screen virgin, Melanie in *Where The Boys Are* (1960) also traumatised by sexual mistreatment, is clearly shown to lose her animation as a result of Marty's attack and thus to have paid a heavy price for her unscrupulous ambition.

Perhaps the media could herald Day's emergence in *Love Me Or Leave Me* as a sexualised star because the well-known real-life story of Ruth Etting suggested the more seamy story of adultery, rather than the film's tale of calculated promises and postponements. Nevertheless, it seems ironic that the film should be taken as evidence of Day's maturity as an actor and a woman when it seems to be largely about the rewards and dangers of what happens when you 'play a man like a fish'.

While the role of Ruth Etting offered the actor a chance to distance herself from her usual parts, this is paradoxically offset by the steps the film takes to distance the modern star, Day, from the earlier star whom she is playing; although MGM announced in its short film *1955 Motion Picture Theatre Celebration* that *Love Me Or Leave Me* had 'the singing sweetheart of the Roaring Twenties portrayed by the singing sweetheart of today,' two main strategies – both musical – are recurrently employed in the picture to minimise the identification of the later star with the earlier. First, although Day works her way through the back catalogue of Etting's famous songs during the movie, she makes no attempt to mimic her vocal qualities, which would still have been familiar to audiences. Perhaps this was either due to the earlier singer's rather undramatic delivery, or her lower-class accent: two factors with which Day might not want to associate herself. Although for her role in *Calamity Jane* Day reportedly altered her singing and acting styles – 'I lowered my voice and stuck out my chin a little', she suggests in her biography (Hotchner, 1976: 148) – here there is no attempt by Day to mimic Etting's vocal delivery. She does, however, mimic her physically: the gesture of clasping her hands together, knitting her fingers, noted in 'Ten Cents A Dance', occurs in all the slow torchy songs and was a direct copy of Etting, as the earlier star's performances in Vitaphone 'soundies' such as *Roseland* (1930) and *A Modern Cinderella* (1932) bear out; it is not in Day's own usual repertoire of gestures.

Second, as noted above, the emotions evoked by Day's voice in the musical numbers most often do not fit with Etting's but with Snyder's. Thus when she sings 'You're Mean To Me', it is at a moment when Etting has again refused to appreciate Snyder. Similarly, in the film's climactic scene when Ruth finally sings the title song, it is his feelings that the lyrics encapsulate. Day as Etting pours out the words of the torch song, but it is Snyder who is carrying the torch, not she. Why then should the film elect to preserve Day's voice in its own familiar timbre, rather than mimic Etting's, and take the even more radical step of having her render Snyder's feelings through the songs, rather than her own? Perhaps this was because of the potentially risky step in casting Doris Day as Ruth Etting; keeping the star's voice recognisable not only maximizes the possibility of album sales[32] but distances a current valuable property from the taint of association with a notorious woman. The problem with this decision is that it makes the Day performance seem even colder, if what she sings is to be discounted, and makes Snyder – a gangster and, as suggested here, rapist – into the emotional focus of the film.

I have already indicated that press response to this film was very much dedicated to evincing surprise and admiration for Day's turn in this more dramatic and adult role. Articles and reviews in the daily newspapers followed the fan magazines in stressing what a departure the role was for Day, and seem largely unanimous in agreeing she was convincing as Etting ('Doris Day gives THE performance of her life and proves she is an actress of note' – Proctor, 1955: 8; 'Miss Day comes through as a subtle and sure emotional actress' – Moffitt, 1955). A couple of pieces testify to media awareness of the novelty of seeing Day in the film's revealing costumes and suggestive situations; the *Los Angeles Times'* weekend magazine, *This Week* ran a story on how the film's producer needed to persuade her to perform the provocative dance routine she assays in the first nightclub scene, noting that the star was usually 'singularly averse to anything resembling cheesecake' (Berg, 1955). This chimes with the views put forward as being those of Day, her husband and son in the 'Sex Isn't Everything' article released in the wake of *Love Me Or Leave Me*, which illustrates that the need was clearly felt to provide the seeming contradiction between Day's well-known beliefs and behaviour in this movie with some sort of explanation. Finally, the Los Angeles-based *Mirror News* overtly commented on the transformation of the film's star:

> ...And in the short haircut and flashy costumes of a nitery chirp of the 20s, La Day also emerges from her cute girl-next-door cocoon as a highly inflammable number.
>
> (Williams, 1955)

While Day's transformation into maturely sexualised star was endlessly commented upon by the media, then, there was no contemporary exegesis on how Etting's behaviour accorded with that of 50s manipulative misses. There was, however, according to Day's co-authored biography, a large amount of negative fan mail evoked by the movie. Some of this seems to have been criticizing her for using the stimulants forbidden by her membership of the Christian Science Church, while other letters found fault with her portraying the woman involved in a notorious love triangle and its associated well-publicised criminal trial.

Perhaps, however, the real impetus behind the chiding mail was audience members' discomfort with the persuasiveness with which Day portrays Etting. Letting viewers see her convincingly play a woman so driven by ambition that she would exploit not only her own talents but anyone else who came near was possibly too close for comfort to the Day who had been, until then, consistently seen as a rarity: a successful star who was also a genuinely nice person (Maynard, 1953: 58). Up to the rift with the press in 1954 she had always been presented in this vein, giving credence to the actual existence of the sunny Day seen in countless musicals; afterwards this was only partially recovered. One fan's testament that Day is 'Hollywood's Nicest Star' seems anachronistic (Mazella, 1957: 46).

Day could now be seen consciously arraying herself against this persona; by indicating the driving ambition of the woman on screen in *Love Me Or Leave Me* she unsettled the usual fantasy of her own niceness, backing up a counter- (and more realistic) image of a different Day: thrice-married, hard working, cleverly marketed; less jolly, more human, more fallible. It is possible to posit that Day at this time in her career, in the mid-1950s, was committed to enlarging her screen persona to accommodate a more adult range of qualities, leaving behind the ingénue characteristics that marked her roles in Warner Bros. musicals. It is ironic, then, that the next film to be examined both took her back to these characteristics *and* consciously set out to copy the one film that did most to establish her as a maturely sexual woman, aware of her desires and confident enough to act on them.

4 *Lover Come Back* (1961)

Between Day's turn as Ruth Etting and her performance as Carol Templeton in the next film analysed here, which came five years later, she took on another nine roles; although now free of her contract at Warners, Day was still working at a fairly hectic rate. While, as noted, she first appeared in three dramas with much darker tones than her usual repertoire, she then returned to the type of film more usually associated with her, with the film version of popular stage musical *The Pajama Game* (1957). Most of the Broadway cast transferred directly to the screen apart from the central female role, that of Katherine 'Babe' Williams, a garment factory worker and union official. It is indicative of Day's box office success by this point that she was picked for this role over the woman who originated the role on Broadway.

Day is convincingly blue-collar and gutsy as Babe, passionately in love with Sid Sorokin (John Raitt) the new factory manager despite the fact he is her natural enemy in workplace terms. Seemingly not a virgin, Babe seeks out and obviously enjoys Sid's affection and caresses, but tells him bluntly that she will always fight for the workers' side no matter what her feelings for him. While sex and romance seem to matter to her, then, remaining true to her beliefs matters more, which marks Babe out as an interestingly active character in a mediascape often filled with more passive women. This spirit of independence is very much in keeping with Day's filmic persona, even if not, perhaps, her off-screen one, and operates in most of her roles throughout the 50s. Although her films are generally romances, Day performs each role as if winning and keeping her man is important but not something for which she will sacrifice her beliefs or core integrity. This is true of her next two vehicles, both black and white lower budget affairs, both released in 1958: *Teacher's Pet* and *The Tunnel Of Love*. The former introduced the 'masquerading male' plotline that was to become such a feature of the Doris Day film in the next decade, while the latter can be credited with initiating the overtly sexual storyline in the star's roster. This spirit of independence seems only lacking in one Day film: *It Happened To Jane* (1959). Day's character Jane Osgood leans on – even leeches off – every man around her, from her beau George (Jack Lemmon), to his uncle and even a newspaper man suddenly introduced into her life via her legal skirmishes with a business magnate. Day weeps and whines through the narrative, behaving quite atypically; although she is given a song to perform, which might be an attempt to boost the film, the resultant performance serves only to prove that musical numbers are not an essential part of what Day brings to the screen, but that the quality of independence is.

It is difficult to over-state the importance of *Pillow Talk* in providing a much needed new impetus to Day's career. It is also difficult to talk about its unofficial sequel, *Lover Come Back*, without frequent reference to the earlier film; therefore in the following analysis of the 1961 movie, examination of elements of *Pillow Talk* will be necessary. Suffice it to say at this point that the film restored and increased Day's box office appeal, taking both her and Hudson to new career heights and making them the most popular movie couple of the moment. Day was nominated for an Academy Award, and the media almost unanimously responded to this 'new Doris' who was seen as having 'gone sexy' (Anon, 1959b: 3) in positive terms which conveyed the convincing nature of her experienced, worldly-wise, self-confident heroine, Jan Morrow. One review which sounded a dissonant note is worth citing here, as it evinces the fact that not everyone saw Jan as a sexually knowing woman, despite the narrative, script, performance and costumes all overwhelmingly pointing to this conclusion (Jeffers McDonald 2006a; 2010).

The review of *Pillow Talk* in *The Hollywood Reporter* clearly situates Jan within maidenly terms; not only does the reviewer comment on Day's 'combination of sophistication and naiveté', without providing evidence for the latter quality, but he goes on further to construct a past history of sexual restraint for Jan which is never hinted in the film itself:

> [Hudson] accuses her of having 'bedroom troubles' that are making her neurotic. A fine healthy young woman, who has so far fought off the passes of many men, Doris now begins to be kept awake by the primary urge [...she meets his Texan persona...] Doris, failing for this like a shooting gallery duck, begins to yearn to surrender to him.
>
> (Anon, 1959a: 3)

The reviewer here is at pains to note that her numerous previous refusals have not been from lack of sexuality: she does not have the 'bedroom problems' hinted at, is not frigid ('a fine healthy young woman'), but has been waiting for the right man ('Doris now begins to be kept awake [...] begins to yearn to surrender') to arouse her dormant sensuality. This reading of the character runs counter to indications in the script that Jan has known other men previously, as with, for example, the moment when she gloatingly reminds herself, eyeing Hudson, 'You've been out with a lot of men in your time, but *this*! This is the jackpot'. Despite the film's motions to the contrary, then, at least one reviewer managed to read Jan as a virgin; this lone reading would multiply after Day's overt portrayal of the mature maiden in *Lover Come Back*.

Pillow Talk was such a hit that it was obvious there would be attempts to repeat its successful formula as soon as possible. Day was already signed to other pictures, however, so work went ahead on two more vehicles while the right script and team were assembled for the follow-up to the big success. Although the first of these filler films puts Day back in the comfortable family-friendly mould she had just proved she could transcend[33], the second actually would have provided ammunition for those, such as Al Capp, who would later claim Day's major work was the incarnation of an untouchable old maid – had anyone noticed. *Midnight Lace* was adapted from the play by Janet Green, *Matilda Shouted Fire*, which features an heiress of about 17 who marries an older man but cannot bring herself to sleep with him. She constantly postpones their 'honeymoon'; then hateful telephone calls begin, tormenting her with threats against her person and life. Crucially, the audience is not permitted to know if the phone calls are actually menacing, as only her side is heard, or if the girl – who has a history of lying – is trying to distract attention from her postponement of the consummation. In the end, the calls and the danger both prove real, and the threat is found to come from the girl's husband; he had married her for her money and planned the calls to make her look so unstable that his eventual murder of her would be taken to be suicide.

What was in the bare bones of this plot that someone found appropriate for Day? Significantly, it was not the sex-aversion, since, although Day's Kit Preston is a virgin, she yearns not to be. Like the young girl in the play, she has not yet had her honeymoon, but she is desperate to do so: it is he who demurs. Other than these two changes, that of the woman's age and which one of the couple is avoiding consummation, the plot remains very much the same. When at the conclusion the husband is proved to be the villain, it is left uncertain whether he was motivated by some sort of misplaced chivalry which made him abstain from sleeping with a woman he did not love; his refusal to have sex with her is, however, made clear, even if his motives are not, as is the relief that Kit finds for her frustrations in two hysterical outbursts which permit her the physical catharsis – after heavy breathing and thrashing limbs – denied by her husband's refusal of sex. While *Lover*

Come Back returned Day to the humorous terrain of *Pillow Talk*, then, *Midnight Lace* should actually perhaps be viewed as being more influential on the later film, as it, rather than the first Day–Hudson comedy, set up the idea of the 40-year-old-virgin character for the star. The tonal shift between the 1960 drama and the 1961 comedy might have made seeing their similarities too difficult, however.

Anxious to emulate the success of its predecessor, *Lover Come Back* takes pains to ensure that it repeats as many of the former film's elements as possible, from larger points such as cast, crew, and narrative, to smaller ones, such as plot hooks and even parallel scenes. It thus includes not only the Day–Hudson pairing, but recruits Tony Randall for another very similar role as the Hudson character's rich best friend/employer. Stanley Shapiro, who had co-written the screenplay for *Pillow Talk*, also returned to co-provide the script. With him as writer of both, then, it is no surprise that *Lover Come Back* repeats the basic plot structure of the earlier film, keeping the enmity between the two lead characters which motivates the man's masquerade. However, the 1961 film not only copies this device but increases the stakes for which the game is being played, by having the Day character's virginity, rather than a relationship, as the prize to be won under false circumstances. That this was a conscious decision has been subsequently confirmed; Delbert Mann, the film's director, is quoted in Hudson's biography saying that, in this film, 'the assault on Doris's fiercely guarded virginity was where the humour came from' (Hudson and Davidson, 1986: 59).

Upping the ante in this way makes the Hudson character more reprehensible this time, as his motives for subterfuge are not romantic, and as Day's character has more to lose. Where the original picture presents the necessity for the masquerade arising from Brad's need to court Jan in a different persona, 'Rex Stetson', since she knows and detests (though she has not *seen*) his real self, in *Lover Come Back* Jerry takes on the 'Linus' persona to humiliate and bed Carol, not in order to win her. Though the ruse is the same, the motivation for the ruse is different, and more immoral. Frequent gleeful script references to his duping of her confirm his underhand intentions, with the audience made complicit by awareness of the real meanings behind seemingly innocent remarks. In this way, Carol is unwittingly made to connive at her own downfall, as when she pleads with 'Linus' to stay in her apartment overnight, since 'for what you have in mind, isn't this the perfect place?'. The narrative thus underlines Carol's naiveté, since she is concerned to provide 'Linus' with a comfortable place to rest, whereas what he actually 'has in mind' is her deflowering.

The newer film thus overtly posits Carol as a virgin, so that, were Jerry Webster's plan to succeed, it would not just be sex but *initiatory* sex into which he manipulates her. Carol is thus made to conform to the *Hollywood Reporter* reviewer's view of the earlier vehicle's heroine, in preserving the illusion that the Day character has so far managed to resist would-be seducers. *Lover Come Back* puts virginity centre stage in a way that *Pillow Talk* does not; it increases the emphasis on virginity since it not only asserts the lack of sexual experience for Carol but also hints at the same – or worse – for 'Linus'. The masquerade plot borrowed from its predecessor here strengthens the trope of the Hudson alias avoiding intimacy with Day's character, moving from the extreme but excusable Southern gentlemanliness of 'Rex' to the unnamed malady from which 'Linus' suffers, variously and murkily insinuated as being anxiety-driven impotence, virginity or homosexuality (Jeffers McDonald, 2006b).

Lover Come Back's title song, which plays over the animated birds-and-bees credits, begins the construction of the virginal Day, but also contains another self-knowing reference to its popular predecessor. The bouncy title tune has her call for her lover to return: Doris Day pleads with Rock Hudson to come back to the cinema for another film. As the song draws to its end, Day sings firmly:

> I've made my conclusion
> I know what I lack
> There's no substitution
> So please hurry back
> Lover, Lover, Lover, Lover, LOVER!
> Come on back.

The film can perhaps further be seen as self-consciously commenting on its own reprising of the popular Day–Hudson pairing in the line 'there's no substitution'. Between *Pillow Talk* and *Lover Come Back*, Hudson had made *Come September* (1961) to Day's two vehicles; besides suggesting Day as a more fitting partner for Hudson than *Come September*'s Gina Lollobrigida, he more right for her than David Niven or Rex Harrison, the line here also suggests that there is no substitute for what the Day character in the new film lacks – a man, and thus by implication, sex.

Within the first few moments of the film, then, the audience has been assured of another sexy skirmish between the popular stars of *Pillow Talk*. The film continues to build on this anticipation of original animosity and eventual romance in a variety of ways in the ensuing scenes, but always reinforcing the newly added fillip that the Day character in this iteration is a virgin.

For example, an early conversation between the two rival advertising executives has them talk on the phone. While this is another of the many conscious nods to *Lover Come Back*'s predecessor, complete with split screen, it also provides the occasion for the script, and Day, to begin the work of establishing Carol as a virgin. The lines of dialogue enable Jerry to accuse Carol of a variety of failings in her femininity:

Jerry: …If you can't stand the competition get out of the advertising profession.

Carol: You aren't even *in* the advertising profession, and if I weren't a lady I'd tell you what profession you are in…

Jerry: Tell me anyway.

Carol: Well, let's just say I don't use sex to land an account.

Jerry: When do you use it?

Carol: I don't.

Jerry: My condolences to your husband.

Carol: I'm not married.

Jerry: It figures…. a husband would be competition. There's only room for one man in the family.

Carol: I wish I were a man right now!

Jerry: Keep trying. I think you'll make it.

The bare lines of dialogue give the outline of the scene, but do nothing to convey its moods and tensions, which are carried through the performances of the two actors. Throughout, Hudson plays Jerry as maddeningly calm and in control, manipulating the increasingly infuriated Carol through the conversation, so that she ends up admitting that she is unmarried and inexperienced. It is Day's performance which really transcends the script, however; the dialogue as written cannot communicate the expressions on her face, her irate gestures, or the emphasis her voice gives to the words. One exchange can act as an example: Jerry asks her, if she doesn't use sex to land an account, when *does* use it. Carol's reply is simple, but Day invests the two words 'I don't' with significance beyond their mere utterance. She lengthens the word 'I' almost musically so that she seems to italicise the word, trying to set herself up in opposition to Webster, while 'don't' is bitten off and closed down, symbolizing her attitude to using scantily-clad women as bribes. The scene works to establish Carol as innocent in both business and sexual terms: the former, because she does not see that 'sex sells' in advertising, and the latter in that she cannot anticipate that Webster will turn her words against her, finding a *double entrendre* in her confession that she doesn't 'use sex'. Actually, Carol's admission should be seen as testimony of her moral rectitude, rather than a slur against her femininity or personal attractiveness, as she does not view sexuality as something that should be exploited. Webster's cynical use of the word 'use' is another gesture towards that mid-century belief in and condemnation of women who did utilise sex as bait for material gain.

While Jerry not only has the upper hand throughout this conversation, constantly able to best Carol's rejoinders, he also has the dominant share of the screen. *Pillow Talk's* equitable division of space, sometimes vertical, sometimes horizontal, is here abandoned in favour of a split which devotes two thirds of the screen space to gloating Jerry, and only the remaining portion to furious Carol (Figure 18).

Although she is overtly set up here and throughout as a virgin, however, there are equally numerous signs that Carol is now learning to feel desire and seeks to attract her man. Her wardrobe shifts at this point from the attractive but business-like suits she

Figure 18.   *Lover Come Back* revises *Pillow Talk's* equitable split screen with a less fair division.

habitually wears, becoming more casual as she starts to teach 'Linus' to swim, dance, sail, play golf, and ride a bicycle, active pursuits which inevitably require tighter clothing emphasising her curves. Her hairstyle, which sets up further overtones of maidenly innocence, has been worn high off her forehead, giving her a very natural, uncontrived look (Figure 19). This not only contrasts with the sensuous glamour of the character of Jan in *Pillow Talk* (Figure 20) but also with the increase that falling in love now brings to Carol's level of allure (Figure 21). Her costumes shift in colour, too, moreover, as she begins to abandon the accent on white, with its inevitable implications of purity and maidenhood, and to sport bright oranges and pinks. That Carol finds 'Linus' more than just a congenial prospective client becomes obvious when at the barber's, a manicurist compliments Carol – 'Your husband is a real doll without the beard' – and the look Carol gives the newly clean shaven man shows that she is excited to picture him in that role. Carol is becoming

Figure 19.   Carol's innocent haircut.

Figure 20.   Jan's sensuous glamour.

prepared for romantic intimacy, then, as long as it is has a serious
commitment to sanction it and will lead eventually to marriage –
a trusting position which Webster nearly manages to manipulate
to his gain and Carol's ruin.

Besides thus having Carol acknowledge herself as single and
inexperienced verbally, and showing her awakening to desire, the
film also seeks to establish Carol's innocence in one further way
made especially interesting as it speaks directly to Day's star
persona outside the movie's narrative. This is the film's extended

Figure 21. 'Today you are a woman!' Increased allure in *Lover Come Back*.

utilisation of alcohol: the star's own well-known abstention is referenced to underline her character's resistance to drinking. But *Lover Come Back* uses liquor as a plot hook as well as a character indicator at four separate points.

The film begins its employment of the motif in the scene where Carol and 'Linus' stroll, chatting, through an aquarium on their first meeting. Carol confides to 'Linus' that although she loves 'the creative challenge of advertising', the *social* challenge of the job is more bothersome. She explains that in her job she needs to entertain clients, and this means drinking: problematically, she does not drink. Mendacious Webster immediately responds that he doesn't either; the film shows him responding spontaneously to Carol's conversation, ad-libbing responses that he assumes, rightly, will make her like and trust him. But the film has a more practical use for this avoidance of alcohol, besides indicating Webster's resourcefulness and Carol's innocence. Her next confession shows Jerry that there might be salacious utility to be gleaned from the point:

Carol: Oh, it's not that I object to it, it's just that I can't tolerate alcohol. Even one little glass of champagne and I become completely irresponsible. I might do anything!.... As a chemist, you probably understand....

'Linus': Yes...I *might* even be able to do something about it...

Jerry's knowing line creates audience expectation that he will later exploit this weakness to seduce Carol, but when the time comes, the film gives a surprising twist to the scenario: it is Carol who wants to make use of her low resistance to drink. The film plays the key scene, set at her apartment as the two dine alone together, as a reversal of customary roles, the *woman* wanting sex and the *man* demurring. This speaks to the contemporary double standard in its subversion of supposed norms no less than other texts do in their maintenance.

I have written elsewhere (2010a) about this scene, considering both the skilful way in which Jerry plays 'Linus' as a sexually inexperienced man in order to manipulate Carol into seducing him, and about the even more skilful way Day plays the scene, managing to create some sympathy for her character. This is no small achievement; Day demonstrates that Carol hovers, trembling, on the brink of a momentous change in her sexual status, even while the script and narrative extort the usual humour about a woman of her age being timorous over losing her virginity, rather than grateful to get rid of it.

That the Day character in *Lover Come Back* is overtly posited as a virgin is indicated by the climactic sung soliloquy scene which now ensues; definitively confirming her maiden state, Carol asks herself, 'Is this the night Love finally defeats me?'. This conscious avowal of virginity seems unique within Day's oeuvre, and is meant to provoke laughter at its confession and enactment by a woman of her age.

The scene is bracketed by two invocations of the dis-inhibiting power of alcohol: at the end, after her song, she swiftly drinks champagne on her own to gain the courage to prove to 'Linus' he is a real man; at the beginning, however, she seeks to share the bottle with him and perhaps encourage a relaxation of their (supposed) mutual shyness.

I want to examine this early part of the sequence in more detail, as it shows Day's voice and body work in delineating Carol's sexual inexperience. She skilfully achieves this via performing her evident eagerness to end her maiden state. Again, while the dialogue is significant for conveying Carol's emotions and desires at this point, it is what she does not overtly state but *enacts* that really matters, and this is revealed though Day's careful acting choices.

Carol:	You know... um... I have a small bottle of champagne that someone gave me once and... um...I debated whether to open it tonight. But knowing how susceptible we both are...
'Linus':	You were absolutely right.
Carol:	In view of the situation... being here, alone as we are, I think we should be especially...
'Linus':	Definitely.

As she initiates this conversation, Carol and her date have finished their meal and sit facing each other drinking coffee. The framing puts Day on the left of the screen, Hudson on the right, and permits both actors to be seen in full so that every gesture registers. As Carol's dining table is glass, too, it means that her legs are visible and this is important, because Day employs her whole body to express how Carol is feeling. Beginning the conversation above, Carol plays with her linen place setting with her left hand, toying with a coffee spoon with her right, and jiggling her leg under the table. This fidgety behaviour suggests Carol's nervousness, and could perhaps be seen as Day conforming to the performance mode for comic virgins, with her excessive energies, not allowed channelling into sex, bursting out in other spontaneous movements. However, Day's voice work, with its 'ums' and ellipses, works against this performance mode as the star's voice is particularly soft, breathy, and slow throughout the scene, connoting both the intensity of her longing and the seriousness of the step she is longing to take. Her delivery of 'alone as we are' is especially attenuated and husky, as she tries to communicate to 'Linus' her desires without having to state them overtly. Carol hopes that 'Linus' will give up his stuffy behaviour and relax a little; when he refuses her second overture she turns her head away from him, her left hand goes to her lips and chin as she props her elbow on the table in a downcast and pensive pose. The tentative nature of this gesture indicates just how out of ideas Carol is; with 'Linus' seeming to have missed all her cues, she does not know how else she can indicate her desires.

Hudson plays Webster here as very much in control and cruelly enjoying his performance as the shy inexperienced scientist, entirely aware of what lies behind Carol's hesitant talk, and resolutely determined not to give her an excuse to blame alcohol for her decisions. He is all stasis to Day's kinesis; as she jiggles and fiddles, he sits straight-backed and polite, staring at her unmoving as she meets his gaze, then drops her eyes, leans forward confidingly, sits back confounded.

When 'Linus' thanks Carol for a delightful evening, he gives the praise she has longed for; in opining she will 'make some man a very fine wife', he seems to be representing his own views on them forming a committed partnership. Glowing with happiness, she returns the compliment, but is then horrified to hear his next words: 'I'm afraid I can *never* get married'. Hinting darkly at a malady that 'a man doesn't discuss with a nice woman', Jerry proceeds to set his ultimate trap for Carol. He implies that unless his sexual doubts are assuaged he will never be able to commit. By the end of the scene, Jerry is ensconced in the darkened bedroom confident that his manipulations of Carol have brought her to the point of capitulation:

'Linus':   ...am I the kind of man a woman could love?
Carol: Oh, of *course* you are!
'Linus':   But I don't know and it's killing me!
Carol: Linus! Don't do this to yourself! *Any* woman would love you!
'Linus':   If only I could be *sure* of that...

Carol now proceeds to the film's penultimate use of alcohol, as she uncorks and drinks some of the champagne to enable her to face her maidenly sacrifice. Although this is prevented in the nick of time, the film has not finished with the motif of stimulants, and indeed, goes on to prove that Carol's initial fear, that alcohol would cause her to commit some kind of indiscretion, was, ironically accurate. The real Linus Tyler finally perfects a product to sell as VIP, what appears to be a form of candy. On ingestion however it hits the bloodstream as 100 per cent alcohol. Jerry Webster brings a carton to the meeting of the Advertising Council to prove the product exists and he, Carol and all the executives try some. Alas, the real Tyler has not warned Jerry about the real nature of the 'mint', and so all of them over-indulge.

Jerry awakens the next morning sharing a motel room bed with a blonde; the film teases the audience for almost a minute before revealing that he is married to her, and waits another six seconds before confirming it is Carol, who is allowed a moment acknowledging how much she finally welcomed her sacrifice. She acknowledges her own sexual fulfilment, when, dreamily, before completely waking up, she sighs: 'Oh Millie, I had the most wonderful dream! Doctor Tyler and I ....' This assures us that Jerry and Carol will eventually, when all the plot exigencies have worked themselves out, be able to have a relationship which can include fulfilling sexualised play even after marriage. While she may have been overtly posited as a virgin by the film, Carol is at least allowed to be one who rejoices in physical love when it finally comes to her.

The film has to go to extreme plot lengths to arrange the saucy situation which brings Jerry and Carol together in bed, but having done so it fully exploits the potential of this moment; being married to Carol, even if only overnight, marks the occasion when Jerry realises he actually cares for her, and also makes Carol pregnant, ensuring that, although she immediately secures an annulment, she is forced to remarry him at the film's end in order to ensure the legitimacy of their baby, as well as bringing about the requisite happy ending for a romantic comedy.

I have spent some time on the film's sustained employment of the alcohol motif in order to show how it both helps metaphorically to signify, and narratively to remove, Carol's virginity. The film works in many ways to suggest that Carol is a virgin, of which her avoidance of drink is just one; using the fact that she is 'susceptible' to stimulants as an indicator of this specific character trait, however, has a crucial side-effect. By referencing an abstention the star herself was known to maintain, the film strengthens the links between character and player. By associating the star's teetotalism with the character's motives for it, it is possible to read Day herself as shunning drink because it might make her behave in an 'uninhibited' manner which she is too prudish to enjoy. Although Carol's physical intolerance of, but moral neutrality to, alcohol is directly contra to Day's religious-inspired avoidance of stimulants, the fact that both actor and character refuse to drink blurs the line differentiating their motives – and them.

Since *Lover Come Back* relentlessly shows the characters who drink becoming amorous, and those who do not remaining primly (even if reluctantly) chaste, Day is further implicated in Carol's aged maiden status because both abstain from liquor and, one abstinence seeming much like another, there is therefore the suggestion that she refrains from sex too. While this reading requires some work to impute Carol's filmic virginity onto the star, once this is accomplished it becomes easier to view other, earlier, Day characters in the same old-maidish light. With *Pillow Talk*, for example, it becomes less problematic to read Jan as the woman the *Hollywood Reporter* asserted was 'healthy' but chaste; if desired, this view can be supported by a reading of the film's narrative which privileges effects (Jan departs from the weekend cottage without sleeping with 'Rex') rather than their causes (Jan has discovered 'Rex' is actually Brad). Coupling her flight with Jan's earlier attempts to fend off Tony's passes, it is possible to see the character as trying to avoid sex, even though the narrative indicates her motives are romantic rather than neurotic. While it thus requires some effort, reading against the natural grain of the text, to see Jan as a prudish maiden, the sex-aversion being imputed to her connects back smoothly enough to the younger women Day had played earlier on in her career, as well as forward to Carol. While a state of innocence in the former seems natural, and in the latter, comically pathetic, it becomes more pathological when applied to Jan, who outwardly behaves as a hip, urban sophisticate.

I noted above that only one reviewer insisted on reading *Pillow Talk* as the story of a virginal heroine. *Lover Come Back*'s Carol was not similarly misunderstood; the combination of overt hints in narrative and script, and Day's expert playing, ensured that reviewers realized the higher sexual stakes for which the game was played on this outing. Margaret Harford in the *Los Angeles Mirror* characterised the story as one in which Hudson comes up with the non-existent product VIP and 'Day mortgages her wit, sanity and ultimately, her honor, to get it away from him' (Harford, 1961). *The Hollywood Reporter* review summed up the two protagonists in terms which conveyed their oppositional qualities: 'she prudish and prim, he a rake...' (Lipkin, 1961: 3), while *Variety*, seeming aware of how close Carol came to losing not just her dignity but her maidenhead, labelled the film as one in which Day's character 'plays brinkmanship with surrender' ('Gene', 1961: 6).

While all these reviewers recognised the initiatory nature of the sex in the narrative, not all of them found this treated in the most tasteful manner. The most negative comment on this, and its sole disapproving note, came in the *Los Angeles Times* review, and was elicited by the crisis scene set in Carol's apartment:

> Hudson's systematic campaign of conquest of Doris' virtue as well as of VIP is symbolized by a delightful scene at the Aquarium wherein one fish gobbles up another. Less to my taste is a seduction sequence in which Hudson diffidently voices doubts as to his manhood and Miss Day, touched by his predicament, asks herself in song, 'Should I Surrender?' Not to such suggestive scripting, my dear.
>
> (Scheuer, 1961: C13)

This review is the sole one in my sample to fix on this moment as problematic. Does this final line imply that Day is out of place in the sequence, or that it is not the subject-matter so much as the way it is written that is at fault? It is difficult to see whether the accent on the problem here is supposed to be with the 'suggestive' or the 'scripting'. It is fascinating that the reviewer finds the symbolic representation of Carol's engulfment by Jerry 'delightful' but is squeamish when the scene has human actors.

It seems paradoxical, then, that the film which presented Day as a maturely and actively sexual woman, *Pillow Talk*, can also be seen setting the scene for the creation of the virgin myth which utterly opposes her possession of any agency and sensuality. Had *Pillow Talk* not relied for its frisson on sexy skirmishes, from which Jan emerged to her own disappointment unbedded, *Lover Come Back* would not have tried to surpass its successful predecessor by magnifying the threat posed to the heroine, making not only her heart, but her hymen, the overt target. *Lover Come Back* thus inaugurated the mature virgin persona which eventually crystalised as the dominant meaning of the star's persona. As Day went into the most financially profitable periods of her career, with more battle-of-the-sexes comedies lined up for her after *Lover Come Back*, this aged maiden character would prove difficult to banish, so that subsequent roles seemed inevitably – and increasingly pathologically – to inherit aspects of Carol's chastity, even when they were married and with children.

5 *The Doris Day Show* (1968–73)

In the final seven years of her film career, Day made a further 11 films, over half of which conform to the template *Lover Come Back* established. These seven films[34] have a sexually suggestive aspect to their plots, even if, as in five of these, the Day character is married to the lead male and the narratives therefore have to work hard to make sex salacious rather than routine. The anomalous films which avoided this pattern – *Billy Rose's Jumbo*

(1962), *The Glass Bottom Boat* (1966), *Caprice* and *The Ballad of Josie* (both 1967) – attempted to take the Day persona away from the sex comedy and place it instead either in a genre which had worked in the star's earlier career, as in the case of family musical *Jumbo* and comedy western *Josie*, or one which had emerged as a contemporary obsession, as with the cycle of spy movies which became rampant after 1962's *Dr No*. *The Glass Bottom Boat* and *Caprice* both try to tap into the popularity of this spy cycle, the former by combining it with other well-worn Day film elements (widow; song; mistaken identity), the latter by fully committing to the familiar tropes of the new cycle and immersing the star in them, to both her own and the film's detriment. Day's sexual status is not a matter for debate in any of these films, and they did not significantly contribute to – or contradict – the virgin myth that was beginning to grow up around her.

As the Al Capp article from December 1962 illustrated, by that time, the 'Doris Day film' was being perceived as a formula with a set of rules which was very specific, and to Capp and other writers like Macdonald and Simon, very outmoded. In writing about the Day product, these popular culture critics discounted the anomalous films mentioned above to concentrate only on those which placed Day in some form of comic sexual jeopardy. *Lover Come Back* had been followed by another movie which seemed to the scornful Capp merely to swap Cary Grant for Rock Hudson and leave all other aspects of the mating ritual unchanged. This is not accurate, however, since although *That Touch Of Mink* preserves the sexual skirmishes, it varies from the Day–Hudson outings in two main ways. Grant's suave millionaire Philip Shayne never pretends to Cathy Timberlake (Day) that he is interested in her for anything other than a sexual relationship, and never courts her in any but his own persona. There is no masquerade plot and no subterfuge on his part. Cathy thus has to decide whether or not she can accept the position he offers her, that of kept woman, or feels that morality or social custom prevents her. The onus is very much on Day's character to make up her own mind, and she is seen to oscillate between doing what she *wants* and what she thinks she *ought*.

While Cathy tries to work out what to do, the film provides her with a more experienced best friend Connie (Audrey Meadows), who expresses the same kind of cynicism towards men that Georgia Garrett evinced back in 1948. The progress – backwards – that Day's film characters have made can be clearly measured by comparing Georgia's relaxed and cheerful attitude towards sex and men, to Cathy's agonised indecision about whether she is conforming to necessary or outmoded mores if she turns down Shayne's offers. Connie, the expert on men, advises against taking the irrevocable step, but her opinion is motivated by mercenary considerations. She urges Cathy to resist, because she believes acquiescence would damage Cathy's ultimate bargaining power, which seems to suggest a woman should dangle the bait of her virginity until the man is so hooked he cannot but marry her. Sacrificing virginity for anything less than marriage would be defeat.

But is Cathy Timberlake a virgin? There is no definitive word on her sexual innocence, as there is in *Lover Come Back*, although it might be imagined that Cathy would not agonise so much over a trip away with Shayne if she had already given up her virginity. Philip Shayne's assistant, Roger (Gig Young, playing the type of second-fiddle role that Tony Randall perfected in the Day–Hudson trilogy) opines that Cathy has 'Something about her: purity, innocence, honour . . . ' but this is the closest that the film comes to an overt statement on her sexual status.

Connie, advising her against the giving out of free samples, asserts that such permissive behaviour does not fit with Cathy's personality – 'You are the husband, four children and a cottage type, this isn't you' – and helps her scheme instead to trap the millionaire into marriage. Presumably she thinks that while the modern young woman who acknowledges and acts on her own sexual desires 'isn't you', Cathy *is* the type of woman to which mid-century American popular culture texts constantly refer, in the person of the manipulative maiden. Although Cathy hesitates at pretending to be seduced by another man, in order to make Philip jealous, Connie delivers her ultimate advice when she warns: 'You have now arrived at the crossroads that every woman eventually arrives at: you can either be an honest old maid or a happy liar.' This pronouncement seems to suggest further workings of the female conspiracy to manipulate men into marriage. *All* women, Connie's words imply, either lie to get married, or stay single, and the opposition set up by 'honest'/ 'liar' similarly sets up 'happy' and 'old maid' as dichotomous to disparage those who might be tempted to choose veracity over conjugality.

Day's next four films all saw her characters married but persisted in maintaining the emphasis on sex postponed, avoided or evaded. In this, they all hark back to the template established by *Please Don't Eat The Daisies*, in which a sexual relationship is something that the married couple used to have but is not something they are enjoying anymore. The plots of all these films revive the threat of adultery which was the invention of the film version of *Daisies*. With Day's character married to her leading man, each film's impetus becomes her blocking of his illicit sex with *other* women. Although post-virginal, Day still tries in these narratives to prevent sexual activity, even if her own activity is both licit and desired. For example, in *Move Over, Darling*, the risk of the Day character's husband having sex with another woman is the motor which drives the film, although here the plot is complicated by the fact that he is legally married to the new woman via strained plot exigencies. *Send Me No Flowers*,

Day's final film with Rock Hudson, underlines the emphasis on the growing pathology of Day's characters by removing any plot necessity for Day's heroine, Judy Kimball, to block intercourse: her husband is not interested in any woman but her, but although married they are somehow still not having sex. *Flowers* is a very odd film; the narrative manoeuvres hypochondriac George into mistakenly believing he has not long to live, whereupon he determines to find his widow-to-be another man before he dies so that she is not lonely. Judy misreads his attempts at introducing her to new men as an attempt to distract her from an affair *he* must be having. The crucial scene comes when Judy fakes desire and propositions her husband. Day employs a repertoire of facial movements which centre around eye and mouth work; she droops her eyes to suggest a relaxed, sensuous state, while her lips alternately broaden in a smile or pout slightly as if yearning to be kissed[35]. Suddenly George's illnesses and aches vanish: he becomes active and energetic again as long as he believes sex is on offer. This incident seems to posit that lack of intercourse is the cause of George's imagined maladies, and imputes this lack to Judy.

In the films before this one, a certain perspective on the narratives and on Day's characters within them can be adduced to support the charge against of her of sex aversion, if effects rather than their causes are privileged. This was true of the reading of Jan in *Pillow Talk*, which, as seen, sustained her as a sex-shy virgin when prizing action (Jan runs away from Brad) over motive (Jan discovers Brad's deception). With the adultery-themed films, Day's characters and thus Day herself can similarly be viewed as preventing sex (effects) even though it is generally because the relations would be within extra-marital relationships (causes). This reading obtains for the 1965 film *Do Not Disturb*, which also features supposedly suspect but actually innocent bed-hopping, but falls to pieces with the final film with Hudson.

Day seems in *Flowers* finally to have become the manipulative wife into which it was always feared the 'conniving maiden' character of mid-century films would evolve. Tasked by society with controlling her husband's sexuality, Judy Kimball keeps such a tight rein on his impulses that he has to find relief in psychosomatic illness. This is very similar to the release Day's character Kit finds in hysteria in *Midnight Lace*, where her virginal longings receive their only physical outlet in the catharsis following her fits of screaming and crying.

By 1965, the mature sexuality intended to be evident in Jan had therefore become so increasingly accreted with pathologies that the woman who had played her now had 'problematic sexuality' as one of her dominant connotations. The 'Doris Day sex comedy' meant a certain kind of film, in which the star would remain chaste though chased; despite her married status in this run of movies, reviews persisted in viewing the narratives and the star in the same framework, so that *Life* magazine's headline for *The Thrill Of It All* labelled the star 'That wolf-chased Day girl' (Anon, 1963 c: 105), even though the narrative shows Day's character being pursued only by her husband.

Day's final film vehicles did nothing to dispel this myth; the last one, labouring under the unwieldy title, *With Six You Get Egg Roll*, had as its alternative title the equally lumbering *A Man In Mommy's Bed* (McGee, 158), which illustrates the insistence on prurience in the later movies. Day has complained in her co-written biography (208) that she despised many of the plots for her later films but found her manager-husband had committed her to them, and this could explain the relentless milking of the suggestive narrative against the interests of the star. Certainly the penultimate film revisits many of the elements that had by this point come to signify the Day movie product. *Where Were You When The Lights Went Out?* is set at the time of the famous 1965 electricity failure in New York City, revolving around the sexual hi-jinks motivated and excused by the blackout. The film has the same adultery subplot of earlier films, although even less palatably, Margaret's husband actually *has* had an affair. Thanks to various machinations, when the lights come back on, Margaret assumes – wrongly of course – that she too has besmirched her marriage vows and thus feels too guilty to seek redress. In the film's coda Margaret, precisely nine months after the blackout, is taken to hospital in the final stages of labour. While the film has shown that no sexual activity took place, it denies this by making its heroine pregnant in the final reel, just as she was in *Lover Come Back*, the first film to establish the 40-year-old-virgin persona openly. In seven years, then, Day's persona had not moved on but instead crystalised, so that what was a one-film joke had become the *only* joke the star seemed to mobilise – and it was at her own expense.

I have dealt with the final films Day made at such length here because the persona evolving during this period seems to have been taken directly into her television series. By this point Day seemed to be accepted as a comedienne whose energy and attractiveness was – *given her age* – quite remarkable[36]. More negatively, her association with being post-, pre-, a- or somehow anti-sexual was entrenched and seemingly unconquerable. Although popular culture was inevitably moving on, the 60s beginning to be recognised as Swinging, Day's later films showed her in situations where she was still struggling to close down sexual opportunities, whether they were hers or those of the many men around her. When Melcher died suddenly in April 1968, the star had been committed to a television show which again rolled out the safely-attractive yet sexually-inactive persona, with her character envisaged as a widow with two young sons. As a widow, the character's sexuality is something safely contained, both by having been within marriage and by now being in the past.

Significantly, it was when Day herself took on producing duties for the show that 'Doris Martin' moved to having a career in the city, rather than just adventures on the farm, and thence by incremental stages to shedding the domestic aspects of her character.

Nevertheless, Day could not single-handedly alter the public perception of who her persona was and what it meant. As was seen in *Mad's* spoof of *The Doris Day Show,* elements from her film career inevitably impacted on the television character; these include the insistence that 'Doris' is constantly being hunted by male-wolves, yet inevitably shuns their attentions since she is 'not that kind of a girl'. Both these factors were in place in *That Touch Of Mink*[37] yet were also regularly used for comic mileage in the television show a decade later. If Doris had been imaginable as *that* kind of a girl in 1948 – as Georgia Garrett certainly seemed to be – why was it so impossible to imagine her that way nearly a quarter of a century later? It is not entirely accurate, however, to insist as the *Mad* article does, that Doris rejects physical contact, and it is never suggested in the show that she withholds her charms until the price is right. Although she is regularly pursued throughout all the seasons of the show, from season 3 onwards she is actively interested in various men, and her dating life increases in intensity and passion as the series go on. Given *Mad's* emphasis in its parody on this trope in the show, it is one to which I will return in a moment. However, the show emphasises not only that men find Doris Martin irresistible but also refers to so many other elements directly taken from Day's past that it is possible to view this trope as just one in a series of meta-critical references, a self-referential quality so marked that it seems the show's dominant characteristic. Many of the episodes across the entire run incorporate publicly-known facets either of Day's own 'real life' or elements from her films, or both.

For example, the episode 'Forward Pass' (S3)[38] not only includes the 'irresistible Doris' motif but also plays knowingly with Day's celebrated enthusiasm for sport, especially basketball and baseball (and, as endlessly rumoured in the press, for baseball players). Audiences in the know could be thus expected to appreciate the humour in hearing Doris Martin announce 'I don't care for football', this being the only sport she was not known to support. A further, but unlinked, reference is that the football player's bachelor pad is an echo of the push-button version possessed by Brad Allen in *Pillow Talk*. Here instead of a couch that turns into a bed while seductive music plays, the couch *itself* plays music whenever anyone sits on it.

Throughout the show its music references Day's career as a singer, as the background tunes, played in restaurants, discos, or bachelor lairs, are instrumental versions of the star's own hit songs[39]. The episode 'Doris, the Model' (S2) includes, in its fashion show sequence, tracks which cover the span of her vocal career; even an instrumental of the *Pillow Talk* theme is used, when Doris models the final outfit. 'Summer Is Gone' from her 1965 album *Latin For Lovers* features in several episodes from S2 and S3. Besides the incidental music, *every* episode of the show reminded listeners of Day's previous film and singing career, since the show's theme tune featured an up-tempo version of 'Que Sera Sera', the Oscar-winning tune she had first sung in 1956's *The Man Who Knew Too Much*, reprised twice in subsequent films, and which had assumed the status of her unofficial theme song, before the television show literalised this.

The 'Cover Girl' episode (S4) acts as a further demonstration of how elements of her past careers could be combined in a single episode. Here an instrumental version of Day's song 'Summer Is Gone', is used again, while the split-screen from *Pillow Talk* is utilised when Doris Martin is on the telephone. The episode thus borrows references to the star's music and film careers before the TV show, but this borrowing is done here and throughout the show's run in a manner that reinforces her personal importance; there is no intended reference to the end of a romance, which the song hints at, or a developing one, as the film presents. The movie and the album are not being referenced for *themselves* so much as for their common factor, Doris Day.

This method of underlining the importance of the star rather than any specific film or music vehicle continues with the show's habit of casting, generally in small roles, but occasionally as series regulars, actors who had been in her films. Thus John Gavin who had appeared beside Day in *Midnight Lace* turns up in 'Skiing, Anyone?' (S3), Mary Wickes, Stella the maid in *On Moonlight Bay* and its follow-up, features in 'The Buddy' (S1), Billy de Wolfe, who had made two films with Day (*Tea For Two* and *Lullaby Of Broadway*) was cast as series regular Mr Jarvis for 12 appearances from S2 to S5, and Patrick O'Neal enjoyed a three-episode arc as Doris Martin's regular beau Jonathan Rusk (S5) having previously played her cheating husband in *Where Were You When The Lights Went Out?* Even bit-parter Barbara Nichols, Poopsie in *Pajama Game*, gets a similarly small role as a criminal's wife ('Have I Got A Fellow For You?', S4) and the Martin family's dog in early episodes is the same one Day worked with in *Please Don't Eat The Daisies* and *The Glass Bottom Boat*. Although it is unlikely that any but the most eagle-eyed viewer would have spotted *all* these returning players, the frequency with which former colleagues were employed still serves as another method of highlighting Day's former film career.

Another trope associated with Day during her film years, 'Clothes', was also persistently revisited in the show. Much press attention was garnered by the film's costumes, often deemed too lavish to be afforded by a secretary/staff writer – as *Mad*'s parody indicates – despite the credit to Magnin's department store at the end of episodes. Day and her team insisted in interviews

(Archerd, 1972: 8; Haber, 1970) that the outfits Doris Martin wore represented affordable glamour, and the series itself seems quite thrifty in reusing garments across different episodes. 'Doris, the Model' provided an opportunity for the star to display on the catwalk many items which then appeared in later episodes, including a blue floor-length coat which reoccurs in 'Col. Fairburn Takes Over' (S2) and a trouser suit and Tyrolean hat sported again in 'The Feminist' (S3). Although as the fan magazine analysis indicated, clothes were associated with Day throughout her career, after *Pillow Talk* they took on a particular resonance celebrating the star as one of the best dressed in Hollywood. This was a radical departure from the earlier press which used the clothes trope to underline Day's relaxed and natural personality; whereas articles then note the absence of evening wear from her wardrobe and her preference for casual clothing, later press pieces after 1959 worked to establish the opposite, and to posit the star as enjoying formal wear. By 1962 one magazine could trumpet that Day and Audrey Hepburn were 'the only Hollywood stars who shine in the world of fashion' (Ritter, 1962: cover and 12).

The sophisticated outfits were highlighted as being one of the aspects of the show likely to give members of the audience pleasure; Day is quoted in a newspaper account of the series changes around S4 that '[now it is] more like one of my movies and I get to wear the kinds of clothes that the viewers like to see' (Laurent, 1971). Although the costume is thus cited as a reason for Doris Martin to leave behind the farm and family and move into the city and single-girl life, there is a lot of play about her clothes *before* she makes this move too. For example, the first episode of S2 where Martin lives on the farm but works in San Francisco, devotes much comedy to the character's search for the perfect outfit for her job-seeking.

Although there are many fascinating aspects of *The Doris Day Show* which reference the star's previous career in various ways, I want to return to the 'irresistible-Doris' motif which *Mad* noticed, as the programme's preoccupation with confronting the star with desirous men and observing her reactions most connects with the pervasive 40-year-old-virgin stereotype that is this book's focus.

While it might seem that the series' change of location, for both character and comedy, from farm to office, might be rooted in the belief that the latter locale would permit more opportunities for the star again being 'that wolf-chased Day girl' (Anon, 1963 c: 105), even before Doris Martin's transformation into a career woman, the show has recourse to the battle of the sexes for its laughs.

At least four of the episodes from the first season provide the woman with a romantic prospect; despite the fact that early press for the show insisted there would be 'No Dates For Doris' (Manners, 1968: 13), analysis of the episodes demonstrates a willingness to revisit the movies' terrain of romantic and comic misapprehensions.

'The Fly Boy' is particularly interesting in this respect since it makes Doris Martin the target of male seductive intent, as in the Day–Hudson films, and also reveals the man – an air force colonel – callously making bets with his fellow officers about 'succeeding' with her. Interestingly, he keeps his language metaphorical: he bets he can thaw 'the iceberg', reducing 'it' to 'a puddle of warm water' and ensuring it is thoroughly 'defrosted'. It is therefore unclear whether he needs to kiss Doris to win his bet, or actually bed her, and this is never made explicit by the show, which prefers to maintain a nebulousness about what his callousness constitutes. Significantly, in the early scenes set on the farm, Doris sees through the colonel's 'pitch' about having grown up in the country, but still accepts his invitations, making him lunch and agreeing to go out with him to a dance. Buck is shown to be taken aback by her willingness to associate with a man who she knows is handing her a line, but the narrative clearly shows she has her own motives, sexual or at least romantic ones. Day enacts Doris's amorous interest in the man: she smiles both openly and more seductively at him during their early conversations; when she realises he is exaggerating his farm experience she permits herself the familiar eye roll at his lines, but maintains her pleasant demeanour. On his return the next day, she has dressed carefully and is especially hospitable. Doris Martin is clearly interested in the man, therefore.

When she learns from her father that her yielding – to whatever degree – has been made the subject of wagers, Doris's response is not to cancel the date but to teach the colonel a lesson. This is reminiscent of the scene in *Lover Come Back* after Carol has discovered that 'Linus' is actually Jerry Webster, but manages to control her anger and revulsion for his subterfuge

Figure 22. Doris Martin's knock-out dress.

long enough to attain a form of revenge. Here the Day character uses her own seductive wiles to get back at the man, similarly pretending to be more compliant than she is. Doris turns up at the dance in a skin-tight gown of brown sequins and marabou, drawing all gazes as she appears to be ready for seduction (Figure 22). Doris dances sensuously with the man (to another of her own tunes as background music[40]), purrs his name, licks the edge of her martini glass and generally behaves in a manner which seems to signal her imminent yielding. However, just when the man thinks he is about to claim his prize, she drops her tipsy seductive act and reveals that she has been pretending all evening, and is far from 'defrosted. I can be, Andy – only *when* I choose and with *whom* I choose.'

Doris Martin here seems to be asserting her rights to having and enjoying a sexual relationship, which is in keeping with contemporary thoughts about women's sexuality but not with the public perception of Day's persona. It must also be admitted that this progressive version of Doris Martin is not maintained throughout the series. It does not wane with time, however, but oscillates strangely across seasons and even within specific episodes, as the character moves from active to passive, from prudish to seductive. Mrs Martin cannot be posited as an actual virgin because she has two very evident children in the first three series; nonetheless, she is oddly shy at times, demurring from going to a man's apartment, for example, to pick up copy for the magazine ('The Woman Hater', S3) but completely happy to be eyed up, picked up and taken out to dinner by a complete stranger ('The Feminist', S3). In 'The Health King' (S2) she is both coy about visiting the man at the start, and then by the end of the episode, completely comfortable to be sitting in his bachelor lair late at night, with a drink, by a cosy fire while wearing only his bath robe. If Doris's virtue is in trouble, it is a trouble she is not trying to avoid, given her relaxed posture and gestures.

The show's presentation of Doris Martin is then strangely fluid, nebulous; at times she seems on very formal terms with 'Mr Nicholson' (McClean Stevenson), her boss at *Today's World,* and at others flirty and playful with him. She is constantly used as bait by her male employers to obtain interviews, and sometimes acquiesces in this, but often objects. The camera, as well as the narratives, often objectifies her also, not just when she parades in elegant outfits for a fashion show, but when she bends down in a tight skirt and the camera, and her male co-star, openly ogle her behind (ironically most overtly in 'The Feminist'). While she is consistently – even relentlessly – presented as an *object* of desire for others, however, Doris Martin is not uniformly permitted to evince desire as a *subject.*

Close analysis of two episodes, both from S3, reveals that, when it comes to her character's attitude to engaging with men, Day can perform both reluctance and enthusiasm with equal skill and with equally comic effect. Building on the foundations of the 'old maid' persona that was now habitually associated with her, however, the reluctance seems to have had more resonance with her existing image, even though her 'desirous Doris' enactments are just as entertaining and, as this study has endeavoured to demonstrate, have just as established a history in her previous roles.

As mentioned, 'Forward Pass' is an episode which exploits the star's own celebrated sports mania and *Pillow Talk's* split-screen technology. It also presents a useful exemplar of Day's enactment of sex-aversion, which could be read as signifying the character and the star's own attitude to matters sensual if this pose were not so readily and frequently thrown off and replaced with its opposite. In the episode, a male work colleague uses Day as bait to get an interview with well-known womanising football player Joe Garrison (Dick Gautier), despite her initial disinclination to see a football game and later dislike of the player himself.

Garrison is shown to be a complete Lothario, keeping at bay many different young women who all desire him as soon as he meets Doris Martin, whose coolness he mistakes for a fitting challenge. This scenario, in which the handsome man prefers the older unwilling Day character to a myriad of younger keen ones, was one noticed and lampooned by Al Capp in his *Show* article, where he observed the recurrent Day movie trope of the attractive bachelor preferring the old maid to the 'love-maddened nineteen year old debutantes' (1962: 72). Convinced that he can win her round, Garrison engineers a situation where Doris has to come to his apartment; when Doris arrives the football player seems entirely prepared to wrest from her what he wants if she will not give it to him willingly. Day enacts her character's dismay at being propositioned initially through a performed stiffness of deportment; she crosses her arms in front of her body defensively while standing, and keeps her handbag strategically in her lap when made to sit. Hauled physically from a straight-backed chair to the (musical) couch, Day manages to maintain her sitting position despite being dragged across the floor, a piece of business that indicates her unease while also being funny. In this part of the scene Doris displays a rectitude of spine that tries to be distancing, and which normal men would read as a warning signal. Garrison is shown to be abnormal, however, in his willingness to take his prey's open rejections as enticement. Doris allows her dislike of Garrison to show facially through eye rolling, sarcastic smiles and slowed down gestures, indicating disbelief at the man's lies. When he actively begins to chase her around his apartment, this slowness and the former stiffness changes to a much more loose slapstick register of speedy, panicky gestures, making 'Ooh!' noises and squeaks of disbelief.

Again, if a reading is utilised which privileges effects over causes, the character played by Day can be read as shunning sex. However, it is not for gain, as *Mad* magazine would suggest, nor from prudery; if motivation can be allowed to count, Doris's actions are consonant with her message to the air force colonel in the 'Fly Boy' episode – that she can happily indulge in sex, but when and with whom she chooses.

Doris Martin demonstrates enthusiastic appreciation for the appearances of many men across the full run of the *Show*, often recounting to a friend or boss the reasons she finds one so attractive[41]. She demonstrates most spectacularly, however, her reaction to Henry Fonda in 'Doris Goes To Hollywood' (S3), an episode of vertiginous self-referentialism in which Doris Day plays Doris Martin winning a Doris Day lookalike competition. This episode is interesting for many reasons, but the performance of Doris's reaction – both physical and vocal – to seeing Henry Fonda is particularly noteworthy in the context of performances of desire. Day had enacted delight at seeing a man before, when first introduced to the Cary Grant character in *That Touch Of Mink*. In 'Doris Goes To Hollywood', however, her reaction to star Henry Fonda is demonstrably more physical, especially since Doris Martin's first response is evoked merely by the sight of the man's name plate on his car parking space. Doris does a double take when she sees the sign, then clutches her stomach and moans excitedly, before rushing over to the spot. She gives another moan with a little physical jiggle, and then tells girlfriend Myrna how wonderful Fonda is: 'Talk about *distinguished*, and *manly*, and *mature*. And so *handsome!*' During this recitation of his fine qualities, Doris can be heard panting, her heavy breathing accompanied by extreme eye rolling over the word 'handsome' (Figure 23). Fonda clearly has a physical effect on the woman, even in absentia. When she actually encounters the man himself and not just his name, Doris's reaction is just as extreme. She sees him, double-takes, narrows her eyes to make sure and then whispers in a high-pitched, excited tone to Myrna that 'It's him!'. When Fonda

Figure 23. The mere idea of Henry Fonda arouses Doris Martin.

assumes Martin is Day, he greets her and she smiles back at him sheepishly. Fonda is called back to the set and Doris follows him, seemingly unable to let him escape, before collapsing into Myrna's arms as she realises she just encountered Fonda. Her eyes bug, bulge and roll, she covers her mouth excitedly when recalling that he talked to her and seems to decide spontaneously that she has to follow the man, before running off to see if she can catch him.

While it is a comic performance then, there seems no doubt that it is one of sexual desire and arousal. Doris merely has to see Fonda's name to become physically hyperactive, her body jiggling and her breathing deepening in excitement. Seeing the man himself results in an equally excessive display of frankly sexual yearning, accompanied by giddy disbelief that the star called to her.

Although it is true, then, that Day continues at times in her show to enact reluctance to engage with men, this is actually only when not attracted to them, as she seems, from the first series onwards, to be entirely comfortable flirting, kissing and making clear her desires as long as she likes the man. Press responses to the show indicate the prevalent belief that it put Day back in the comedy role of pursued virgin; *Variety* was especially scathing with its review of the premiere of the fifth and final series:

> This premiere show was a hark-back to those days when Miss Day labored in the Hollywood vineyards with Rock Hudson. There was in the show the veiled implication that Lawford might be bedding the liberated Miss Day [...]. It is indicative of the febrile plotting that Miss Day's ambiguous virginity looms important at all in these times.
>
> (Anon, 1972: 34)

The review fixes on 'Miss Day's ambiguous virginity', but actually the ambiguity lies in the reviewer's own response to the show; seeing Doris Martin as 'liberated' but also a virgin, the review seems confused over its own reaction to the series, and whether it is sneering at the implication of chastity maintained in such a mature woman, or anxious over the fact it is not maintained at all. As analysed, Day does not consistently play Doris Martin as a mature virgin; her enactment of desire and enjoyment of kisses and embraces from her vast variety of partners means that a virginal reading of her has to work hard to ignore the suggestions to the contrary.

While, then, the *Mad* magazine spoof could attempt to score points by suggesting Day must be an extreme narcissist, insisting every man in the show must fall in love with her character, when analysed alongside other recurrent elements of the series, the 'irresistible-Doris' motif seems more like a further meta-textual reference, one which works to gesture back to Day's past history of films and songs. Given that it occurs in nearly every episode, the motif seems to exist in the show to mock the inevitability of the heterosexual coupling in romantic comedy films and love songs, rather than to play up the star's maintained glamour and attractiveness.

What is so interesting and so noticeable about the constant quotations in the series of other Day films, songs, factoids, is that they are evoked not for what they might mean themselves but only because they point back to publicly-known elements of the Day persona. In several episodes, for example, Doris Martin is taken to a restaurant by a date or client, and much byplay is made of the huge order she makes or her insatiable appetite for sweet things (see 'The Woman Hater' and 'Forward Pass'). Her appetite is not however referenced for any narrative reason, her sweet tooth does not impact on the story: they are just aspects concerning the star that are included *because* they concern the star. Quotations from songs, films and life facts therefore find inclusion in the show not for what they can contribute to the plot per se but because they constitute 'Dorisness'. In this way the television series seems to act as a form of weekly helping of Doris lore, in a very similar manner to the mode of the star's frequent presentation in the film fan magazines studied earlier, which rehashed information on Day when it had no new items, just in order to keep her in the public eye. It is easy to see why *Mad* felt her show needed to be parodied; the one vital factor which qualifies the star for this is that she be perceived as part of the popular culture. With weekly reminders of her position in the zeitgeist serving to provide regular rehearsals of her various meanings, Day was assured topical currency, even if for reasons that dismayed her. While she struggled to include narrative opportunities for her character to evince desire, the show's equal emphasis on her shunning unwelcome male attention derived comedy mileage from the perpetuation of the aged maiden persona.

And it was this persona that the series seemed to perpetuate, despite press awareness of the various attempts to keep the series current through format changes. A brief look at the *Los Angeles Times*' reactions to the different seasons indicates the key aspects of the show focused on by reviewers and makers alike. Before the show was launched, and while Melcher was still alive and in charge of production, the newspaper interviewed him and learned his feeling that the show would maintain the sense of integrity represented by the star: 'she will still stand for morality. Everything will be wholesome, as it is in her movies' (Humphrey, 1968: D17). The reviewer notes that 'Melcher doesn't count all of those risqué and double-entendre situations Doris usually finds herself involved in with Rock Hudson and others,' and concludes the preview of the show by opining it sounds 'too darned wholesome – even for Doris Day' (Humphrey, 1968: D17).

By July 1969, Doris Day was commenting on the changing aspects of the show, as the series encompassed her change from farmer's daughter to secretary. Making the alterations seem called for by fans, Day highlights the net result of the evolution will be better outfits and more men: 'people complained I never wore pretty clothes and had no romance in my life' (Smith, 1969: C21). Commenting on these changes from the other end of the series run, another reviewer cites an agent on the lack of fit between Day and the farm scenario; he insists 'She's actually a big city girl, not a country girl. That's what she played in the movies that did so well' (Haber, 1970: V21). Although focusing on the locale of the action here, the review seems to acknowledge that it is the sexy skirmishes enjoyed by Day's career women in the big city which were both the most noticeable aspect of later films and the one copied for the show. The 'adult comedy' angle was noticed by the paper when the series attempted its final revamp, but highlighting that 'romance [was] to be added' (Henniger, 1971) overlooks how prevalent this had actually been as a theme since the very first season, even if it perhaps tries to gesture towards the more liberated persona Day was portraying.

Altogether, press response to the show throughout its run seemed to be that, in it, Day kept on playing 'those virginal sexy roles' (Mackin, 1971); sadly, the seeming paradox enshrined in this oxymoron does not seem to have alerted contemporary or subsequent critics to the fact that Day continued to perform desirous female characters, as she had in her film roles. By the end of her regular television series it seemed as if nothing could rupture the presumption of her maiden state, whether maintained for gain or by fear.

6 Performance Analysis – Conclusion

This section of the book has had as its main labour the task of putting Day herself back in the centre of the frame. Since the previous portion had shown what an immense impact the film fan magazine and other press had on the presentation of Day's star persona, it was important to look at what the star herself contributed as an actor and performer to the ways in which she could be perceived. Because it has become habitual since the early 1960s for Day to stand for a negative type of female sexuality which included, to various degrees, elements of the prudish, coy, manipulative and pathological, examining whether she contributed to this viewpoint by consciously setting out to perform such a sexuality was an essential task. Four specific performances were closely examined for signs of how Day worked to build her characters and establish their sexual statuses. In addition to these four texts, the films between these key points were briefly explored to see how more gradual changes developed the star's image, as elements were added and sloughed off over time.

In each of the four works closely examined in this section, Day makes the performance of her character's sexual status part of what she is conveying through her voice and body work; sexual inexperience or knowledge is a one facet within the whole portrayal of the character she is building. The significance given to sexual status varies from text to text, attaining most importance in *Lover Come Back*, but even there still only acting as a part of Carol's overall personality, not as its only aspect. Analysing how the actor's labour helped to create characters in this section has helped regain some sense of Day's own agency, even if, as has been shown, the dominant meanings that have accrued about her over time are ones which she manifestly was not setting out to initiate. Day's performances as analysed above show her – *for the most part* – acting the role of a fully desirous woman, even if not always an experienced one, yet she was received from early 1960 onwards as perpetually playing the opposite part. This divergence, this contradiction, between what she herself performed and how those performances were perceived, illustrates the might of external media in creating lasting perceptions of players, and thoroughly underlines the importance of historical context, since *when* Day was being assumed to play the virgin was the vital contributory factor to *why*.

The Day character in *Romance On The High Seas*, Georgia Garrett, is not a virgin but a worldly-wise young woman who knows what she wants, and is relaxed and confident enough to try for it. Although her sexual status is not foregrounded, or at issue in this, her first screen role, Georgia is performed by Day with sufficient sass and self-assurance to be post-virginal. There is never a moment where she seem to experience anxiety over the morality of consummating her desires with the man she wants, only over the method of attaining this when he seems so subject to troublesome principles. At the other end of Day's career, her performances as Doris Martin across the five seasons of *The Doris Day Show* see the star evincing similar sexual desire, although the blue-collar brashness and street-wise sass of Georgia have long been smoothed away. Day imbues the part of Doris Martin with a sexual confidence which is increasingly foregrounded as the series develops and the format changes to take her from the farm to the big city, but even in the first season she experiences desire. As the show evolves, Day has more and more opportunities to show her character reacting to and flirting with a large number of men, as well as avoiding the over-zealous attentions of many others whom she clearly does not consider desirable. And as she makes clear in 'The Fly Boy' episode, she can yield, she can 'be defrosted', when she wants to and when she has the right, both sexually attractive and properly respectful, partner. This is not a departure from the sexualised career woman Day played in *Pillow Talk*; there her reluctance to have sex is caused solely because of the Hudson character's mendacity, rather than any lack of desire. In 'The Fly Boy' too, and in other subsequent episodes of her television show, Doris Martin indicates that she will enter into a sexualised liaison outside or before marriage, but only when the man is attractive to her, honest enough to court her in his own person, and realises that sex will be set within a proper relationship. Day enacts Martin's desire through careful use of her voice and body, which persuasively suggests her sexual yearnings even while keeping within the comic mode of the show.

There is a significant paradox central to the understanding of Day's star persona contained within the other two performances analysed here, Day's turn as Ruth Etting in *Love Me Or Leave Me* and her overt portrayal of the virginal old maid, Carol, in *Lover Come Back*, even though both parts are skilfully played by the actor. The former looks sexually alluring and available, but the performance Day gives is as a cold calculator, carefully withholding intimacies while insinuating they will soon be granted. The latter works the paradox the opposite way, with the character looking virginal but being desirous, inexperienced but eager for physical love. Reduced to the baldest formula, Ruth looks hot but is *cold*; Carol looks cold but is *hot*. Yet the 40-year-old-virgin myth was created by the second role, where Day clearly performs the longing for sexual congress, and not by the first, despite the actor there most evidently enacting the 1950s stereotype of the manipulative maiden.

Day's performances in both can therefore be seen to be out of step with the readings contemporaneously imposed on them, not because her acting is unskilful or ineffectual in those roles but rather because their opposing contexts were so overwhelmingly set up to read her in the modes they did. The Ruth Etting role was hailed from the first as marking a complete alteration from those usually assayed by the actor, specifically because of its increased sexuality; but, as has been shown, an earlier role like that of 1948's Georgia Garrett was entirely consonant with the overt sexualisation being posited as innovative in 1955. With the media-milieu positing Day as newly playing a torrid role, her acting choices which actually present Ruth conforming to the wily maiden motif of mid-century went unnoticed.

As such a contemporaneous obsession with the uninitiated female was set raging by Kinsey's second 'Report', when Day eventually played an overt virgin in 1961's *Lover Came Back*, the character was inevitably given more significance than she might otherwise have possessed, as she chimed so well with topical interests in the inexperienced maiden. In the prevailing cross-media environment of mingled excitement and anxiety created by the unmarried woman who was tempted and *might* succumb, the character of Carol, expertly played by Day, suddenly crystallised as the dominant version of the star's persona, ensuring this role became the lens through which others were read, even when the actor later played wives, mothers, sexually mature widows.

Carol's personal inexperience, along with her principled stand against using sexual bribery at work, clearly echoed characteristics evinced in earlier Day roles: those possessed by her range of women like Georgia, Judy, Martha, Calam, Babe Williams and Erica Stone, all plucky, independent, self-reliant women, even if also starting out their movies as yet untouched by an *important* love affair. Instead of reading Carol positively in the light of these positive characterisations, however, she is reduced to her naivety which resonates not with other movie heroines played by Day but with connotations within the star's *own*, largely media-created, persona. The accent was thus placed on a misplaced 'Energy' mocked by the film as a maidenly zeal, on her pristine, twinkling prettiness and spotless apartment which seem to reaffirm the 'Clean' motif, shading into the 'Pathology' trope. Day's own 'Age' combines with her character's explicit virgin condition to create a character wholly designed to be mocked.

Despite the overwhelmingly potent context of the media's virgin frenzy, which easily read lack of sexual experience in Carol and then forced the same onto other Day characters too, in creating her *Lover Come Back* heroine the actor was not using the same tactics as the other, younger, women employed to make their sexual status visible in movies in the 'virginity dilemma' cycle. Other contemporary actors such as Shirley MacLaine, Jane Fonda, Carole Lynley and Natalie Wood were enacting sexual innocence using a performance rubric which aligned comedy with kinesis and virginity maintained, melodrama with stasis and innocence lost (Jeffers McDonald, 2006a). Day by contrast presents Carol's inexperience through performing the character's overwhelming desire to *lose* that inexperience, through a skilful enactment of desire, rather than by the options of knockabout slapstick style or contrasting tense stillness.

As analysed above, the sequence where the amorous Carol attempts to encourage 'Linus' to seduce her, or at least allow her to seduce him, features Day performing her character's nervousness through fidgety movements, but crucially here the comic excess of energy is the conscious method by which the character seeks to control her anxieties. The clumsy mugging of comic virgins such as Meg in *Ask Any Girl* (1959), Eileen in *Sunday In New York* (1962), Robin in *Under The Yum Yum Tree* (1963) or Helen in *Sex And The Single Girl* (1964)[42] by contrast is innate to them and outside of their control, the inevitable consequence of their maiden state and dangerous unmarried desires.

The implications these two key roles in particular had for the evolution of Day's persona highlight the importance of going back to the original film texts and analysing the voice and body work of the performer anew, in order to see what the actor is actually achieving, rather than relying on vague memories of roles enacted or other authors' accounts. After the role of Carol, the die seems cast and the figure of the aged maiden inevitably affixed to Day, no matter how married, or swinging, or salacious later roles were. Day became gradually more associated with and implicated in perpetuating the safely-sexy content of her works; beginning with the intellectual writers around 1960, the movement to blame Day for the perceived cloying coyness of her characters and outmoded, hypocritical portrayals of sexual mores gathered momentum, with the fan magazines catching on to this by mid-decade.

Although *Screenplay* tried to blame Melcher for foisting this persona on Day, in truth it was never wholly there, and never wholly derived from her movie roles; this did not stop the magazines from disseminating it, however. I think that, in the later episodes of her television show, after the first season, Day herself attempted to comment on the absurdity of this by trying to remind viewers that she was a person whose *job* was pretending to be other people. Thus within the series 'Doris pretends to be a...' (feminist, go-go dancer, dance instructor) becomes a trope so regularised as to foreground its own metafictional intent. In the same way that Doris Martin pretends to be a model, Doris Day was pretending to be this brash chanteuse, that amorous virgin, this cold manipulator, that swinging widow. In one of those self-reflexive moments that seem to have regularly occurred in Day's careers, she chose to engage with this notion most overtly in her co-written biography and in a series of articles – published in the very magazines she was criticising – which acted as pre-publicity for the book.[43] In his review of 'Her Own Story' in the *Los Angeles Times*, Robert Kirsch acknowledges awareness of a division between the actor and her roles, but interestingly, insists that he does not feel there is as extensive a gap as Day would have her readers believe:

> Somehow, I don't think that the revelations here will really shatter the image because I am not so sure after reading this candid account that films and appearance aside, Doris Day is really very different from her image.
>
> (Kirsch, 1976: K1)

This is an intriguing sentence. What is Kirsch saying about Day's 'films and appearance' here? That they do not fit with the virginal goody-goody image Day rails about at the start of her book, as quoted similarly at the start of his review? In which case, is he choosing to prioritise the off-screen meanings of Day over what she personally contributed to her persona through her film work? Kirsch does seem to state here his belief that Day herself actually *is* the 'Miss Goody Two-Shoes' which the biography's whole confessional approach, taking in broken home, car accident, marriages and affairs, malfeasance by husband and lawyer, wildness of son and horror of the Manson gang attacks, had set out to destroy with its accretion of details. In a further twist of logic, the review itself contains a metafictional turn, implying that the biography 'will make a fascinating movie with lots of intriguing material' (Kirsch, 1976: K1). If it had been Day's intent to educate fans and viewers that she had been playing other characters throughout her career, as my reading of *The Doris Day Show*'s overarching 'pretence' metaphor argues, she had obviously failed, at least in Kirsch's case. Ignoring the variety of women with a variety of sexual pasts, experiences and longings that the star had played, he insists on the authenticity of the inviolate version advanced not by her work or life but by other journalists like him.

Conclusion

I began this examination of the star persona of Doris Day with a close look at a moment from one of her films. In closing, I want to look at another such moment. The very brief 'fame montage' sequence from *My Dream Is Yours* analysed in the introduction provided a useful introduction to the varied yet intermingled sources of power in Hollywood, all of whom, in combination with the performer – agent, movie magazines, newspapers columnists, and audiences – had a part to play in her elevation to stardom. A similarly isolated moment considered here, from *Midnight Lace*, confirms, just at the turning point of Day's career, the importance of ancillary forces. Whereas Martha Gibson's labours were supported by these external agents, however, Day's own labours in the later film were undercut by them, specifically in the framing given her work by the media. While Martha is raised up to a new level of stardom by the mingled forces of the Hollywood machine, Day is pulled down from improving or altering her range, blocked from being accepted as a serious actor. Examining *Midnight Lace* here reveals again the vital role played by the printed reviews in circumscribing Day's persona, keeping perceptions of her work in the usual round. But it has a further utility: highlighting the general laziness of critics who have called Day a perpetual virgin. The films that are usually adduced as displaying Day in this role, when the writer can be bothered to provide any, are those career woman movies, in only one of which she overtly played the maiden. *Midnight Lace* by contrast would have provided ammunition for the myth-supporters, had Day's work been recognised.

Midnight Lace fits into the Gothic subgenre of thrillers, films which show off the dark side of the marital relationship and in which the heroine can usually say, in the apt summary of Joanna Russ, 'Somebody's trying to kill me and I think it's my husband' (Russ, 1973). Day plays Kit Preston, a wealthy American who has married an Englishman and is struggling to come to terms with her new life. It is made clear by Day's performance that although Kit is experiencing some culture shock adapting to Britain, she is most bewildered by the fact that her marriage has not been consummated. Rex Harrison's portrayal of Tony Preston makes the husband seem plausibly fond but just terribly busy, but Day's performance works to show that there is actually something seriously wrong with the marriage and it is this rather than threatening telephone calls which is making her desperate.

In a few key scenes, Day acts out Kit's frustrated attempts to interest her husband; she clings to him when he embraces her, demands 'More!' when he kisses her, and works hard to entice him through the purchase of seductive lingerie: a delicate laced top over clinging silk pyjamas actually gives the film its title. But Tony resists her advances through all of this; and Day's careful acting choices then convey the consequence for her character. Convinced that she is being stalked by a potential killer, Kit tries to flee the apartment building where she lives but the lift gets stalled. Trapped in the darkness Kit can hear a man's relentless footsteps approaching as she cowers, at first terrified and silent, then gasping and moaning (Figure 24).

Day's performance of Kit's hysteria works skilfully to indicate that the outburst is both a result of and an outlet for her pent-up

Figure 24.   Kit is terrified in the elevator in *Midnight Lace*.

sexual tensions, with her audible panting echoing the deep breathing of arousal. The filming of the sequence enhances this reading, as the shots of the man's hands pulling at the elevator roof, the opening up of a small space into which he inserts himself bodily, become very suggestive in the context of her panting and rhythmic moans.

I have mentioned Day's performance choices here to emphasise how skilful her work is in conveying the symptoms being manifested by her character, and the central problem provoking them, her unwilling continued celibacy. By contrast, contemporary audiences did not, for much of the film's release window, have a sponsor arguing for the seriousness of Day's work in the movie. How then was the performance contextualised, positioned, in the material surrounding the film?

The earliest piece to mention Day's more melodramatic role is 'Emotions Rise In Elevator', an article published 7 May 1960 in the *Los Angeles Examiner*. Staff writer Neil Rau reports from the set of the movie as it is being filmed, relating that he sees – or rather, *hears* – Day giving a performance of a woman in terror: he recounts the filming of the elevator scene described above. Rau relates that the sequence is claustrophobically shot in a space no bigger than an actual elevator, with director and camera-man poised on beams outside the compartment, which really does elevate and descend. Due to this tight set-up Rau cannot see Day, but he can hear her 'calling for help, reasonably calm at first but with her voice gradually rising in volume and intensity as her fear increases'. So far Rau's account seems a fairly neutral one, but the end of the article changes this:

> When the elevator again reaches the stage floor, Doris' own husband, Marty Melcher, is there to help her off. It is obvious her play-acting has gotten the best of her, because she falls into his arms and starts sobbing.
>
> (Rau, 1960: 11)

Rau here couches Day's endeavours in the elevator in terms not of a *performance*, a job of work for an actor, but as an *ordeal* for the star paralleling that of the woman in the narrative. It is Day and not Kit who has been suffering in the elevator. The word 'play-acting' too has rather patronising overtones, downgrading the actor's job of work to an episode of dressing up and let's-pretend. Rau's article had the material necessary for paying tribute to the star's talents, with her working in a tightly confined space, needing to deliver a controlled performance conveying lack of control. By concluding his story, however, with Day an emotional wreck, needing to be comforted by her husband, Rau undermines Day's labour and talent, and reduces her work to an emotional outburst.

In the immediate responses on the film's release in November 1960, other reviewers followed this general line, tending to belittle Day's achievement in the role by insistently framing it in light of her more usual offerings. The writer for the *Southern California Prompter*, for example, noted that Rex Harrison should be replaced as Day's co-star, since 'with Jack Carson and a song or two, it could easily turn into more typical, and welcome, fare.' (Anon, 1960 f). *Photoplay*'s review of the film similarly framed Day's dramatic performance in the context of her more usual vehicles:

> her helpless-heroine role is full of hysterics that give her a dandy chance for emoting. (No songs for Doris).
>
> (Anon, 1960 h: 5)

The detachment which sees the role offer the *actor* 'a dandy chance for emoting' works against an involvement with the narrative that would foster sympathy with its central *character*. Instead of dwelling on Kit's suffering, the review comments on the mixed deal the film offers to the woman playing her: on the upside, a chance to chew the scenery, on the downside, none of the usual songs for extra promotional value and tie-in revenue.

By contrast, a review then appeared in the *Hollywood Citizen News* which was more positive about Day's performance and what she was trying to do. Lowell Redelings found that, as Kit, Day

> registers her finest dramatic performance to date, a completely convincing portrait of a woman driven to the point of insanity.
>
> (Redelings, 1960)

Praising Day's performance thus, Redelings suggested that Day's acting might one day earn her an Academy Award, although asserting that *Midnight Lace* would not be the film to do it, because of the poor quality of its script. Despite this denial of the film's overall value, Redelings' more positive comment about the merit of Day's performance seems to have started a rumour in Hollywood that she was being considered for an Oscar nomination. I think it is highly suggestive that what Day is doing in the film is not what determines later publications' enthusiasm for her work; it is not her skilful enactment of hysteria that earns their interest, but the work of another journalist. Day herself seems to have been unable to convince in the serious role until one rogue reviewer viewed her in this light. This is typical of the self-reflexive nature of the press which I found accompanied Day's entire career, and which was a major surprise in the research for this monograph. Here Day's work as Kit is read entirely within the confines of her earlier roles and accepted persona, regardless of her efforts, until one journalist reframes it. From late November onwards, up to the announce-ment of Academy Award nominations in February 1961, a consensus that Day would be officially recognised for her work in the role of Kit spreads through the trade periodicals and other press and media outlets.

For example, although she had been a big star for a long while at this point, it *was* at this point that Day received an invitation to put her handprints and footprints in the concrete outside Grauman's Chinese theatre. Reporting the event, which took place on 19 January 1961, *The Hollywood Reporter* made sure to note that Day had drawn the biggest crowd since the tradition started in 1927, and that she was also presented at the ceremony with a Hollywood Chamber of Commerce 'Star of Stars' trophy which was:

> in tribute to the actress' noteworthy performances in both comedy and drama, climaxed by her award-winning portrayal in 'Midnight Lace'.
>
> (Anon, 1961 a: 3)

This *Hollywood Reporter* piece does its overt job in relating the news event and testifying to Day's eminence at the box office, her popularity and worthiness to be Star of Stars. But perhaps its covert job is given away in the intriguing phrase 'award-winning portrayal'. This almost seems placed as a subliminal hint to Academy members to remember her, since her portrayal had not at this point been nominated for or won any awards.

The same month, *Motion Picture* contained an article about the star, 'The Giggly World Of Doris Day', which, despite its self-consciously kooky title and presentation of the star as kittenish and fun-loving, diverged from this main focus, in one specific area:

> There's a thing some people don't realise about Doris Day. Because she looks like she just stepped out of a bath or is about to enter a tennis game, because she always looks like the most casual, friendly girl in town, many are unaware that this is an actress who is deadly serious about her craft.
>
> (Wilkie, 1961: 60)

Day was now being presented across the trades, fan magazines and newspapers as a serious actor worthy of serious attention and rewards. The film's studio, Universal, began a campaign in *The Hollywood Reporter* pairing full page stills of dramatic moments of the film with capsule extracts of positive reviews, each proclaiming Day's fitness for a nomination. The image of Kit suffering in the elevator was reproduced on 3 January 1961 with a quote from columnist Jimmy Starr (. . . 'among the front runners for the big award'), the reel and scene numbers and the stage direction, 'Her terror mounts as she hears a man's footsteps grow closer and closer!'.

By contrast, June 1961's issue of *Look* magazine dealt with the after-story. In the end, not only had Day's work *not* been recognised by the Academy, she had been eclipsed in the nominations by the film's *costumes* – which then did not win.

The headline on the cover of *Look* indicates the media's reversion to typical fare about the star:

> The surprising story of her three marriages, her grown son, her moods, drives and successes, her millions and her Christian Science faith.
>
> (Davidson, 1961: cover)

Inside, the five-page story provides the usual information about Day's family and personal life; although her most recent film is also mentioned, in the wake of Day's failure to be recognised *institutionally* as a serious actor for *Midnight Lace*, a negative slant is put on her work in the film once more. The journalist returns to the story of the on-set breakdown Neil Rau mentioned. *Look* too attributes its power not to the actor's 'craft' but to the woman's feelings:

> In the big scene in the picture, she worked herself into a state of near collapse. She continued with such frenzy of emotion [...]. When the scene was over, the frightened cast and crew rushed over to the prostrate, sobbing form...
>
> (Davidson, 1961: 42)

Day is clearly positioned here to deny her labour, to reject the idea that she offers a carefully thought-through performance using her bodily and vocal talents. Kit's hysteria, created through Day's skills, is read as not performed but lived.

I have spent some time looking at the press reception of this film as it seems to me to sum up usefully many of the findings this book has made. If I began my research into the myth of the 40-year-old-virgin mystified as to its origins and its seemingly inevitable application to a woman who was never, during her film and television career, not a mother, and not married or dating, what became clear was the fact that there were signs in

Day's performances that could contribute to this notion; yet they were not in the films that were regularly used as evidence of this. Furthermore, while Day's romantic and marital status – regularly highlighted in magazines – never seemed indicative of a lack of interest in or aversion to sex, some of the connotations which arose and became affixed to her persona did prove to be interpretable in this light. Her well-known devotion to her religion, which forbade her drinking, created the idea that the star was some kind of a 'goody-goody' or killjoy, which was quite at odds with her initial presentation as a bouncy, cheerful young woman who enjoyed life.

With some explanation, if not support, for the aged maiden myth provided by the researches, then, what has come to fascinate me is both Day's contribution to this persona, at times unconscious and at times overt, and the fact that at the moments when she most seems to be working in accordance with this image her work is not picked up on. *Love Me Or Leave Me*, as has been discussed, could easily have been used to support the mid-century aversion to the manipulative maiden; Ruth Etting can clearly be seen, like other young women in films around this time, following the advice of one calculating mother initiating her naive daughter into the ways of man-management with the dictum, 'Never say No to a man – simply avoid saying Yes to him'.[44]

Day's performances as Etting and as Kit Preston both provide evidence of her maintained celibacy, even if the second character finds herself in that state unwillingly, rather than by a careful calculation. It seems so ironic that Etting, and Day once she had played her, were read as conforming to a 'sexpot' mould, when the actor can so obviously be seen fulfilling the stereotype of the 'Shirley', the woman who subjugates her own desires and parcels out her favours 'on a carefully graduated scale' in order to get what she wants from her man.[45] By contrast, when Day assays the part of a truly sophisticated, sexually mature woman, in

Pillow Talk, the film's very success paradoxically sets in train the implications and inferences which cemented her into the perpetual virgin image, by establishing the terms and terrain of the comedy which *Lover Come Back* attempted to match and outdo. Although Day's alterations to the format of her television show have been read by me as indicating her intent to emphasise to viewers that both what Doris Martin and Doris Day do is *pretend* to be someone other than they are, in order to underline the division between person and persona, her TV series seems to have had no major impact on the way in which the image was read; by the time *The Doris Day Show* finished in the early 1970s, the virgin myth had been fixed, and withstood the star's own, and any subsequent, efforts to alter or ameliorate it.

It has been this book's intention to show the crucial impact of external publications on contemporaneous, and current, understanding of what 'Doris Day' means. This dictated the decisions to examine, in both depth and number, the film fan magazines which made up the majority of the material on the star. By returning to the original sources on Day, rather than relying on second-hand accounts, it has been possible to chart the development of her persona and the evolution of the connotations circulating around it. Tracing these connotations as they arrived, persisted and declined frequently revealed that tropes initially employed to imply positive qualities in the star corroded over time until their employment became part of the method of criticising the actor and confirming her old maid image. Hands-on study not merely of many magazine articles in order to find these tropes, but the magazine copies themselves, proved important because of the revelations gained about the significance of article placement. Different methods of framing the reading experience for magazine users emerged that were comparable to the different modes of framing Day's own performances, although it was very noticeable that the film fan magazines were, at least in the 1950s, much more invested in celebrating and praising the star. Newspaper reviews of her roles and performances were always more likely to find fault; by the 60s this detachment had both grown to dislike and had spread to other publications. Starting with the highbrow press, it became fashionable to disparage Day; as seen, by mid-decade notes of dissent began to filter into the popular film periodicals until, with Melcher's death in 1968, the star began to be openly mocked and questioned, while yet remaining the subject of intense interest. Despite Day's own attempts, in both her television series and in written articles and her book, to engage with the media on the subject of her image and its lack of fit with how she herself believed she appeared and acted, the media seemed to have decided how Day should be perceived. Attempts to establish alternative or dissenting views have been made, and it is the ultimate aim of this book to encourage further acts of dissent.

I acknowledge that it is entirely possible that other Hollywood stars might not have had their stardom so conditioned by and mediated through the medium of print, but, as I hope this study has demonstrated, Day's stardom was. This needs to be recognised, no less than the skilful multiplicity of the roles she played and the contemporaneous importance of her star persona. By returning to Day appreciation of her agency in making acting choices to build character, yet foregrounding those choices in the social and historical contexts of the times she made those choices, I want to return to the image of Day's face on magazines all over the news-stand in *My Dream Is Yours* with which I began this book. The multiplicity of her character's faces on a variety of magazine covers echoes the very large number of periodical stories which fixated on her with such intensity for 30 years. If the same sense of the multiple can be restored to contemporary understanding of the roles Doris Day played, this book will have achieved its aim.

Notes

Introduction

1   The 479 pieces on Day comprising my sample are randomly compiled, in the sense that I was dependent on the periodical holdings of the British Film Institute Library, the British Library, the Margaret Herrick Library of the Academy of Motion Picture Arts and Sciences, Los Angeles, the Library of Congress in Washington DC, and the Boston, Denver, Los Angeles, New York and San Francisco Public Libraries in building the collection. Ebay.com also proved a source of material on occasion. In this way I want to stress that the first occurrence of a key term is only the first occurrence *in my sample*; I am not claiming that it should be considered the first usage in material on the star ever.

2   'The will to knowledge noted by Foucault aptly describes the fan's intense and insistent involvement in discovering the truth of the star's identity. And, as I hope I have demonstrated, that truth is, at its limit, the truth of sexuality. The sexual scandal is the primal scene of all star discourse, the only scenario that offers the promise a full and satisfying disclosure of the star's identity' (deCordova, 1990: 141).

Section 1 – Contexts

3   It seems evident this was a phrase much used in the contemporary press; Joseph Folsom uses the phrase 'K bomb' with a feeling of custom the year after the Report's publication (Folsom, 1954: 168).

Section 2 – Film Fan Magazines

4   I have taken this period to be from 1948–73, the dates that bracket Day's first and last regular film and television show appearances. Slide provides a comprehensive list of the film fan magazines operating from the beginning of the medium through to its end in his *Inside The Hollywood Fan Magazine* (2010).

5   The 48 items not from film magazines come from women's service magazines such as *Good Housekeeping, Ladies Home Journal,* and *McCalls;* lifestyle publications such as *American Weekly, Collier's, Coronet, Cosmopolitan, Life, Look* and *Pageant;* scandal rags such as *Inside Story;* specialist magazines such as *Esquire, Mad, Newsweek,* and *Show;* and newspaper reports about Day from such dallies or weeklies as *Beverly Hills Citizen News, Los Angeles Examiner, Los Angeles Herald Express, Los Angeles Mirror News, Los Angeles Times, New York Herald Tribune, New York Journal American, New York Morning Telegraph* and *New York Post Weekend Magazine.*

6   More work is needed on this, but analysis of magazines within my sample indicates that the shared coverage method of star promotion operates most often. For example, in *Photoplay* February 1938, one star, Myrna Loy, is featured five times in adverts, photographs and editorial copy; Shirley Temple receives four separate mentions, Ginger Rogers, Joan Crawford, Claudette Colbert and Alice Faye three, and four other stars two each. In *Filmland* June 1953, similarly, Virginia Mayo and Lana Turner have four separate inclusions each, June Haver and Rita Hayworth get three each, but nine further female stars, including Day, receive two mentions.

7   Day's contract is preserved in the Warner Bros.' archive at the University of Southern California.

8   According to the American Film Institute website, see www.afi.com.

9   'Isn't Doris Day's secret romance on the volcanic side? We're just asking, Doris...' (Anon, 1949 e: 10).

10   Stanley Shapiro returned for *Lover Come Back,* but Paul Henning replaced *Pillow Talk*'s Maurice Richlin as Shapiro's co-writer for the second film.

11   Or was admitting to be: most biographies and magazine accounts published before Kaufmann's *Untold Story* (2008) give Day's birth year as 1924, whereas it was actually two years earlier.

12   (See McGee, 2005: 72.) The lawsuit against the magazine was withdrawn after it printed a public apology.

13   This trope lay dormant in Day's persona even after 1955; in 1962's *That Touch Of Mink*, Cary Grant's millionaire playboy calls Day's character 'an atom bomb...I should have dropped her over the desert'.

14   (See Manners, 1949) (no page – in clipping file on Doris Day for 1949 in Margaret Herrick Library, Los Angeles).

15   'The boys made the fire for the coffee while the girls spread out the food'...'Picnic In The Park' (Mulvey, 1948: 61).

16   A breakfast cereal of wheat and bran flakes.

17   For example, she is reported as having gone shopping for food but only buys 'hard candies [...] marshmallows, tootsies pops, cookies...' (Wilkie, 1961: 59).

18   Such as *Tea For Two* (1950), *On Moonlight Bay, I'll See You In My Dreams* (both 1951), *The Winning Team* (1952) and *By The Light Of The Silvery Moon* (1953).

19   Day's roles in *Tunnel Of Love* and *Teacher's Pet* (both 1958) could also be seen in this light, arguably, as both involve battle of the sexes banter and situations. *Tunnel Of Love* indeed involves, overtly, sex, although sex-for-procreation rather than sex-for-recreation. It is possible that those contemporary sex comedies that end with the announcement of a pregnancy or delivery (*Pillow Talk, Lover Come Back, That Touch Of Mink*) are attempting to recuperate sex by underlining its role in the propagation of the species and downplaying its fun aspects.

20   The term 'out at home' does not, as it might now, imply that Day was a lesbian who could acknowledge her true sexuality at home (be 'out of the closet') but uses – pointedly, given the tenor of the article – a baseball metaphor to suggest there is disharmony in the Day–Melcher household. Day is 'out' of Melcher's favour at home because of her – alleged – relationship with baseball player Wills.

21   In examining the piece, the author will be designated as 'Day' in acknowledgement both that it is supposed to be the star and that the identity cannot be now proven.

22   The May 1956 issue of *Motion Picture* analysed in the previous section was used for these comparisons. Its dimensions and cost (in 1956) are average for the other film fan magazines of the time. This put *Show* on a par with other lifestyle magazines in size and cost, (such as *Ladies Home Journal* and *Life* magazine) but bigger and up to 10 cents more expensive than most of the film fan magazines.

23   But answering to 38...

24 'No one realised that under all those dirndls lurked one of the wildest asses in Hollywood' (Hotchner: 188).

25 Examination of fan magazine covers illustrates this; see http://www.moviemags.com/. Anthony Slide also notes that Taylor was 'the dominant star from the world of movies' (197).

Section 3 – Performance Analysis

26 See Leff and Simmons, 2001: 197–205.

27 These lists are still compiled by the company which owned and edited *MPH*, Quigley Publishing Inc. See http://www.quigleypublishing.com/index.html

28 The *New York Star* reporter mentions the need to be at the movies because of air conditioning (cited in *The Hollywood Reporter* article, 30 June 1948: 14); *Film Daily* notes in its rave review that Day is 'the Warner answer to the effect of the Summer meteorology on the box office and its attendant slump' (9 June 1948: 6).

29 Four (1960, 1962, 1963 and 1964); in this she ties with Shirley Temple. If a points system is implemented, however, which gives ten points for appearing in the number one spot and one for appearing at number ten, with equivalent weightings to the other places, Day's total is 72, which is the highest ever achieved by a female star (for comparison, Julia Roberts, who also appears ten times in the list, has a score of 60).

30 This is Noel Airman to Marjorie, in *Marjorie Morningstar* (1958). Noel spends most of the film attempting to seduce Marjorie through various means; here he uses misogyny and cynicism to goad her into proving herself different.

31 Another 'virginity dilemma' movie quotation, this time from *A Summer Place* (1959). The virgin's mother tells her daughter that she must learn how to manipulate men and deny her own desires.

32 Day's *Love Me Or Leave Me* soundtrack album 'spent 17 weeks at number one on the album charts, and was the third most successful album of the 1950s' (McGee, 2005: 218).

33 *Please Don't Eat The Daisies*, 1960.

34 *That Touch Of Mink* (1962), *The Thrill Of It All* and *Move Over, Darling* (both 1963), *Send Me No Flowers* (1964), *Do Not Disturb* (1965), *Where Were You When The Lights Went Out?* and *With Six You Get Egg Roll* (both 1968).

35 It is interesting to note that here Day is acting Judy acting desire, since the character is actually angry with her husband and, as Day's Carol did in *Lover Come Back*'s revenge scene, is feigning readiness for sex to trap him.

36 'Miss Day is not as young as she used to be for this sort of caper but she does have the energy...' Judith Crist, *Today* programme (quoted in McGee: 145).

37 Connie of Cathy: 'She's gonna spend the rest of her life saying, "I'm not that kind of a girl." I'm only afraid that someday, before she can finish saying it, she will be.'

38 The series from which episodes come will be marked in brackets on first mention; thus S3 is series 3, etc.

39 Since *The Doris Day Show* was a CBS show, it could use her Columbia recordings without rights problems, as the two were part of the same parent company.

40 'Hold Me In Your Arms' which Day sang in 1954's *Young At Heart*.

41 Compare her account of David Cowley's charms to Myrna in 'The Feminist' (S3) with a similar rendition of why she likes Dr Peter Lawrence in 'Doris At Sea' (S4).

42 Played, respectively, by the same four women listed above, MacLaine, Fonda, Lynley and Wood. These same actors also performed in the melodramatic version of the 'virginity dilemma' film.

43 See 'Bold, Bra-less and Brassy' (Dahl, 1975); 'I love being free and single' (Ardmore, 1976a); 'Doris Day Finds True Love At Last' (Ardmore, 1976b); 'Love Should Be Free' (West, 1977).

Conclusion

44 So sung by the young woman's mother, in the 1962 version of *State Fair*.

45 Again, these sneering lines are spoken by Noel Airman in *Marjorie Morningstar*. 'Shirley' is the name he gives to the type of young woman who pays out her favours gradually.

Synopses

Romance On The High Seas

Mrs Elvira Kent (Janis Paige) suspects her husband Michael (Don DeFore) of adultery and, with the blessing of her rich uncle (S.Z. Sakall), recruits nightclub singer Georgia Garrett (Doris Day) to impersonate her on a cruise from New York to the Caribbean so that she herself can actually stay at home and spy on her spouse. At the same time, Michael Kent has become suspicious of his wife's behaviour and hires a private detective Peter Virgil (Jack Carson) to follow her and report on her activities. Not having seen Mrs Kent before, Virgil does not realise that the woman on board the ship is an imposter; the pair are attracted to each other, but each has reasons for not pursuing the romance, she because she is masquerading as a married woman, and he because he believes he is falling in love with his client's wife. When the boat docks, the real Mrs Kent and her husband arrive, and eventually, at a concert organised to launch 'Mrs Kent' as a society singer, all identities are made known, subterfuge forgiven and couples joined.

Love Me Or Leave Me

Chicago in the 1920s: dancehall hostess Ruth Etting (Doris Day) is fired from her job for slapping a grabby customer. Outside the club, she is propositioned by local hoodlum and racketeer Marty Snyder (James Cagney); he asserts he can help launch her desired singing career. Ruth is suspicious but Marty makes good on his claims by getting her a job at a nightclub. The club's pianist, Johnny Alderman (Cameron Mitchell), meets Ruth but he is warned not to pursue her since she 'belongs' to Snyder. Ruth, however, refuses to pay off her debt in the way Snyder wants – by becoming his mistress – instead using Marty to negotiate for her until she has her own nightclub act. Alderman tells Ruth that she does not need Snyder since her own talent would take her to stardom, but she dismisses him, despite their mutual attraction, and he leaves for Hollywood. Ruth continues to succeed with Snyder's help, and he eventually gets her a role in the Ziegfeld Follies. Payment can no longer be deferred, however, and although Ruth resists, Snyder forcibly claims what he insists she owes him. The pair marry. Ruth continues to perform, and Snyder to manage her, but the joy has gone out of her performances and she turns to alcohol. Eventually she too goes to Hollywood and meets Alderman again; they realise they love each other, but Ruth says they can never be together. Despite this, she begins divorce proceedings against Snyder. Furious and convinced the pianist is to blame, Snyder shoots Alderman and wounds him. Ruth visits Snyder in prison and tries to convey that she will always be grateful to him. Snyder scorns her sympathy, but when he is released, finds her singing at his new night club as a thank you.

Lover Come Back

Carol Templeton (Doris Day), an ambitious advertising executive, seems blocked at every turn by an unscrupulous playboy rival, Jerry Webster (Rock Hudson), whom she has never met. Attempting to poach a potential client from Webster, Templeton wines and dines shy chemist Linus Tyler hoping to secure the campaign to promote his new mystery product, 'VIP', for her agency. In showing Linus around New York Carol begins to fall in love with the handsome, if gauche, young man; moreover, he is so shy with women that she finds herself taking the romantic initiative with him, finally inviting him to an intimate dinner in her apartment. Tortured by his feelings of inadequacy, Linus tells Carol to forget him and find a real man. Carol debates the problem with herself. Deciding to 'Surrender!' she is about to don a lacy negligee when her phone rings, the cruel plot is exploded, and she learns 'Linus' is actually Jerry Webster. To have her revenge, Carol goes to the Advertising Standards Council claiming that there is no VIP, but Jerry turns up with a box of mints – alcoholic mints. After over-indulging, they wake up in a motel to find they have got married whilst drunk. Carol has the marriage annulled, but cannot annul the pregnancy that resulted from her one night with Jerry. Nine months later he finally learns the news and flies to her side, marrying her again in the elevator on the way to the delivery room.

Bibliography

Allen, Don. 1952. 'I Know This Is Love', *Movie Stars Parade*, January: 30–31, 76–77.

Anderson, Consuelo. 1950. 'Why Men Love Doris Day', *Modern Screen*, August: 44–45, 81–82.

Anon. 1948, a. 'Inside Stuff', *Photoplay*, January: 12.

———. 1948, b. 'Duet For 1948', *Photoplay*, June: 72–73.

———. 1948, c. 'Review Of The New Films' – *Romance On The High Seas*. *Film Daily*, 9 June: 6.

———. 1948, d. 'Sure Fire'. *Movie Life*, July: 90–91.

———. 1948, e. Review – *Romance On The High Seas*, *Screenland*, July: 14.

———. 1948, f. 'Screenland salutes Doris Day in 'Romance On The High Seas'. *Screenland*, July: 50.

———. 1948, g. 'Day and Date', *Movie Life*, August: 50–53.

———. 1948, h. 'Choose Your Star', *Photoplay*, August: 66–67, 103.

———. 1948, i. Letters page, *Motion Picture*, November: 14.

———. 1948, j. 'Gay Day', *Movie Life*, December: 62–65.

———. 1949, a. 'Day In A Boy-Filled House', *Movie Life*, March: 28–33.

———. 1949, b. 'Doris Day: Miss Huck Finn', *Look*, June: 105.

———. 1949, c. 'How Wet Can You Get?', *Movie Life*, June: 34–37.

———. 1949, d. 'She's Got What It Takes', *Screen Guide*, August: 66.

———. 1949, e. 'Hollywood's Whispering', *Screen Guide*, December: 10.

———. 1950. 'Busy Day', *Radio Album*, Spring: 30–31.

———. 1951, a. 'What A Dish!', *Movie Life*, February: 85.

———. 1951, b. 'Sunny Day', *Movie Life*, May: 25–26, 78–79.

———. 1951, c. 'Honeymoon Daze', *Movie Life*, July: 16–19.

———. 1951, d. 'Kitchen Cut Up', *Movieland*, September: 24.

———. 1952, a. 'No Cookee, No Washee', *Movie Life*, February: 28–31.

———. 1952, b. 'Old-Fashioned Girl', *Movie Stars Parade*, February: 34–37.

———. 1952, c. 'Dream Girl', *Movie Stars Parade*, March: 62–63.

———. 1952, d. 'What Makes Doris Tick', *Movie Stars Parade*, May: 34–37.

———. 1952, e. 'Be Pretty While You Play', *Movie Stars Parade*, July: 62–63.

———. 1952, f. 'Doris Day', *Photoplay*, October: 41.

———. 1952, g. 'Letters', *Movie Stars Parade*, December: 85.

———. 1953, a. 'His Girl Friday', *Movie Stars Parade*, February: 34–37.

———. 1953, b. 'Calamity Jane Rides Again', *Filmland*, June: 12–13.

———. 1954, a. 'You Can Help Doris Get Well!', *Photoplay*, February: 34–36, 104.

———. 1954, b. 'Two Sweet For Her Own Good', *Movieland*, March: 30–33, 77–78.

———. 1954, c. 'Man Bait!', *Movie Life*, July 1954: 32–33.

———. 1954, d. 'A Day At The Ball Park', *Movie Fan*, November: 32–35.

———. 1955, a. 'Some Wives Have Secrets', *Photoplay*, May 1955: 46–47, 111–113.

———. 1955, b. 'Daffy About Dodo', *Movie Life*, August: 26–27, 66–67.

———. 1959, a. Review of *Pillow Talk*. *The Hollywood Reporter*, 12 August: 3.

———. 1959, b. Review of *Pillow Talk*. *Cleveland Plain Dealer*, quoted in advertisement for the film in *The Hollywood Reporter*, 16 September: 3.

———. 1960, a. 'The Big Change In Doris Day', *Movie World*, March: 32–33, 60–61.

———. 1960, b. 'Movies – Where Hollywood Begins', *Newsweek*, 11 April: 121.

———. 1960, c. 'What Makes Doris Run?', *Movie Mirror*, July: 34–35, 62.

———. 1960, d. 'Box Office Bonanza: Sunny Doris Day In A Shivery Role', *Life*, September: Cover and 136–138.

———. 1960, e. 'Is Doris Sick Of Being A Good Wife?', *Photoplay*, September: Cover; 48–49, 69–71.

———. 1960, f. 'At The Movies: Bad Humor Man Is A Bit Of A Bore', *Southern California Prompter*, November: *Midnight Lace* Production File, Margaret Herrick Library, Los Angeles.

———. 1960, g. 'Doris Day Will Divorce in 61', *Movie TV Secrets*, December: 32–33, 62–63.

———. 1960, h. 'Movies', review of *Midnight Lace*, *Photoplay*, December: 5.

———. 1961, a. 'Doris Day Foot-Printing Revives Glamour Days At Grauman's Chinese', *The Hollywood Reporter*, 20 January: 3.

———. 1961, b. 'Doris Day: The Rumors And The Facts!', *Movie Life*, May: 30–31, 60–62.

———. 1961, c. 'The Trouble Doris Day Has Had Since The Mixed Marriage', *Movie TV Secret*, October: 24–25, 50, 52.

————. 1963, a. 'Gold Medal Movie Of The Month' – review of *Jumbo*. *Photoplay*, February: 6–12.

————. 1963, b. 'Wedding Bells For Doris Day', *Movie TV Secrets*, May: 22–25, 58, 60.

————. 1963, c. 'The Tomato On Top Is Doris' – review of *The Thrill Of It All*. *Life*, 27 September: 105–107.

————. 1963, d. 'Magic of the Movies', *Life*, 20 December.

————. 1964, a. 'The Oldest Teenager In The World', *Motion Picture*, August: 34–35.

————. 1968. 'What Doris Day Will Never Know About Her Husband's Shocking Death', *Screenplay*, July: 9–11, 72–75.

————. 1969. 'How Doris Day Became A "Virgin" After Marriage!', *Movie Life*, August: 48–49, 72.

————. 1970. 'What Doris Day Wants That Only Her Son Can Give Her!', *Movie Life*, December: 40–41, 74–77.

————. 1972, a. 'Doris Day + Fashions – Fads = The Elegant Look', *Motion Picture*, April. Constance McCormick Collection.

————. 1972, b. Review of *The Doris Day Show*. *Variety*, 20 September: 34.

————. 1973. 'Doris Day's New Man – Strictly On The Sly', *Movie Stars*, July: cover.

Archer, Jules. 1956. 'Will she or won't she?', *Playboy*, January: 13 and 64.

Archerd, Amy. 1972. 'Hollywood Style', *Variety*, 31 July: 8.

Ardmore, Jane. 1957. 'I'm On My Way By Doris Day', *The American Weekly*, 17 November. Constance McCormick Collection.

————. 1968. 'Why Doris Day Rides By Night – Hides By Day', *Photoplay*, January: 52–53, 60.

————. 1976, a. 'I Love Being Free And Single', *Photoplay*, February: 8, 24–25.

————. 1976, b. 'Doris Day Finds True Love At Last', *Photoplay*, May: 50–52.

Asher, Jerry. 1952. 'An Unharried Day', *Movieland*, August: 40–43, 70.

Banes, Sally. 1993. *Greenwich Village, 1963: Avant-garde Performance and the Effervescent Body*. Durham, NC: Duke University Press.

Barnett, Hoyt and Alice. 1950. 'She's A Real Warm Day', *Collier's*, January: 16–17, 73.

Bascombe, Laura. 1968. 'Doris Day's Last Words To Her Dying Husband', *Photoplay*, July: 46–47, 86–88.

Benedict, Paul. 1954. 'Doris Day Is Not A Snob!', *Screenland and TVLand*, August: 30–31, 62–63.

Berg, Louis. 1955. 'Doris Wouldn't Dance', *Los Angeles Times – This Week Magazine*, 15 June: I17.

Brown, Helen Gurley. 1962. *Sex And The Single Girl*, New York: Bernard Geis and Associates.

Burke, Paul. 2002. *Father Frank*. Cannock, UK: Flame.

Caldwell, Darin. 1969. 'Is Doris Day Playing Sick To Stop Her Son's Wedding?', *Screen Stars*, July: 50–51, 94–96.

Cameron, Kala. 1971. 'Doris Day's Son Forced Into Hospital', *TV Star Parade*, November: 28–29, 68–69.

Capp, Al. 1961. 'All That Doris Day Wanted Was To Get Wed To The Guy', *Los Angeles Mirror*, 27 July. Doris Day clippings file, Margaret Herrick Library, Los Angeles.

——. 1962. 'The Day Dream', *Show*, December: 72–73, 136–137.

Carleton, Jane. 1954. 'What Really Happened To Doris Day', *Modern Screen*, January: 2–3, 80–81.

Churchill, Reba and Bonnie. 1957. 'Her Best Friends Wouldn't Tell Her', *Silver Screen*, June: 14–19.

Collins, Felicity and Davis, Therese. 2004. *Australian Cinema After Mabo*. Cambridge: Cambridge University Press.

Connolly, Mike. 1955. 'Impertinent Interview', *Photoplay*, September: 4.

Crist, Judith. 1965. 'And Dori$ Day Led All The Rest', *New York Herald Tribune*, 24 January: 27.

Cronin, Steve. 1952. 'Happy Talk', *Modern Screen*, December: 54–55, 84–86.

Crowther, Bosley. 1948. Review of *Romance On The High Seas*, *The New York Times*, 26 June: 10.

——. 1955. Review of *The Tender Trap*, *New York Times*, 11 November 1955: 29.

Dahl, Barbara. 1975. 'Bold, Bra-less and Brassy', *Screen Stars*, January: 34–35, 50–51, 52–53.

Davidson, Bill. 1961. 'Doris Day', *Look*, 20 June: 39–47.

'Day, Doris'. 1953. 'My Home Is My Castle', *Movieland*, March: 52–53, 60.

——. 1956. 'Sex Isn't Everything', *Motion Picture*, May: 26, 27 (picture) & 67.

——. 1958. 'Doris Day Tells Why Marty Calls Her "Goofiddity"', *Screen Stars*, January: 32–33, 63.

deCordova, Richard. *Picture Personalities, The Emergence Of The Star System In America*, Champagne IL: University of Illinois Press, 1990.

Doniger, Wendy. 2006. *The Woman Who Pretended To Be Who She Was – Myths Of Self-Imitation*, Oxford and New York: Oxford University Press.

Dyer, Richard. 1979. *Stars*, London: British Film Institute.

———. 1986. *Heavenly Bodies. Film Stars And Society,* Basingstoke: Macmillan.

Edgerton, Lane. 1971. 'Doris Day Stunned! Wife Of The Man She's Been Linked With Mysteriously Dies', *Modern Screen,* May: 59–60, 81.

Evans, Sara. 1989. *Born For Liberty: A History Of Women In America,* New York: Free Press.

Feinstein, Elaine. 2003. *Ted Hughes, The Life of a Poet,* New York: W.W. Norton & Co.

Flagg, Fannie. 2010. *I Still Dream About You,* London: Chatto and Windus.

Folsom, Joseph K. 1954. 'Kinsey's Challenge To Ethics And Religion', *Social Problems,* i/4 April: 164–168.

Friedman, Flavius. 1960. 'Everyone's Favorite Day', *Pageant,* September: 26–32.

Garner, Joe. 2004. *Made You Laugh! The Funniest Moments In Radio, Television, Stand-Up, And Movie Comedy,* Riverside, NJ: Andrews McMeel Publishing.

Gehman, Richard. 1963. 'The Girl Next Door', *The American Weekly,* June 9: 3–5, 14–15.

'Gene'. 1961. 'Film Review. Lover Come Back', *Variety,* 12 December: 6.

Goodwin, Mary. 1953. 'And Along Came Dodo', *Photoplay,* February: 42–43, 103–105.

Graham, Sheilah. 1956. 'Sounding Off', *Motion Picture,* May: 50, 53.

Green, Janet. 1961. *Matilda Shouted Fire!* London: Evans Brothers.

Greer, Lorrayne Jo. 1959. 'I'd Like To Be Different', *Photoplay,* March: 57–59, 100–101.

Haber, Joyce. 1970. 'Doris Day: She's More Than Just Apple Pie', *Los Angeles Times* – Calendar, 15 November: V21.

Hale, Anne. 1948. 'Bright Day', *Screen Stories,* May: 32–33.

Hall, Gladys. 1953. 'What Doris Day Thinks Of Doris Day', *Motion Picture,* September: 28–29, 76.

Hansen, Miriam. 1991. *Babel And Babylon: Spectatorship In American Silent Film,* Cambridge and London: Harvard University Press.

Harford, Margaret. 1961. '"Lover, Come Back" Ribs Madison Ave', *Los Angeles Mirror,* 25 December: *Lover Come Back* Production File, Margaret Herrick Library, Los Angeles.

Haskell, Molly. 1974. *From Reverence To Rape: The Treatment Of Women In The Movies,* New York: Penguin.

Hayward, Susan. 2006. *Cinema Studies: Key Concepts,* 3rd edition, London: Routledge.

Henaghan, Jim. 1951. 'Love Sneaked In', *Modern Screen*, June: 32–33, 73–76.

Henniger, Paul. 1971. 'Romance To Be Added – Doris Day Series Gets "Adult" Image', *Los Angeles Times*, 10 September: F22.

Hoffman, Irving. 1948. '"High Seas" Suffers From Brushoff By NY Critics', *The Hollywood Reporter*, 30 June: 14.

Holland, Jack. 1953. 'If You Were Doris' Friend', *Movies*, October: 38–41.

Hotchner, A. E. 1976. *Doris Day: Her Own Story*, New York: William Morrow and Company, Inc.

Hudson, Rock and Davidson, Sara. 1986. *Rock Hudson: His Story*, New York: Morrow.

Humphrey, Hal. 1968. 'Wholesome Series For Doris Day', *Los Angeles Times*, 7 February: D17.

'Hunter, Ross', 1964. 'The Most Misunderstood Girl In Hollywood', *Modern Screen*, October 1964: 34–35, 64–65.

Jacobi, Ernst. 1955. 'You're In Luck', *Photoplay*, February: 48–49, 103–104.

Jeffers McDonald, Tamar. 2005. '"Under All Those Dirndls': *Pillow Talk's* Repackaging of Doris Day', in Rachel Moseley (ed) *Fashioning Stars: Dress, Culture, Identity*, London: British Film Institute. 50–61.

———. 2006 a. 'Visible virgins: How Hollywood showed the unshowable in late 1950s films', in Kylo-Patrick R. Hart (ed), *Film and Sexual Politics: A Critical Reader*, Newcastle Upon Tyne, UK: Cambridge Scholars Press. 73–83.

———. 2006 b. 'Very little wrist movement': Rock Hudson acts out sexual heterodoxy. *Canadian Journal of Communication*, Special Issue on 'Sex/Sexualities', Vol xxxi, 843–860.

———. 2007. 'Carrying concealed weapons: gendered makeover in *Calamity Jane*'. *Journal of Popular Film and Television*. Winter, Vol 35, 179–186.

———. 2010 a. *Virgin Territory: Representing Sexual Innocence In Film*, Detroit: Wayne State University Press.

———. 2010 b. *Hollywood Catwalk: Reading Costume And Transformation In American Film*, London: I.B.Tauris.

Johnson, Nora. 1959. 'Sex And The College Girl', *The Atlantic Monthly*, November, 56–60.

Jones, James. 1997. *Alfred Charles Kinsey. A Public Private Life*, New York: Norton.

Joseph, Joe. 1998. 'Sex Aplenty, But Little Sensibility', *The Times*, 21 October, 47.

Kahn, Roger, 1963. 'Is there A Doris Day?', *Ladies Home Journal*, July/August: 62–65.

Kappel, Paul. 1955. 'If You Knew Doris – ', *Silver Screen*, August: 12–17.

Kaufman, David. 2008. *Doris Day: The Untold Story Of The Girl Next Door*, New York: Virgin Books USA.

Kinsey, Alfred C., Pomeroy, Wardell B., Martin, Clyde E., and Gebhard, Paul H. 1953. *Sexual Behavior In The Human Female*, Philadelphia and London: W. B. Saunders Company.

Kirsch, Robert. 1976. 'Miss Goody Two Shoes Kicks Back', *Los Angeles Times*, 17 January: K11.

Larkin, Lou. 1952. 'The Honeymoon Is Over', *Motion Picture and TV Magazine*, February: 42–43, 54.

Laurent, Lawrence. 1971. Review of *The Doris Day Show*, *The Washington Post*, reprinted in *The Courier-Journal and Times*, Louisville, Kentucky, 31 October (New York Public Library Doris Day cutting file, MWEZ + nc 26734).

Leff, Leonard J. and Simmons, Jerold H. 2001. *The Dame In The Kimono: Hollywood, Censorship And The Production Code*, Lexington, KT: University of Kentucky Press.

Levine, Ralph. 1963. 'Why Doris Day Was Out At Home', *Inside Story*, May: 14–17, 54.

Lipkin, Lawrence H. 1961. 'Lover Come Back Top Fun Geared For Big Boxoffice', *The Hollywood Reporter*, 12 December: 3.

Lippert, Gene. 1962. 'Why Doris Hides Her Secret Love', *Screen World & TV*, July 1960: 20–22, 6.

Lynch Vallee, William. 1948. 'Day Break For Doris', *Silver Screen*, March: 45, 80–81.

Macdonald, Dwight. 1962. 'The Doris Day Cycle II and III', *Esquire*, November: 58, 60.

Mackin, Tom. 1971. 'Say It Ain't So, Doris!', *Newark Evening News*, 7 May: (New York Public Library Doris Day cutting file, MWEZ + nc 26734).

Madison, Jim. 1960. 'Hollywood's Oldest Teenager', *Modern Screen*, March: 30–31, 76–78.

Maier, Thomas. 2009. *Masters of Sex: The Life and Times of William Masters and Virginia Johnson, the Couple Who Taught America How to Love*, New York: Basic Books.

Manners, Dorothy. 1949. 'Snappy Shots – Doris Day', *Los Angeles Examiner*, 14 August. Doris Day Clipping File, Margaret Herrick Library, Los Angeles.

———. 1968. 'No Dates For Doris', *Modern Screen*, December: 13.

Mathews, John. 1954. 'This Is Doris', *Motion Picture*, October: 46–47, 49–50.

Maynard, John. 1953. 'Doris Day: her gimmick is – YOU!', *Motion Picture and TV Magazine*, July 1953: 34–35, 58.

Mazella, Sally. 1957. 'I Trailed Doris Day....', *Modern Screen*, November, 46–7, 68.

McCracken, Ellen. 1993. *Decoding Women's Magazines: From Mademoiselle to Ms*, Basingstoke, UK: Palgrave Macmillan.

McGee, Garry. 2005. *Doris Day: Sentimental Journey*, Jefferson NC: McFarland and Company.

'Melcher, Martin'. 1951. 'My Wife – And The Other Man', *Motion Picture*, August: 26–27, 50.

Miller, Chris. 2007. *The Real 'Animal House': The Saga of the Fraternity That Inspired the Movie*, New York: Little, Brown and Company.

Miller, Eugene L., Arnold, Edwin T. 2004. *Robert Aldrich Interviews*, Jackson MS: University Press of Mississippi.

Mills Goode, Bud and Betty. 1953. 'Change Of Face – In Hollywood', *Photoplay*, February: 58–59, 74–75.

Miron, Charles. 1969. 'Doris Day Interferes In Son's Love Life! Is Candy Bergen Fed Up?', *TV Star Parade*, August: 34–35, 64.

Moffitt, Jack. 1955. '"Love Or Leave Me" Tops As Musical With Story', *The Hollywood Reporter*, 23 May: 3.

Monroe, Barbara. 1994. 'Courtship, Comedy and African-American expressive culture in Zora Neale Hurston's fiction' in Gail Finney, (ed.), *Look Who's Laughing: Gender And Comedy*, London and New York: Routledge, 173–188.

Mulvey, Kay. 1948. 'Picnic In The Park', *Photoplay*, November: 60–61.

Murphy, Bernice M. 2009. *The Suburban Gothic in American Culture*, Basingstoke UK: Palgrave Macmillan.

Night, Noonie. 1972. 'Doris Day In Tears Over The Grandchild She'll Never See', *TV Star Parade*, January: 34–35, 62–64.

O'Hea, Shamus. 1965. 'Doris Day Speaks Out About Love, Marriage & Movie Magazines', *Modern Screen*, November: 28–29, 68.

O'Leary, Dorothy. 1955. '"Mind Your Marriage Manners" Says Doris Day', *Filmland*, September: 28–29, 58, 60.

Oppenheimer, Peer J. 1957. 'Dodo's Very Practical Summer Wardrobe', *Modern Screen*, 52–53, 74–76.

Ott, Beverly. 1956. 'Whistle Bait', *Photoplay*, May: 48–49, 110–111.

Paglia, Camille. 1992. *Sex, Art and American Culture*, London: Vintage.

Parsons, Louella. 1955. 'Louella Parsons In Hollywood', *Modern Screen*, July: 16.

Paul, Jasmine and Kauffman, Bette J. 1995. 'Missing persons: working class women and the movies, 1940–1990' in Angharad N. Valdivia, *Feminism, Multiculturalism, and the Media: Global Diversities*, Thousand Oaks CA: Sage Inc. 163–184.

Peterson, Marva. 1956. 'The Lady In Pink', *Modern Screen*, January: 40–41, 75–77.

Polykoff, Shirley. 1975. *Does She Or Doesn't She – And How She Did It*, New York: Doubleday and Company, Inc.

Pomeroy, Laura. 1948. 'The "Most Everything" Girl In Hollywood', *Motion Picture*, August: 38–39, 76.

Powell, Lynn. 1969. 'Doris Day's Son Rebels: "You Can't Force Me To Take Marty's Place"', *Screen Stars*, February: 50–51, 66–67.

Proctor, Kay. 1955. '"Love Me" Story Factual', *Los Angeles Examiner*, 16 June: 8.

Quart, Leonard and Auster Albert. 2001. *American Film and Society since 1945*, Westport CT: Praeger.

Ransom, Julie. 1952. 'Doris – Today And Yesterday', *Movie Stars Parade*, April: 62–63.

Rau, Neil. 1960. 'Emotions Rise In Elevator', *Los Angeles Examiner*, 7 May: 11.

Redelings, Lowell E. 1960. 'Doris' Acting Wins Praise', *Los Angeles Citizen News*, 17 November: *Midnight Lace* Production File, Margaret Herrick Library, Los Angeles.

Rilley, Vicky. 1952. 'Four Smart Girls', *Photoplay*, May: 43–44, 88–90.

Ritter, Monica. 1962. 'Why Our Stars Don't Shine', *Movieland and TV Time*, June: Cover and 12–17.

Roberts, Wynn. 1955. 'Atom Blonde', *Photoplay*, June: 39–40, 80–84.

Roddy, Joseph. 1950. 'Record Guide', *Look*, 11 April: 109.

Rowland, Ruth. C, 'Is Glamor A Plunging Neckline?', *Screen Stars*, January: 26–27, 68–69.

Russ, Joanna. 1973/1995. '"Somebody's trying to kill me and I think it's my husband": The Modern Gothic.' Reprinted in *To Write Like A Woman: Essays in Feminism and Science Fiction*, Bloomington and Indianapolis: Indiana University Press: 94–119.

Sammis, Fred. 1952. 'Announcing *Photoplay*'s Gold Medal Award Winners for 1951', *Photoplay*, March: 33–36.

Scheuer, Philip K. 1961. '"Lover Come Back" Brisk, Gay Farce', *Los Angeles Times*, 25 December: C13.

Schroeder, Carl. 1953. 'Sentimental Journey', *Modern Screen*, September: 40–43, 62–65.

Scullin, George, a. 1957. 'Escape To Happiness', *Photoplay.* April: 68–69, 70–71, 105-107.

———. 1957. 'Escape To Happiness', *Photoplay.* June: 68–69, 111–113.

Shelly, Elizabeth. 1948. 'Happy Day', *Movieland*, November: 36–37, 88–89.

Shipp, Cameron. 1956. 'Hollywood's Girl Next Door', *Cosmopolitan*, April: 58–63.

Shteir, Rachel. 2010. *Gypsy: The Art of the Tease*, New Have CT and London: Yale University Press.

Simon, John. 1967. 'Infantilism Revisited' In *Private Screenings: Views Of The Cinema Of The Sixties.* London: Macmillan: 101–102.

Simpson, Paul. 2010. *Rough Guide To Cult Movies*, London: Rough Guides.

Skolsky, Sidney. 1948. 'Tintype: Doris Day', *Los Angeles Citizen News*, 16 September: 22, 28 E.

Slide, Anthony. 2010. *Inside The Hollywood Fan Magazine*, Jackson, MI: University of Mississippi Press.

Smith, Cecil. 1969. 'Doris Day Show To Commute To City', *Los Angeles Times*, 28 July: C21.

'Smith, Frankenstein'. 1954. 'Virginity: An Important Treatise On A Very Important Subject', *Playboy,* September: 9, 40, 50.

Smith, Gay. 2010. *Lady Macbeth In America: From The Stage To The White House*, Basingstoke: Palgrave Macmillan.

Solemn, Sean. 1970. 'Doris Day And Lucille Ball: How Their Sons Are Breaking Their Hearts!', *TV Star Parade*, October: 28–29, 58, 62.

Stein, Sally. 1992. 'The Graphic Ordering of Desire: Modernization Of A Middle-Class Women's Magazine, 1919–1939', in Richard Bolton, (ed.), *Contest Of Meaning, Critical Histories Of Photography,* Cambridge MA: MIT Press.

Stephens, Shelby. 1970. 'Doris Day's Son Asks: "Mom, Why Don't You Leave Me Alone?"', *Photo Screen*, September: 26–27, 70, 72.

Swisher, Vi. 1959. 'Dodo In Yankeeland', *Screenland Plus TVLand*, January: 14–17, 77.

Torres, Angelo and Hart, Stan. 1971. 'The Doris Daze Show', *Mad*, January: 43–47.

Trent, Susan. 1952. 'She Doesn't Like Her Type!', *Modern Screen*, February: 34–35, 91–93.

Tusher, William. 1960. 'Doris Day – Sexy But Nice!', *TV Picture Life*, July: 26–27, 50–52.

Walker, Alexander. 1968. 'The Great American Massacre: Rock Hudson and Co.' in: *Sex In The Movies*, London: Penguin, 231–251.

Waterbury, Ruth. 1952. 'Life Is For Living', *Photoplay*, March: 42–45, 87–90.

———. 1968. 'A New Day For Doris', *Coronet*, September: 44–49.

Weaver, William. 1948. 'Nation's Showmen Select The Stars Of Tomorrow', *Motion Picture Herald*, 11 September: 11–14.

Weissman, Len. 1956. 'Here Are Some Of My Answers, by Doris Day', *Modern Screen*, May: 48–49, 64–65.

West, Bonnie. 1977. 'Love Should Be Free', *Movie Life*, January: 28–29, 58–59.

Wheeler, Joan. 1972. 'Two Hollywood Mothers Comfort Each Other: Lucille Ball And Doris Day's Agony: We Can't Let Our Wild Sons' Sins Ruin Our Lives!', *Movie Life*, May: 46–47, 57–58.

Wheeler, Lyle. 1952. 'Sunny Side Up', *Photoplay*, April: 54–55, 104–105.

Wilkie, Jane. 1961. 'The Giggly World Of Doris Day', *Motion Picture*, January: 44–45, 59–60.

Williams, Dick. 1955. 'Movies Finally Create A Believable Biography', *Los Angeles Mirror News*, 1 June: *Love Me Or Leave Me* Production File, Margaret Herrick Library, Los Angeles.

Williams, John. 1954. 'Sitting On Dynamite', *Movie Life*, March: 26–29.

'X', Suzy. 1970. 'How Doris Day's Son Escaped "Tate Murder" Hippies!', *Movie Life*, March: 10–11, 14, 18.

Other resources

American Film Institute, www.afi.com. Accessed 2 September 2012.

The site of movie magazines, www.moviemags.com/. Accessed 2 September 2012.

Filmography

Annie Hall (Woody Allen, Jack Rollins–Charles H. Joffe Productions, 1977).

April In Paris (David Butler, Warner Bros. Pictures, Inc., 1953).

Ask Any Girl (Charles Walters, Metro-Goldwyn-Mayer Corp; Euterpe, Inc., 1959).

The Ballad of Josie (Andrew V. McLaglen, Universal Pictures, 1967).

By The Light Of The Silvery Moon (David Butler, Warner Bros. Pictures, Inc., 1953).

Calamity Jane (David Butler, Warner Bros. Pictures, Inc., 1953).

Caprice (Frank Tashlin, Melcher-Arcola Productions, 1967).

Come September (Robert Mulligan, 7 Pictures; Raoul Walsh Enterprises, 1961).

Do Not Disturb (Ralph Levy, Martin Melcher Productions, 1965).

The Doris Day Show (CBS, 1968–1973).

Dr No (Terence Young, Eon Productions, Ltd., 1962).

Four Daughters (Michael Curtiz, Warner Bros. Pictures, Inc., 1938).

The Glass Bottom Boat (Frank Tashlin, Arwin Productions, 1966).

Hugo The Hippo (William Feigenbaum, Brut Productions, 1973/1976).

I'll See You In My Dreams (Michael Curtiz, Warner Bros. Pictures, Inc., 1952).

It Happened To Jane (Richard Quine, Arwin Productions, Inc., 1959).

It's A Great Feeling (David Butler, Michael Curtiz Productions, Inc., 1949).

Julie (Andrew L Stone, Metro-Goldwyn-Mayer Corp., 1956).

Jumbo (Charles Walters, Euterpe, Inc., 1962).

Love Me Or Leave Me (Charles Vidor, Metro-Goldwyn-Mayer Corp., 1955).

Lover Come Back (Delbert Mann, 7 Pictures, 1961).

Lucky Me (Jack Donohue, Warner Bros. Pictures, Inc., 1954).

Lullaby Of Broadway (David Butler, Warner Bros. Pictures, Inc., 1951).

The Man Who Knew Too Much (Alfred Hitchcock, Paramount Pictures Corp., 1956).

Marjorie Morningstar (Irving Rapper, Beachwold Pictures, Inc., 1958).

Midnight Lace (David Miller, Universal-International-Pictures Co., Inc., 1960).

A Modern Cinderella (Roy Mack, Vitaphone Corporation, 1932).

Move Over, Darling (Michael Gordon, Melcher-Arcola Productions, 1963).

My Dream Is Yours (Michael Curtiz, Michael Curtiz Productions Inc., 1949).

On Moonlight Bay (Roy Del Ruth, Warner Bros. Pictures, Inc., 1951).

On The Stage, Or Melodrama From The Bowery (no director given, Vitagraph Corporation, 1907).

The Pajama Game (George Abbott and Stanley Donen, Warner Bros. Pictures, Inc., 1957).

Pillow Talk (Michael Gordon, Universal-International-Pictures Co. Inc., 1959).

Please Don't Eat The Daisies (Charles Walters, Metro-Goldwyn-Mayer Corp., 1960).

Romance On The High Seas (Michael Curtiz, Michael Curtiz Productions, Inc., 1948).

Roseland (Roy Mack, Vitaphone Corporation, 1930).

Send Me No Flowers (Norman Jewison, Martin Melcher Productions, 1964).

Sex And The Single Girl (Richard Quine, Reynard Productions, 1964).

State Fair (José Ferrer, Twentieth Century Fox Film Corp., 1962).

Storm Warning (Stuart Heisler, Warner Bros. Pictures, Inc., 1951).

A Summer Place (Delmer Daves, Warner Bros. Pictures, Inc., 1959).

Sunday In New York (Peter Tewksbury, Seven Arts Productions, 1962).

Tea For Two (David Butler, Warner Bros. Pictures, Inc., 1950).

Teacher's Pet (George Seaton, Perlsea Co., 1958).

The Tender Trap (Charles Walters, Metro-Goldwyn-Mayer Corp., 1955).

That Touch Of Mink (Delbert Mann, Granley Co., 1962).

The Thrill Of It All (Norman Jewison, Ross Hunter Productions, Inc., 1963).

The Tunnel Of Love (Gene Kelly, Fields Productions, Inc., 1958).

Under The Yum Yum Tree (David Swift, Sonnis-Swift Productions, 1963).

The West Point Story (Roy Del Ruth, Warner Bros. Pictures, Inc., 1950).

Where The Boys Are (Henry Levin Metro-Goldwyn-Mayer, Inc., 1960).

Where Were You When The Lights Went Out? (Hy Haverback, Metro-Goldwyn-Mayer, Inc., 1968).

The Winning Team (Lewis Seiler, Warner Bros. Pictures, Inc., 1952).

With Six You Get Egg Roll (Howard Morris, Arwin Productions, Inc., 1968).

Yellow Submarine (George Dunning, King Features, 1968).

Young At Heart (Gordon Douglas, Warner Bros. Pictures, Inc., 1955).

Young Man With A Horn (Michael Curtiz, Warner Bros. Pictures, Inc., 1950).

Index